EXPERIENCE AND CONDUCT

A PHILOSOPHICAL ENQUIRY INTO
PRACTICAL THINKING

EXPERIENCE AND CONDUCT

A PHILOSOPHICAL ENQUIRY INTO PRACTICAL THINKING

STEPHAN KÖRNER

EMERITUS PROFESSOR OF PHILOSOPHY,
UNIVERSITY OF BRISTOL, AND PROFESSOR OF PHILOSOPHY,
YALE UNIVERSITY

CAMBRIDGE UNIVERSITY PRESS

CAMBRIDGE

LONDON   NEW YORK   NEW ROCHELLE

MELBOURNE   SYDNEY

Published by the Press Syndicate of the University of Cambridge
The Pitt Building, Trumpington Street, Cambridge CB2 1RP
32 East 57th Street, New York, NY 10022, USA
296 Beaconsfield Parade, Middle Park, Melbourne 3206, Australia

First published 1976
First paperback edition 1980

Printed in Great Britain at the
University Press, Cambridge

British Library Cataloguing in Publication Data

Körner, Stephan
Experience and conduct.
1. Reasoning   2. Practice (Philosophy)
I. Title
160   BC177   75-44578
ISBN 0 521 29943 8 paperback

TO THE MEMORY OF MY PARENTS
EMIL AND ERNA KÖRNER

Die Hölle selbst hat ihre Rechte?
Das find ich gut...

Goethe, *Faust*, part I

Statt heissem Wünschen, wildem Wollen
Statt lästgem Fordern, strengem Sollen
Sich aufzugeben ist Genuss.

Goethe, *Eins und Alles*

CONTENTS

PREFACE

Since the topics of this essay may be of interest not only to philosophers, but also to social scientists, lawyers and others, every conflict between its systematic and its expository aims was deliberately solved in favour of the latter. Part I, which contains a discussion of the formal structure of practical thinking, might seem an exception to this policy. It is, however, written with a minimum of technical detail and in such a manner that – except perhaps for an occasional backward glance – the second and third parts can be read independently of it. I have not discussed the works of contemporary moral philosophers because an adequate examination of their views would transcend the scope of this enquiry, while random references could not do them justice.

My thanks are due to the editors of *Mind*, the *Proceedings of the Aristotelian Society* and the *American Philosophical Quarterly* for permission to use material from previously published papers, to my friend Dr John Cleave for checking some of the logico-mathematical arguments and to my wife for a critical reading of the whole book.

S.K.

THE PLACE AND PLAN OF THE ENQUIRY

This introduction is, first of all, intended to demarcate the field which is to be investigated and to draw some general distinctions which will be used or presupposed throughout the enquiry. Its second aim is to describe the strategy of the enquiry and, in the light of it, to outline the topics which will be discussed as well as the order in which this will be done.

A preliminary description of practical thinking

Practical thinking consists, at least *prima facie*, in a narrowing down of possibilities and in evaluating the result of this process. The narrowing down starts with the determination of a set of logically possible courses of nature, proceeds to the determination of a set of factually possible courses of nature and hence to the determination of a set of constructively or practically possible courses of nature, that is to say of possible courses of action. Each of these sets is meant to consist of mutually exclusive and jointly exhaustive possibilities of the appropriate kind. The evaluation of the courses of action is either axiological, consisting in their preferential ordering, grading or measurement, or else deontological, consisting in the attribution to them of deontic attributes such as 'being obligatory' or 'being permitted'. While the moral evaluation of courses of action may be of over-riding philosophical interest, it cannot be properly understood without being compared to other species of practical evaluation, for example prudential gradings or deontic characterizations from the point of view of a legal or professional code of conduct.

To think about factually possible courses of nature is, at least *prima facie*, to hold, acquire or abandon commonsense, scientific or metaphysical beliefs about facts and future possibilities. To think about constructively possible courses of nature or courses of action is, in addition, to think in a commonsense, scientific or metaphysical way about the part played by human action in apparently realizing one course of action and, thus, one course of nature rather than another. To evaluate practical options is – at least sometimes – to apply various types of evaluative or deontic standards of consistency, coherence, prudence, morality, etc., whose nature demands and will receive detailed discussion, as will the other key-concepts used in this preliminary description of practical thinking.

Of the components which can be discerned in practical thinking, factual thinking, i.e. thinking about factually possible courses of nature, seems to be presupposed by constructive thinking, i.e. thinking about practicable courses of action, which in turn seems to be presupposed by evaluative thinking, i.e. the axiological or deontic characterization of courses of action. This *prima facie* relationship does not prejudge any results which a 'deeper enquiry' may yield. Thus one cannot from the outset exclude as absurd a constructivist position according to which all factual thinking is in the 'last analysis' constructive or a pragmatist position according to which all thinking is in the 'last analysis' evaluative. Since, however, in philosophy a 'deeper enquiry' more often than not means philosophical speculation and the 'last analysis' the results of such speculation and since, moreover, the confusion of speculation and analysis tends to breed all kinds of other confusion, a few remarks about the difference between analysis and speculation may be desirable. They are all the more appropriate at the outset of an essay which engages in both kinds of philosophy.

On the separation of the analysis of practical thinking from speculation about it

The analytical task of this essay is to exhibit the general structure of systems of practical attitudes or, briefly, of practical systems and to exhibit various specific aspects and kinds of practical thinking and of practical systems. This kind of analysis must be distinguished from another philosophical activity which, though largely reconstructive, is also often called analysis. To avoid confusion it is advisable to refer to these two kinds of philosophical activity by different names, for example, to call the exhibition of the structure of practical or cognitive systems or of whatever is described without being modified 'exhibition analysis' and to call any analysis which involves reconstruction 'replacement analysis'. To draw this distinction is not to deny that it is sometimes difficult to apply or that perhaps 'in the last analysis' all description is reconstruction.

2

Without going into detail one may explain the nature of replacement analysis by assuming that the result of an exhibition analysis, say an exhibited system of beliefs or practical attitudes is considered to be defective by some accepted criterion and thus to stand in need of modification, reconstruction or analysis and in this sense to be an 'analysandum'. The task of a replacement analysis is then to replace the defective analysandum by an 'analysans' which while fulfilling the function of the analysandum is yet free from its defects.† The criteria of defectiveness vary greatly and may include ambiguity, logical inconsistency, incompatibility with certain adopted standards of scientific or ontological adequacy or with a speculative view of the nature of reality as a whole. But – and this is here of the greatest importance – a replacement analysis presupposes the prior acceptance of the criteria of defectiveness. It does not propose or try to justify them. Indeed it is, even among philosophers, quite usual that the acceptance of these criteria is taken so much for granted that one is not even aware of them – at least not without a special effort at making them explicit.

Both exhibition analysis which, at most, exhibits accepted speculative assumptions and replacement analysis which, at most, presupposes them, differ from speculative philosophy which proposes and defends speculative assumptions about reality as a whole. The first and main task of this essay is exhibition analysis. But there is no reason to shy away from speculative proposals especially if, after the analytical task is concluded, its results suggest a possible conception of reality as a whole. To examine such a conception with care is in the tradition or the great philosophers and satisfies a need felt by many. It is, moreover, unlikely to do harm – so long as one does not confuse what the analysis implies with what it merely suggests.

On the distinction between form and content in practical thinking

The distinction between the form and content of practical thinking is largely a matter of convenience and convention, especially if one regards the class of formal principles as wider than the class of logical principles. Yet even the definition and demarcation of logic or a logic is to some extent a matter of convention. Here a logic will be understood as embracing a propositional calculus, a quantification theory

† For details see, for example, Körner (1971b: ch. 2).

and a theory of identity, but no principles for the quantification of predicates. We shall, moreover, acknowledge and make use of more than one logic, namely of classical, non-constructive 'factual' logic, as developed by Frege and his successors, of intuitionist or constructive logic as developed by the intuitionist mathematicians and first formalized by Heyting, and of extensions of these systems which admit not only exact but also inexact predicates (see chapter 1). Although the factual and the constructive logic – and their extensions – can each be interpreted in the other and be considered as fundamental, the former is particularly useful in the analysis of factual and the latter in the analysis of constructive thinking.

From the constraints which are based on the acceptance of a logic, one must distinguish the constraints based on the acceptance of an ontology, i.e. of a set of assumptions about the ultimate kinds of entities which exist in the actual world (atoms, monads, causally determined events, etc.). While a person's substantive ontological assumptions express some of his beliefs about the actual world, his formal ontological principles express the requirement that all his beliefs about the actual world be consistent with his substantive ontological assumptions and be in this sense ontologically possible. The reason for calling these principles 'formal' is that they presuppose the adoption of an ontology, but not of a particular ontology.

To the ontological constraints in a person's sphere of factual thinking there correspond analogous constraints in the practical sphere. Some – though by no means all – of these may be implied by his acceptance of a code of conduct which determines what is deontically possible, or permissible, conduct. If so, one can, as before, distinguish between substantive deontic principles which determine the content of a particular code of conduct and formal deontic principles which presuppose the adoption of a code of conduct, but not of a particular code of conduct. (Formal deontic and formal ontological principles resemble each other sufficiently in their structure to justify their being discussed together, see chapter 2.)

In considering factually possible courses of nature and practicable courses of nature or courses of action it is often important to determine, as best as can be done, the probability with which they can be assumed to occur with or without an agent's intervention. The principles for doing so consist on the one hand in the so-called calculus of probability, on the other in general criteria for its application to courses of nature or of action. The system of these principles, which is sometimes called the 'logic of probability' will also be regarded as formal – at least in the sense of an important formality which must be clarified before dealing with more substantive issues. The same applies to the principles which are sometimes said to constitute the 'logic of preference', i.e. the principles of measuring, ordering and grading practical preferences, in particular their trichotomizing into pro-attitudes, anti-attitudes and attitudes of indifference. The presentation and discussion of the logics of factual and constructive thinking and of the formal systems of ontological, deontological, probabilistic and evaluative reasoning will not aim at completeness. Their purpose is on the one hand to make some results of the relevant formal inquiries readily available, on the other hand to indicate where these results need to be modified or supplemented.

On commonsense and specialist thinking

In the analysis of practical thinking the contrast between commonsense and specialist thought and language will prove no less important than it has proved in the analysis of factual thinking. Although it is not feasible to repeat in detail the results of an earlier enquiry into the relation between commonsense and theoretical thought about the course of nature (Körner 1966), a general understanding of their differences and interrelations is in at least two ways relevant to our purpose. The first is that practical involves factual thinking as one of its components; and the second, that the contrast between commonsense and specialist thought which manifests itself in thinking about nature, also manifests itself in analogous ways in thinking about conduct. Roughly speaking, a person's commonsense propositions and his scientific theories – however rudimentary – describe, or are true of, different worlds containing different particulars, different characteristics and different regularities.

In our culture an educated person's commonsense world may, for example, contain material objects, persons and an indefinite variety of physical and mental phenomena. These are located in perceptual space and time or time only, possess an indefinite variety of attributes and exhibit an indefinite variety of regularities and irregularities. The same person's physical theory may be, for example, a more or less faithful version of Newtonian dynamics describing a world which contains material particles as its only particulars. These particles are located in Euclidean space and Newtonian time, possess momentum and position as their only primitive attributes and move with perfect regularity according to the three laws of motion.

A convenient way of comparing the person's theory with his commonsense factual beliefs is to regard the former as resulting from modifications of the latter – modifications which can be summarized under the headings of deductive unification, deductive abstraction and theoretical innovation. Deductive unification consists in organizing the believed factual propositions into premises and conclusions, ideally in such a manner that the transition from premises to conclusions is made in accordance with transparent formal, especially logical and mathematical principles. In so far as these principles are foreign to commonsense reasoning they enforce the replacement of commonsense propositions, particulars and attributes which do not conform to them by theoretical propositions which do. In the case of our example indefinite commonsense propositions are replaced by definite propositions, inexact commonsense attributes are replaced by exact attributes, and commonsense relations between quantities which are not isomorphic with certain mathematical relations are replaced by relations which are.

Whereas deductive unification modifies the formal structure of commonsense factual thought, deductive abstraction and theoretical innovation modify its content. Deductive abstraction is, roughly speaking, the severing of deductive connections between the concepts of the theory and other concepts which are irrelevant to the special purpose for which the theory is used. For example, if a particle of classical dynamics is comparable to a billiard ball, it is a billiard ball which possesses *only* momentum and position and lacks any other attributes not definable in terms of momentum and position. Theoretical innovation is, again roughly speaking, the introduction of new concepts and deductive connections into the theory, for example of instantaneous acceleration and its connection with kinetic energy. Comparing the system of commonsense concepts which a person employs in his factual thinking to a net – the intersections representing concepts and the connecting strands deductive relations – we might compare deductive unification to a tightening of the net, deductive abstraction to removing some of its strands and theoretical innovation to adding new strands to it.

To apply a theory describing a world which may differ radically from the world of commonsense to this latter world, is to identify the theory's (description of its) world with the commonsense (description of its) world within the relevant special contexts and for the relevant special purposes for which the theory has been designed. Clearly, the world as described by classical physics and the world as described by some economic theory will be identifiable with different parts of the world of commonsense. The limits of such identifiability will depend mainly on the success of these identifications in predicting and explaining the course of nature.

The rôle played by deductive unification, deductive abstraction and theoretical innovation in opposing various special or specialist worlds to the world of commonsense, and the rôle played by limited identifications of these opposing worlds with each other, are not peculiar to factual thinking and thus to the factual component of practical thinking. They are equally effective in thinking about practicabilities, preferences and obligations. Yet, just as within the factual sphere an understanding of the particular modifications leading from commonsense to, say, a physical theory, demand a detailed analysis of the structure and content of commonsense beliefs and specialist systems; so an understanding of the particular modifications leading from commonsense to, say, a code of professional conduct or a legal system will require similarly detailed analyses. It will, moreover, be seen that the analyses which have yet to be given are by no means trivial variations of those provided already.

The content and the formal structure both of commonsense and of specialist thinking, as here conceived, are both subject to change. And we must not confuse specialist factual or practical thinking with Platonic or rationalist ways of theorizing, which allegedly yield descriptions of an unchanging Reality, or self-evident intersubjective intuition. Factual or practical commonsense must equally not be confused with the unchanging *sensus communis* of Aristotle, the *bon sens* of Descartes or the 'commonsense' of British empiricism from Locke to Moore. The opposition of commonsense to specialist thinking raises the question whether one should, after the manner of some empiricists, judge the truth claims of specialist thinking by its agreement with commonsense; whether in rationalist fashion one should judge commonsense thinking by the standard of some specialist system; or whether one should consider neither kind of thinking as subordinate to the other. This is one of the questions which will be answered by a speculative proposal, after the analytical task has been completed.

The strategy and plan of the enquiry

In the light of the preceding distinctions, whether drawn for convenience or deeper reasons, the following strategy seems appropriate. In order to separate problems of exhibition analysis from other issues, especially speculative proposals, part I and part II will be almost exclusively devoted to the exhibition analysis of practical thinking. Part III will be mainly concerned with problems arising from the plurality of mutually incompatible practical and cognitive systems, more particularly the problem of the relations between these different systems to each other and to reality as a whole. In accordance with the distinction between the form and content of practical thinking, part I contains an examination of the formal structure of practical thinking, whereas part II examines specific kinds and aspects of practical thinking and systems of practical attitudes.

Within the topics discussed in part I and part II the distinction between commonsense and specialist practical principles and systems will be observed and encounter the familiar obstacles. One of them is that while the syntax and semantics of the artificial languages or the restricted and standardized parts of some natural language expressing specialist practical thinking are comparatively well understood, the syntax and semantics of natural languages are comparatively obscure. It is nevertheless possible – as has been done in comparing commonsense and specialist factual thinking – to draw attention to features of commonsense thinking which are not expressible in a given artificial language and sometimes even to construct a new artificial language in which these features become expressible. Examples are inexact attributes which though inexpressible in classical logic becomes expressible in an extension of it (see chapter 1 on the relation between the logics L and L^*). Whether the construction of such an extension represents a step towards the formulation of the 'deep structure' of a particular natural language or of every member of a group of such languages is impossible to decide, until one is told more clearly what the deep structure of a language (i.e. of all its well-formed sentences) is, why every language must have one and only one deep structure, and what the criteria are for distinguishing the legitimate contender for the title from the pretenders to it. However, for the purposes of this essay one may regard an artificial, logical language as a fragment of any natural language in which its sentences can be paraphrased.

In progressing from the exhibition of logical principles at the beginning of part I to the exhibition of principles of practical rationality and moral coherence, one proceeds not only from more general principles to less general ones, but also from more generally accepted to less generally accepted principles. There is, clearly, more agreement about conditions of mere consistency between, say, a set of practical preferences than about more specific conditions of their systematic interdependence. As the principles which are accepted by some and rejected by others increase in number and variety, two questions arise with increasing insistence. One is the epistemological question of the nature of the evidence for or against one particular system of practical principles. The other is the related, but different question about the relation between alternative systems of practical principles and a reality which transcends human existence. From what has been said about the nature of exhibition analysis and its relation to other types of philosophy these questions are best discussed in the third, and last, part of this essay.

Once the division of the essay into its three main parts has been determined little choice is left for their appropriate subdivision. Part I, devoted to the formal structure of practical thinking, deals with the logical foundations, the formal ontological and deontic constraints of practical thinking, the 'logic' of probabilistic reasoning and, lastly, the 'logic' of preferential ordering and grading. Part II, devoted to the investigation of various aspects and kinds of practical systems and evaluation, begins with the analysis of some concepts whose applicability is presupposed by any practical evaluation, in particular the concepts of an intervention in the course of nature, of action and agent, and of practical attitudes of different kinds and levels. It turns to the analysis of the principles of evaluation, the relation between axiological and regulative standards of conduct, and then to the analysis of morality, justice, prudence, legality and the rôle of practical idealizations and ideals. Part III, devoted to the questions of the epistemology and speculative metaphysics of practical thinking, inquires into the relation between cognitive and practical rationality, the nature of argument and evidence in morals, of understanding an alien morality and the limits of moral pluralism. It ends by considering moral systems as a topic for speculation and a source of moral guidance.

Although the plan as outlined seems justified from the point of view of a systematic exposition, it will not suit all classes of readers equally well. *As indicated in the Preface those with little interest in logical matters and those who are well versed in them will not be prevented from understanding parts II and III if they peruse the first part rather quickly.* The former are advised to do so in order to make sure where they can find more detailed logical explanations should they feel the need for them in order to follow the more substantive parts of the essay; the latter in order to become aware of logical innovations, deviations and idiosyncrasies which might otherwise become a hindrance rather than the help they are meant to be

PART I

ON THE FORMAL STRUCTURE OF PRACTICAL THINKING

CHAPTER 1

THE LOGICAL FOUNDATIONS OF PRACTICAL THINKING

The purpose of this chapter is to examine the logical principles which govern the factual and the constructive component of practical thinking, that is to say thinking about what is (was, will be) the case and thinking about what can be made the case or brought about. The discussion will proceed by examining some interrelated logical systems each of which governs at least a part or aspect of practical thinking. Since these systems have for the most part been thoroughly investigated, it will be possible and appropriate to put the main emphasis on examining their rôle in practical thinking, to omit the proof of theorems and in general to subordinate mathematical rigour to explanatory clarity. From the point of view of our enquiry the most important distinction between logical systems is that between non-constructive and constructive systems. However, the distinctions between finite and infinite as well as between exact (extensionally definite) and inexact logical systems will also prove relevant.

The logical systems which will be discussed are the infinite, definite, non-constructive logic L, which was first axiomatized by Frege; the infinite, definite constructive logic I which was first axiomatized by Heyting; the finite restrictions L_0 and I_0 of L and I respectively; and the indefinite extensions L_0^*, L^*, I_0^* and I^* of these systems. The chapter begins with a heuristic discussion of the finite, definite logical systems L_0 and I_0 which because of their simplicity clearly exhibit the contrast between non-constructive and constructive logical systems. There follow outlines of the syntax and semantics of L_0 and L and of I_0 and I as well as of the indefinite extensions of these systems which are arrived at by allowing predicates with neutral or borderline cases. The chapter ends with some remarks on the relation of the various logical systems to each other.†

---

† Most textbooks on mathematical logic contain competent discussions of L and L_0. The interpretation of the constructive systems I and I_0 is essentially due to Grzegorczyk (1964). For a discussion of inexact logical systems, see e.g. Körner (1966: ch. 3). For their metamathematical investigation see Cleave (1974).

Heuristic considerations of L_0 and I_0

Let us assume a person, say S, who finds himself in a situation α and who is wondering about the sequences of situations which might follow α. Let us further assume that S regards the number of sequences and of situations as finite and that each situation is describable by a finite number of atomic statements. If so he might represent his predicament by a tree diagram of which the following might be an example.

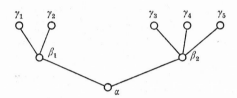

To each node of the tree there corresponds a consistent set of atomic sentences describing S's original situation and – except in the case of the original situation – the situations which temporally precede it. If in order to simplify this illustration we assume that for our purpose a temporal division into days is sufficient, it might, for example, be that $\alpha = \{$On Monday: S is at London airport, S has lost his ticket, S is phoning his wife...$\}$; $\beta_1 = \{$On Monday: S is at London airport, S has lost his ticket, S is phoning his wife... On Tuesday: S is in New York...$\}$: $\beta_2 = \{$On Monday: S is at London airport, S has lost his ticket, S is phoning his wife... On Tuesday: S is at London airport...$\}$ etc. The statements that S is at London airport on Monday and that he is at London airport on Tuesday are clearly different.

About such a tree one can ask a variety of questions, including 'factual' questions whose systematic treatment leads to the development of factual logical systems and 'constructive' questions whose systematic treatment leads to the development of constructive logical systems. The simplest factual and constructive questions concern the factual or constructive truth of atomic statements in the sense of the following definitions: An atomic statement (a statement not containing either a quantifier or a statement connective) is factually satisfied by a tree if, and only if, it is contained in one of its nodal sets. If one of the paths of the tree is singled out as actual, then an atomic statement is factually true if, and only if, it is contained in a nodal set lying on

14

the actual path. An atomic statement is constructively satisfied by a tree if, and only if, however one proceeds from the origin of the tree along any of its paths one reaches a nodal set containing it. If all the paths of the tree correspond to realizable options, then a statement which is constructively satisfied by the tree is also constructively true on it. Let us assume, as we do when making plans, that any tree has an actual path and that all paths are realizable. If so, then 'On Monday S is at London airport' is both factually and constructively true, while 'On Tuesday S is in New York' is not constructively true and is factually true only if β_1 rather than β_2 lies on the actual path of our tree.

The difference between factual and constructive satisfaction or truth extends from atomic to non-atomic statements, e.g. to disjunctions and negations. A disjunction of two statements is factually satisfied on a tree if, and only if, at least one statement is factually satisfied on it; whereas a disjunction of two statements is constructively satisfied on a tree if, and only if, at least one of them is constructively satisfied (i.e. if a nodal set containing it is reached, however we proceed from the origin along any path on the tree). The negation of a statement is factually satisfied on a tree if, and only if, there is a path on the tree no set of which contains the statement; and it is factually true if the actual path contains no nodal set containing the statement. The negation of a statement is constructively satisfied on a tree if, and only if, however we proceed from the original set along any path we do not reach a set containing the statement. It follows that while the disjunction of a statement and its negation is factually satisfied on every tree, it is not also constructively satisfied on every tree. Thus if we consider the tree of our example and cut off its γ-sets so that the new tree contains only the paths $\alpha\beta_1$ and $\alpha\beta_2$ the disjunction 'On Tuesday S is in New York or on Tuesday S is not in New York' is factually, but not also constructively true on this tree.

The next and most fundamental heuristic step towards formulating the finite, definite factual logic L_0 and the finite, definite factual logic I_0 is to ask which finite and definite statements (i.e. statements containing only exact predicates applied to a finite number of particulars) are factually satisfied and which of them are constructively satisfied on all trees of the kind illustrated by our example (i.e. trees with a finite number of nodal sets containing a finite number of atomic statements). It turns out that the statements which are factually satisfied on all trees are precisely the finite theorems of classical logic

15

and that the statements which are constructively satisfied on all finite trees are precisely the finite theorems of constructive logic. Thus, calling the finite theorems of classical and of constructive logic respectively L_0-theorems and I_0-theorems and calling the statements which are factually and constructively satisfied on all trees respectively L_0-valid and I_0-valid, it can be proved that a statement is an L_0-theorem if, and only if, it is L_0-valid; and that a statement is an I_0-theorem if, and only if, it is I_0-valid.†

This result is philosophically interesting because planning and practical thinking generally involves thinking about what is the case and what can be made to be the case on finite, definite possibility trees reflecting a person's practical position more or less completely and more or less precisely. It also prepares the way for an understanding of more complex logical systems which can be regarded as extensions of L_0 and I_0.

On the logical systems L_0 and L

Before comparing the various logical systems mentioned, it is worth noting that all of them can, and will be, expressed in the same language. This language contains signs for the propositional connectives of conjunction, disjunction, negation and the conditional, namely '$\wedge$', '$\vee$', '$\neg$', '$\rightarrow$'; for propositional variables, namely f, g, h, ...; for individual variables, namely x, y, z, ...; for predicate variables, namely P, Q, R, ...; and for the universal and existential quantifiers, namely $\forall$ and $\exists$. In order to distinguish propositional, individual and predicate constants from the corresponding variables one may, where this is necessary to avoid misunderstandings, use letters without subscripts for variables and letters with subscripts for constants so that f_0, x_1, P_2 are respectively a propositional, an individual and a predicate constant. The common language also contains a (recursive) definition of a well-formed formula, which will be taken for granted – e.g. '$f \wedge g$' being well formed and '$f \wedge \wedge g$' being ill formed.

In order to characterize the definite, finite, non-constructive logic L_0 we consider a domain of n particulars, designated for simplicity by the numerals 1 to n, and the set of all extensional predicates applicable to these individuals – a predicate being extensional if, and only if, it is determined solely by the class of individuals of which it is true.

---

† The first statement is proved by noting that it is a special case of the completeness theorem of classical logic, the second by pointing out that it is a special case of the completeness theorem for intuitionist logic, given by Grzegorczyk (1964).

The atomic statements formed by the application of the predicates to the individuals will be all statements in which a one-place extensional predicate is applied to an individual, e.g. $P_0(2)$; all statements in which a two-place extensional predicate is applied to an ordered couple of individuals, e.g. $Q_2(7, 9)$ or $Q_1(9, 7)$, ...; all statements in which an n-place extensional predicate is applied to an ordered n-tuple, e.g. $R_2(1, ..., n)$. Assuming all atomic statements to be either true or false, we define a conjunction $f \wedge g$ as true if, and only if, both conjuncts are true; a disjunction $f \vee g$ as true if, and only if, at least one of the disjuncts is true; a negated statement $\neg f$ as true if, and only if, f is false (i.e. not true); a conditional statement $f \rightarrow g$ as true if, and only if, it is not the case that f is true and g is false; an existentially quantified statement $(\exists x) P(x)$ as true if, and only if, at least one statement derived from $P(x)$ by replacing the variable by an individual constant from the finite domain is true; a universally quantified statement $(\forall x) P(x)$ as true if, and only if, all statements derived from $P(x)$ by replacing the variables by an individual constant from the finite domain are true. In formulating these definitions one should, strictly speaking, qualify the truth of the statements as factual. But where the context leaves no doubt about the appropriate qualification it is permissible, and often convenient, to omit it.

In considering the definitions of the quantified statements for a finite domain of individuals it is obvious that they are mere abbreviations of quantifier-free statements. Thus for a domain of n individuals designated by 1, 2, ..., n, $(\exists x) P(x)$ can be *defined* as true if, and only if, the finite disjunction $P(1) \vee P(2) \vee ... \vee P(n)$ is true; and $(\forall x) P(x)$ if, and only if, the finite conjunction $P(1) \wedge P(2) \wedge ... \wedge P(n)$ is true.

It is now possible to characterize the logic L_0 semantically by defining the L_0-valid statements; and syntactically by indicating a formal theory whose theorems are precisely the L_0-valid statements. As regards the semantic characterization of L_0 we define a statement as (factually) valid in L_0 or L_0-valid if, and only if, it is true whether its component atomic statements are true or false. Thus

$$\text{`}R(7, 4) \vee \neg R(7, 4)\text{'} \quad \text{or} \quad \text{`}R(7, 4) \rightarrow R(7, 4)\text{'}$$

are L_0-valid. It may be worth noting that since the L_0-validity of these and other valid statements is independent of the truth or falsehood of their atomic components, it also does not depend on the nature of the particulars designated by the numerals 1, 2, ..., n (or any other names). L_0-validity over a finite domain of particulars trivially coincides with validity in the sense of factual truth on all trees whose nodal sets comprise the atomic statements which are true or false of the particulars of this domain. Indeed, the only point of defining factual or non-constructive validity by reference to trees is its comparison with constructive validity.

As regards the syntactic characterization of L_0, it can be demonstrated (as is done in most textbooks of elementary mathematical logic) that a statement is L_0-valid if, and only if, it is a theorem of classical propositional logic. That is to say any set of axioms and inference rules of classical propositional logic constitutes a syntactic characterization of the finite, definite logic L_0.

We arrive at the infinite, definite logic L by allowing not only finite domains of individuals but also infinite domains and with them infinite conjunctions and disjunctions. In such a system $(\forall x)\, P(x)$ and $(\exists x)\, P(x)$ are no longer reducible to compound statements. The syntax of L is characterized by the so-called first order predicate calculus, its semantics by an extension of the notion of L_0-validity, due to Tarski (as is again shown in most textbooks of elementary mathematical logic). The assumption of actually infinite domains of objects is metaphysically highly controversial. It is nevertheless made in any mathematical theory presupposing L and in any scientific theory using such mathematics. However, most of our concerns with definite factual thinking in this essay will be served by considering L_0 (i.e. classical propositional logic) as governing it. And there is hardly any simpler or more transparent logical system.

On the logical systems I_0 and I

In characterizing the valid statements and theorems of the finite, definite, constructive logic I_0 the same primitive symbols and the same definition of a well-formed formula may be used as were used in characterizing L_0. Atomic statements, in particular, consist of n-placed predicates applied to ordered n-tuples of individuals. However, though every atomic statement is either factually true or factually false, it is *not* also either constructively true or constructively false. The constructive truth of atomic and compound statements can be defined in terms of certain constructions and constructibilities, in particular in terms of proceeding along the branches of a tree as described when interpreting the diagram on p. 14. Proceeding along the branches of such a tree may be a merely mental procedure. But it may represent

procedures which are not merely mental, especially possible interventions in the course of nature and possible courses of action. This is
worth keeping in mind when considering the following definitions.

We consider a finite set of individuals and a finite set of atomic statements about them. We further assume that these atomic statements
are properly assigned to the nodal sets of a tree, say T_0. The (recursive)
definition of constructive truth consists of the following clauses: (1) An
atomic formula f is constructively true with respect to T_0 or, more
briefly, is constructively true on T_0 if, and only if, however we proceed
on it (along the branches of T_0) we reach a nodal set containing f.
(2) A negation $\daleth f$ is constructively true on T_0 if, and only if, however
we proceed on it, we do not reach a nodal set containing f. (3) A conjunction $f \wedge g$ is constructively true on T_0 if, and only if, however we
proceed on it we reach a nodal set containing both f and g. (4) A disjunction $f \vee g$ is constructively true on T_0 if, and only if, however we
proceed on it, we reach a nodal set containing f or if, however we
proceed on it, we reach a nodal set containing g. (5) A conditional
$f \rightarrow g$ is constructively true on T_0 if, and only if, either f is not constructively true on it or g is constructively true on it. (6) $(\exists x) P(x)$ is
constructively true on T_0 if, and only if, however we proceed on it we
reach a nodal set containing $P(x_0)$, where x_0 is one of the individual
constants occurring in the atomic statements assigned to T_0. (If we
think of the individual objects as designated by the numerals $1, 2, ..., n$,
then the place of x_0 must be taken by one of them.) (7) $(\forall x) P(x)$ is
constructively true on T_0 if, and only if, however we proceed on it we
reach a nodal set which contains every statement which consists in
applying $P(x)$ to an individual constant which occurs in at least one
atomic statement assigned to the tree.

As was the case with the factual logic L_0 the quantified statements
of I_0 are merely abbreviations of compound statements. If the individual constants are designated by $1, 2, ..., n$ then we can *define* the
constructive truth of $(\exists x) P(x)$ as the constructive truth of the disjunction $P(1) \vee P(2) \vee ... \vee P(n)$ and the constructive truth of $(\forall x) P(x)$
as the constructive truth of $P(1) \wedge P(2) \wedge ... \wedge P(n)$. Thus I_0 like L_0
contains no separate quantification theory; and this greatly simplifies
the task of its semantic and syntactic characterization.

As regards its semantic characterization, a statement can be defined
as valid in I_0 or as I_0-valid if, and only if, it is constructively true
on every finite tree. For example, $R(1, 2) \rightarrow R(1, 2)$ is I_0-valid, while
$R(1, 2) \vee \daleth R(1, 2)$ is not I_0-valid, as was pointed out in considering

19

the tree diagram on p.14. In these expressions the numerals 1 and 2 are names of distinct individuals whatever their nature and R the name of a two-place relation whatever its nature.

As regards the syntactic characterization of I_0 it can be demonstrated that a statement is I_0-valid if, and only if, it is a theorem of intuitionist propositional logic (see e.g. Grzegorczyk 1964). The structure of an intuitionist propositional calculus is best explained by comparing it with a classical propositional calculus, from which it is derived by eliminating that axiom or conjunction of axioms which is deductively equivalent to the principle of excluded middle. (Two statements are deductively equivalent with respect to a set of axioms if, and only if, neither is deducible from the set but each becomes deducible if the other is added.) In other words an intuitionist propositional calculus or a calculus for I_0 is any set of axioms and inferences rule in which the principle of excluded middle is not derivable and which becomes a classical propositional calculus if the principle is added to the axioms.

We arrive at the infinite, definite logic I by allowing not only finite possibility trees, but trees on which at least one branch is allowed to grow *ad infinitum*. In such a system $(\forall x)\,P(x)$ and $(\exists x)\,P(x)$ are no longer reducible to compound statements. The syntax of I is derived from that of L in the same way as the syntax of I_0 is derived from that of L_0, that is to say by eliminating from a classical first order calculus any axiom or conjunction of axioms which is deductively equivalent to the law of excluded middle. The semantical characterization of I-valid statements is the same as that of I_0-valid statements – except that the possibility trees may have branches growing *ad infinitum*. (The number of branches issuing from any node must still be finite.) The assumption of infinitely growing branches is a version of the metaphysical assumption of potential infinities which, though in some ways weaker than the assumption of actual infinities, is still controversial. However, most of our concerns with definite, constructive thinking will be served by considering I_0 (i.e. intuitionist propositional logic) as governing it. And this logic of the mental climbing of finite possibility trees is not much more complex than the classical logic L_0 of truth-functional combination.

On the logical systems $L_0{}^*$, $I_0{}^*$, L^* and I^*

The logical principles which govern our ordinary, commonsense thinking – factual as well as constructive – allow for the possibility of inexact attributes some of whose instances are borderline cases and thus for the possibility of indefinite statements. An object o is a border-line instance of a one-place predicate P if, in accordance with the rules governing P, one may choose to regard o as a positive instance of P or to regard it as a negative instance of P. Neutrality is thus a third truth-value, but differs from truth and falsehood in that one may without inconsistency or incorrectness decide to promote a neutral case to a positive case, and thus the corresponding neutral statement to a true statement or to demote a neutral case to a negative case and thus the corresponding neutral statement to a false statement. Replac-ing neutral by definite statements is one of the simplest idealizations of scientific and legal reasoning.

If we acknowledge neutral instances, inexact predicates (one- as well as many-placed) and indefinite statements in our finite factual thinking then we must modify its underlying logic L_0. Clearly, the admission of neutral atomic statements influences the truth-value of compound statements which have to be redefined as follows: (1) A con-junction $f \wedge g$ is true if, and only if, both conjuncts are true; false if, and only if, one conjunct is false; neutral if, and only if, no conjunct is false but one or both are neutral. (2) A disjunction $f \vee g$ is true if, and only if, at least, one disjunct is true; false, if and only if, both disjuncts are false; neutral in all other cases. (3) A negation $7f$ is true if, and only if, f is false; false if, and only if, f is true; neutral in all other cases. (4) A conditional $f \rightarrow g$ is true if, and only if, f is false or g is true; false if, and only if, f is true and g is false; neutral in all other cases. As with L_0 and I_0 the quantified statements $(\forall x) P(x)$ and $(\exists x) P(x)$ are respectively equivalent to $P(1) \wedge P(2) \wedge \ldots \wedge P(n)$ and $P(1) \vee P(2) \vee \ldots \vee P(n)$ so that once again quantification becomes a merely abbreviatory device which does not lead beyond L_0.

Turning to the semantic characterization of L_0^* it is immediately obvious that it does not coincide with the semantic characterization of L_0. Thus, for example, while any statement of form $7(f \wedge 7f)$ is L_0-valid, i.e. true independently of the truth-value of its components, a statement of this form, say $7(f_0 \wedge 7f_0)$, is neutral if f_0 is neutral. (By the above definitions if f_0 is neutral, $7f_0$ is also neutral and so are $f_0 \vee 7f_0$ and its negation $7(f_0 \wedge 7f_0)$.) However, the following stipula-tions amount to a reasonable definition of L_0^*-validity.

Let us consider a compound statement α and let us define its 'definite core', briefly, $[\alpha]$ as the statement derived from α by eliminat-ing from it all its neutral atomic components together with the connectives which thereby become superfluous. For example, if in $(f_0 \vee 7f_0 \vee g_0)$, g_0 is neutral and f_0 definite (i.e. true or false), then its definite core $[f_0 \vee 7f_0 \vee g_0]$ is $f_0 \vee 7f_0$; if f_0 and g_0 are neutral, then the definite core is the empty statement Λ. We define the 'definite evaluation' of α, briefly, $[[\alpha]]$ as the statement derived from α by assigning a definite truth-value, say truth, to all its neutral atomic components. For example, if in $(f_0 \vee 7f \vee g_0)$ f_0 is neutral and g_0 false, we assign truth to f_0, whereby $[[f_0 \vee 7f_0 \vee g_0]]$ becomes true.

We are now ready to define L_0^*-validity: A statement α is L_0^*-valid if, and only if, its definite core and its definite evaluation are L_0-valid. For example if in $(f_0 \vee 7f_0 \vee g_0 \vee 7g_0)$ f_0 is definite and g_0 neutral, then the statement is L_0-valid. If, however, both f_0 and g_0 are neutral, then the statement is not L_0-valid, since its definite core is the empty statement which is not L_0-valid. It is worth noting that L_0^*-validity is defined only for compounds whose atomic components are constant statements and that it is defined in terms of L_0-validity, more precisely the L_0-validity of the definite core and the definite evaluation which are associated with any statement of L_0^*.

The syntax of L_0^* is the propositional calculus included in the infinite, indefinite predicate calculus L^* (see Cleave 1974). L^* is, of course, like L based on the assumption of infinite totalities. For our purposes, however, it will, on the whole be sufficient to regard the fairly simple and transparent logic L_0^* as underlying our finite, indefinite, factual thinking.

The steps leading from I_0 to I_0^* and from I_0^* to I^* are analogous to the steps from L_0 to L_0^* and from L_0^* to L^*. For our purposes it will be sufficient to indicate the transition from I_0 to I_0^*. One first defines an atomic statement $P(o)$ as constructively neutral with respect to a tree if, and only if, however one proceeds on it, one reaches a nodal set which comprises $P(o)$ or a nodal set which can with equal correctness be judged to comprise $P(o)$ or not to comprise it – provided that at least one nodal set of the latter kind lies on the tree. One secondly defines compound statements considering, as in the case of L_0^*, the influence of constructively neutral atomic components on compound statements. Lastly, one defines the I_0^*-validity of any statement in terms of the I_0-validity of its associated definite core and its associated definite evaluation.

The syntactical characterization of I_0^* and I^* by a system of axioms and inference rules which yields as theorems precisely the statements which are respectively I_0^*- and I^*-valid also presents no difficulty of

22

principle. For just as any valid statement of each of these indefinite systems is associated with two valid statements of the corresponding definite system (namely its definite core and its definite evaluation), so any theorem of each of these indefinite systems would be associated with two corresponding theorems of the corresponding definite system. However, so long as we remain within the sphere of *finite* factual and constructive thinking there is no need for any syntactical systems because the semantic characterization of L_0-, L_0*-, I_0- and I_0*-validity *ipso facto* describes a finite procedure for deciding whether a given statement is or is not valid.

On the relation of the various logical systems to each other

In discussing the various systems of actual and constructive logic – whether finite or infinite, definite, or indefinite – the question as to which, if any, of them is fundamental was left open. While at this stage of the inquiry no answer can be properly proposed, it is appropriate to indicate how any such proposal could be implemented. If the decision is in favour of logical pluralism nothing has to be done. If it is in favour of the supremacy of one logic over the others, then it must be shown how the others can be interpreted in the supreme logic. For L and I it is known how either of these systems can be interpreted in terms of the other.† Because of the association of the indefinite with the definite systems these interpretations can be extended to L* and I* and, hence, to their finite subsystems L_0* and I_0*. However, the possibility of implementing the various metaphysical proposals about the supremacy or otherwise of any logic over the others, does not in any way establish the adequacy of any of them.

The technical problem of distinguishing between the various logical systems can be solved either by expressing each of them in a different language or, as has been done, expressing them all in the same language and taking care to avoid ambiguities. This is usually done by relying on the context. Where doubt may arise the following method commends itself. If f is a formula considered, say, from the point of view of L or I, one may indicate this by a preceding 'L:' or 'I:'. Thus L: $\vdash P(1) \vee \neg P(1)$ indicates that the statement is an L-theorem or L-valid, and I: not $\vdash P(1) \vee \neg P(1)$ that it is not an I-theorem or I-valid. Strictly speaking one would have to distinguish between 'being

† For Interpretations of I in L see e.g. Mostowski (1966: ch. 10); for an interpretation of L in I see Gödel (1933).

a theorem' and 'being valid' e.g. by indicating the former by ⊢ and the latter by ⊨. Since, however, all the systems here considered are complete in the sense that for each of them the class of theorems and the class of valid statements coincide, the sign ⊢ can be used to indicate membership in either class.

CHAPTER 2

ON THE FORMAL
STRUCTURE OF ONTOLOGICAL AND
DEONTOLOGICAL CONSTRAINTS

Apart from the logical constraints to which factual and practical thinking are subject, they may also be subject to domination by non-logical cognitive and deontic standards or systems of them. A cognitive standard is a belief which dominates a class of beliefs in the sense that any belief which belongs to the class and is inconsistent with the cognitive standard is considered cognitively inadequate. In so far as we shall be concerned with cognitive standards and cognitive domination we shall be mainly interested in ontological standards, i.e. cognitive standards which dominate all other beliefs but are themselves undominated. Examples of ontological standards are particular beliefs, such as Moore's belief that the earth existed before he was born, or general principles such as Kant's principle of causality. A deontic standard is a regulative maxim which dominates a class of a person's practical attitudes in the sense that any action which implements a practical attitude belonging to the class and conflicts with the deontic standard is ruled out as deontically inadequate or impermissible. A deontic standard is deontically dominated by a higher deontic standard if an action, though implementing the former, is nevertheless ruled out as inadequate because it conflicts with the latter. In what follows we shall be concerned both with dominated deontic standards (such as rules of professional conduct) and with undominated ones (such as moral regulations).

The chapter begins with a discussion of the nature of ontological constraints, taking the structure of ontologies for granted. It proceeds to a formal analysis of deontic systems or codes of conduct, in particular their deontic consistency, their adequacy to the actual world, the manner in which this adequacy can be lost, and the manner in which it can be restored. The basic connection between standard logical necessity on the one hand and ontological and deontic necessity on the other seems fairly obvious and has been used in earlier analyses of ontological and deontic constraints.†

Ontological necessity and related notions

Let us assume that a person has explicitly or implicitly adopted a consistent conjunction of ontological assumptions N which constrain his factual thinking in such a way that N cognitively dominates all his other beliefs while not being dominated by any of them. Being cognitively dominating, but itself undominated, N will in this sense be necessary or, more precisely, ontologically necessary. Acknowledging this non-logical, ontological necessity leads to a distinction between three kinds of true propositions, namely true propositions which are neither logically nor ontologically necessary, true propositions which are ontologically, but not also logically necessary and true propositions which are logically necessary. It leads, consequently, to the corresponding distinction between false propositions which are neither logically nor ontologically impossible, false propositions which are ontologically, but not logically impossible, and false propositions which are logically impossible. Since the notions of ontological necessity and possibility are defined with respect to a particular N they are relative concepts. For example the statement that somebody was miraculously raised from the dead is ontologically impossible with respect to the ontology of a determinist, materialist ontology, and ontologically possible with respect to the ontology formulated by Thomas Aquinas.

Abbreviating 'The statement f is ontologically necessary with respect to the conjunction of ontological assumptions N' by '$\Box_N f$' we can define the ontological necessity of f with respect to N by

(1) $\Box_N f \underset{D}{=} (N \vdash f) \wedge f,$

where f ranges over all statements which are well formed in accordance with an underlying logic and where $\vdash$ expresses deducibility according to this logic. We may similarly define ontological possibility or cognitive coherence with respect to N by

(2) $\Diamond_N f \underset{D}{=} \neg \Box_N \neg f$

or more explicitly by

(3) $\Diamond_N f \underset{D}{=} \neg (N \vdash \neg f) \vee f.$

† See e.g. Körner (1955: pp. 19ff. and *passim*). Richard Montague (1960) adopts a similar approach. But he does not consider the rôle of domination in making a belief ontologically necessary or the rôle of a code's adequacy to the world in making it the ground of code-dependent obligations.

The definitions of ontological necessity and of ontological possibility or coherence with respect to a set of ontological assumptions can be used to provide a natural interpretation of some formal systems of modal logic (see Körner 1973). For our purposes, however, the transparent definitions containing familiar and well-tried semantic concepts are preferable.

Since the examination of deontological necessity or obligation and of other deontic concepts, to which the rest of this chapter is devoted, will also exhibit them as relative (to a system of regulations) and as analysable in terms of familiar semantic concepts, it may be useful to emphasize some important similarities and differences between ontological and deontological necessity and the conceptual families to which they belong. Both kinds of necessity are analysed in terms of logical deducibility from, or logical implication by, some wider system of propositions – the notion of deducibility being the familiar one (of L or one of the other systems explained in the preceding chapter). This notion is sometimes diagnosed as the source of paradoxes which, if the diagnosis were justified, would affect both the analysis of ontological and of deontological necessity. The paradoxes will be considered in our analysis of deontological reasoning where they appear most obnoxious. The main difference between the two types of necessity is that while what is ontologically necessary is *eo ipso* the case, what is deontologically necessary or obligatory may or may not be, or ever be made to be, the case.

Systems of regulative maxims and their formal adequacy

Before going into detail it may be useful to consider in a very general way the case of a legislator, charged with devising a code of conduct in the service of some purposes or ideals. He would have to possess a fairly clear idea of the world for which he is legislating, especially of the contingencies which can arise in it. Being human, his description of the world, or rather those of its features which are relevant to his legislative task, will necessarily be finite. In the light of his factual beliefs he will have to decide which of the possible contingencies are to be embodied into regulative maxims – either as conditions requiring actions of a certain kind, or as actions required by certain conditions.

A regulative maxim or regulation requires of an individual who finds himself in a situation having certain characteristics that he brings about by his action – i.e. his deliberate intervention or non-intervention in the course of nature – another situation with the same or different characteristics. The formal features of maxims which concern us here, are schematically represented by expressions of form $f \underset{i}{\rightarrow} g$! where i, f, g are variables, with i ranging over persons, and f and g over propositions referring to situations at a certain time and place (to objects at a certain time and place, to four-dimensional events etc.) such that the time referred to in f is not preceded by the time referred to in g. This restriction, which excludes regulative maxims ordering that something be done in the past, could – like the law of non-decreasing entropy and other physical laws – with equal propriety be incorporated in the description of the world for which the maxims are intended. It will henceforth be taken for granted and as implicit in the context. We might read a regulative maxim m of form $f \underset{i}{\rightarrow} g$! as 'It is required of i to conduct himself in such a manner (see to it, cause, bring about, make sure etc.) that if the situation described by f is the case, then the situation described by g is the case (i.e. that the situation described by $\neg f \lor g$ is the case).'

Whenever it is necessary explicitly to distinguish between constants and variables the former will, as agreed earlier, be given subscripts, so that $f_1 \underset{i_0}{\rightarrow} g_2$! is a constant maxim, in which f_1 and g_2 are constant statements and i_0 a constant individual. If the regulative maxim $f_1 \underset{i_0}{\rightarrow} g_2$! were addressed not only to the individual i_0, but also to the individuals i_1 and i_2 or to every individual i belonging to a class I_0, we could express this by substituting for i_0 respectively $\{i_0, i_1, i_2\}$ or $\{i : i \in I_0\}$. Yet although the range of a maxim's addressees and their relations to each other are important for a more detailed analysis, it will for our present purpose often be possible to rely on context, rather than explicit reference to the addressees. It will also be convenient to use m without subscript for a variable ranging over maxims and m_0, m_1 etc. for constant maxims. Two maxims of form $f \rightarrow g$! and $f \rightarrow \neg g$! briefly m and $\overline{m}$ will be called conjugate. If M is a system of maxims, it is important to distinguish the statement that the conjugate of m belongs to it, briefly $\overline{m} \in M$, from the statement that m does *not* belong to it, briefly $\neg (m \in M)$. In legal theory and practice it is often considered advisable to state explicitly that a certain maxim is not part of the law.

In explaining the deontic adequacy of a code of maxims to a world, the following – obvious and natural – terminology will be useful: if $m_0 = f_1 \rightarrow g_1$! is a maxim, let us call f_1 the descriptive antecedent of m_0, g_1! the regulative consequent of m_0, g_1 the descriptive (counterpart of the regulative) consequent of m_0 and $f_1 \to g_1$ the descriptive counterpart of m_0.

If $K_0 = (f_1 \to g_1!) \wedge (f_2 \to g_2!) \wedge \ldots$ is a conjunction of maxims, let us call $F_0 = f_1 \wedge f_2 \wedge \ldots$ the conjunction of the descriptive antecedents of K_0, $G_0! = g_1! \wedge g_2! \wedge \ldots$ the conjunction of the regulative consequents of K_0, $G_0 = g_1 \wedge g_2 \wedge \ldots$ the conjunction of the descriptive (counterparts of the regulative) consequents of K_0,

$$D(K_0) = (f_1 \to g_1) \wedge (f_2 \to g_2) \wedge \ldots$$

the descriptive counterpart of K_0. The last preliminary before turning to the analysis of deontic adequacy is a reminder of the classical definition of logical consistency: A statement, say, p_0 is logically consistent if, and only if, there is at least one other statement which is not deducible from it – schematically Cons (p_0) iff $(\exists q) \, 7 \, (p_0 \vdash q)$. A statement, say, p_0 is logically consistent with another statement, say, q_0 if, and only if, $(p_0 \wedge q_0)$ is logically consistent – schematically

$$p_0 \,\text{Cons}\, q_0 \,\text{iff}\, \text{Cons}\, (p_0 \wedge q_0).$$

A system of maxims as represented by the conjunction of all its maxims, M, is deontically consistent if, and only if, (1) the descriptive counterpart of M, i.e. $D(M)$ is logically consistent and if (2) in the case of any subconjunction K of M for which the conjunction F of its descriptive antecedents is logically consistent the conjunction G of its descriptive consequents is also logically consistent. A simple example illustrating the need for the second condition is the system consisting of the two conjugate maxims $(f_1 \to g_1!)$ and $(f_1 \to 7 \, g_1!)$. The descriptive counterpart of this conjunction $(f_1 \to g_1) \wedge (f_1 \to 7 \, g_1)$, i.e.

$$(7f_1 \vee g_1) \wedge (7f_1 \vee 7 \, g_1),$$

satisfies the first condition; but two conjugate maxims are in a clear legal or other normative sense obviously contradictory.

A first step towards the definition of the adequacy of a (deontically consistent) system of maxims M to a world, as described by a finite conjunction of statements W, consists in defining for a single maxim of form $m = (f \to g!)$ its applicability to, its practicability in, and its adequacy to this world. The maxim is (1) applicable if, and only if, f is logically consistent with W(f Cons W, i.e. Cons $f \wedge W$); (2) practicable if, and only if, when the maxim is applicable, g is logically consistent with the conjunction of f and W

$$(7 \, (f \,\text{Cons}\, W) \vee g \,\text{Cons}\, f \wedge W,$$

i.e.
$$\neg\, \mathrm{Cons} f \wedge W \vee \mathrm{Cons} f \wedge g \wedge W);$$

(3) adequate if, and only if, it is both, applicable and practicable ($\mathrm{Cons} f \wedge W \wedge (\neg\, \mathrm{Cons} f \wedge W \vee \mathrm{Cons} f \wedge g \wedge W)$, i.e. $\mathrm{Cons} f \wedge g \wedge W$). A maxim may be applicable and impracticable or inapplicable and practicable. For example, the maxim which requires of John that if he is healthy on Monday he should spend the day working in his office, is applicable and impracticable in a world in which John is always healthy, but has no office or in a world in which John is always healthy except whenever he works in his office. The same maxim is inapplicable and practicable in a world in which John is never healthy. It is for no world both inapplicable and impracticable.

The generalization of the definitions just proposed for single maxims, to systems of maxims is more or less obvious. A system of maxims M is (1) applicable to W if, and only if, the descriptive antecedent f of every maxim m of M is logically consistent with W (for every f – $f \mathrm{Cons}\, W$); it is (2) practicable in W if, and only if, for every conjunction K of maxims belonging to M it is the case that if the conjunction F of the descriptive antecedents of K is logically consistent with W, the corresponding conjunction G of the descriptive consequents of K is logically consistent with the conjunction of F and W (for every conjunction K of maxims belonging to M –

$$\neg(F \mathrm{Cons}\, W) \vee G \mathrm{Cons}\, F \wedge W,$$

i.e.
$$\neg\, \mathrm{Cons}\, F \wedge W \vee \mathrm{Cons}\, F \wedge G \wedge W);$$

it is (3) adequate to W if, and only if, it is both applicable to, and practicable in W

(for every f – $\mathrm{Cons} f \wedge W$) $\wedge$ (for every K –
$$\neg\, \mathrm{Cons}\, F \wedge W \vee \mathrm{Cons}\, F \wedge G \wedge W).$$

A deontically consistent system of maxims may be deontically adequate to some worlds, but not to others. Consider the system of maxims consisting of

$$m_1 = f_1 \to g_1! = \text{'If it rains, open your umbrella!'}$$
and
$$m_2 = f_2 \to g_2! = \text{'If it is windy, wear your raincoat!'}$$

The system $m_1 \wedge m_2$ is deontically consistent since its descriptive counterpart, i.e. $(f_1 \to g_1) \wedge (f_2 \to g_2)$ is logically consistent and since

$F_0 = f_1 \wedge f_2$ as well as $G_0 = g_1 \wedge g_2$ are both logically consistent. The system is deontically adequate to our world, as described, say, by W_0 since f_1 Cons W_0, f_2 Cons W_0, F_0 Cons W_0 and G_0 Cons $F_0 \wedge W_0$. But it is not deontically adequate to a world as described, say, by W_1 in which F_0 Cons W_1 and $\daleth\, (G_0$ Cons $F_0 \wedge W_1)$ because, for example, its winds are so strong that it is physically impossible (logically incompatible with its laws of nature) to open an umbrella when a wind is blowing.

While M may be a wholly imaginary system of maxims which is deontically adequate to a purely imaginary world, described by W, it may also be an actually accepted legal system which is deontically adequate to an actually existing society or one that has existed in the past. However, the concepts of the *de iure* or *de facto* validity of a legal system in a society are narrower than the relation of deontic adequacy, which is logically implied by either. A system of maxims may include categorical maxims of form $g!$ which may be regarded as defined by $t \to g!$, t being a statement which is logically or empirically true.

A natural interpretation of the so-called standard deontic logic
in terms of deontically adequate systems of maxims

If a system of maxims M is adequate to a world W, if a person i accepts M and believes W to be the case, then M and W determine a sphere of obligations and permissions for this person. By speaking of a sphere, rather than *the* sphere, of a person's obligations one admits the possibility of different spheres, as well as of orders of priority and conflicts between them. It will be assumed that our deductive reasonings are governed by the classical elementary logic, whose deducibility relation is customarily symbolized by $\vdash_L$ which for simplicity we shall write simply as $\vdash$. (Replacing L by any of the other systems discussed in chapter 1 raises no question of principle.)

We now introduce the locutions 'On the basis of the system of maxims M (conduct ensuring the situation described by the proposition) f is obligatory', briefly $O_M f$, and 'On the basis of the system of maxims M (conduct ensuring the situation described by the proposition) f is permitted', briefly $\mathrm{Perm}_M f$, and define (a) $O_M f \underset{D}{=} D(M) \vdash f$ and (b) $\mathrm{Perm}_M f \underset{D}{=} \daleth\,(D(M) \vdash \daleth f)$. In other words, $O_M f$ and $\mathrm{Perm}_M f$ are conceived as, and translated into, metalogical statements to the effect that a statement f is, or is not, logically deducible from a conjunction of implications $D(M)$ (derived as indicated from an M which is adequate to a W). The syntax and semantics of logical deducibility in

31

classical logic is well understood and will be taken for granted. Whenever the system of maxims on which an obligation or permission is based need not be specified, or can be determined from the context, subscripts may be omitted.

An obligation may be positive (prescriptive, a prescription) or negative (proscriptive, a prohibition). The distinction depends, however on, extralogical circumstances, such as linguistic accident or psychological emphasis. The positive obligation to be silent and the negative obligation *not* to talk are logically equivalent. Although it is pointless, and often misleading, to select from any such pair of obligations one as absolutely positive and one as absolutely negative, no great harm would come from such a practice, at least not for our present purpose.

If one adopts definitions (*a*) and (*b*) the following three propositions are obvious truths of logic.

(1) $Of \rightarrow {\scriptstyle 7} O {\scriptstyle 7} f$ (or $Of \rightarrow \text{Perm} f$)

(2) $O(f \wedge g) \rightarrow Of$

(3) $O(f \vee {\scriptstyle 7} f)$

This is so because (1) is another way of stating that if $D(M)$ logically implies f then it does not logically imply ${\scriptstyle 7}f$; (2) is another way of stating that if $D(M)$ logically implies f and g then $D(M)$ logically implies f; and (3) is another way of stating that $D(M) \vdash f \vee {\scriptstyle 7} f$ (i.e. a special case of *verum ex quolibet*). Propositions (1)–(3) will be called the axioms of the standard system of deontic logic.† In (1) the symbol ${\scriptstyle 7}$ is used indifferently, first for metalinguistic and then for intralinguistic negation. No harm will come from this economy and there is no objection to using two different negation signs.

Because of the interpretation of (1)–(3) as logical truths of L, more precisely as metatheorems of L, it is obvious that any application of the following rule of inference to the axioms (1)–(3), or to propositions derived from (1)–(3) by means of this rule of inference again yields logical truths of L. The rule of inference is

(4) the so-called rule of extensionality, that if f and g are logically equivalent then so are Of and Og (or equivalently, $\text{Perm} f$ and $\text{Perm} g$). The propositions (1)–(3) and the rule of inference (4) together constitute the standard system of deontic logic. briefly SDL.

† See Føllesdal & Hilpinnen (1971). The book contains, apart from some important papers on deontic logic, a comprehensive bibliography. Strictly speaking, (1)–(3) are axiom schemata with f and g ranging over the well formed formulae of classical logic.

Our interpretation of SDL is based on two fairly simple and familiar ideas. One is the logical notion of deducibility. The other is the juridical relation of adequacy which holds between a system of maxims and a world to which the system is applicable and in which it is practicable. The more usual interpretations of SDL are based on the idea of systems of ideal worlds such that any action which is obligatory in the actual world is performed in all of them and such that any action which is permitted in the actual world is performed in at least one of them (for details see Føllesdal & Hilpinnen 1971). While interpretations of this kind have the advantage of being extendable to formally more complex systems of deontic logic, they have little relevance to commonsense practical thinking or its theoretical refinements in jurisprudence, decision theory and other disciplines concerned with proposing, modifying and applying normative systems.

Soon after its inception, von Wright's first deontic logic, of which SDL is a variant, was criticized for a variety of reasons. And it was mainly because of these criticisms that the merely intuitive justifications of deontic logic were replaced by rigorous semantic interpretations. It will be useful to consider some of these criticisms of SDL in the light of the general $M-W$ interpretation, as we might call our interpretation. The objections which are of particular interest to us amount to the allegation that SDL has paradoxical consequences and to the allegation that its expressive power is insufficient for its purpose.

Alleged paradoxes based on deontically inessential components

The formula $Of \rightarrow O\,(f \vee g)$ is a theorem of SDL as can be seen by means of a formal proof. In the $M-W$ interpretation the formula becomes the trivial metalogical statement that if $D(M) \vdash f$ then $D(M) \vdash (f \vee g)$ whatever g may be. Thus by substituting in our formula 'I am paying my debt' for f and 'I am going for a walk' for g, we arrive at the statement that if it is obligatory that I pay my debt, then it is obligatory that I pay my debt or go for a walk. And such a statement might in many contexts seem pointless or even paradoxical. This impression may become even stronger if for g one substitutes 'I am doing my best to avoid paying my debt'. The substitution instances of $Of \rightarrow O(f \vee g)$ which tend to make an impression of paradoxicality are usually called Ross's paradoxes after Alf Ross who drew attention to them (see the bibliography of Føllesdal & Hilpinnen 1971).

The alleged deontic paradoxes can by means of the $M-W$ interpretation be translated into deductive statements, which may give a similar impression of pointlessness and paradoxicality. Indeed the deontic paradoxes are on this interpretation merely a species of the so-called paradoxes of deducibility (strict implication, entailment) which were widely discussed after C. I. Lewis proposed his systems of strict implication. In either case – the special deontic and the general deductive – the source of the paradoxical impression is the same, namely the occurrence in the offending statements of components which are inessential to their correctness. It will be best to show this first in the case of the alleged deductive paradoxes.†

Let us call any correct statement of form '(...⊢...)' or of form '*not* (...⊢...)' a deductive statement – more precisely an *L*-deductive statement – and any statement which occurs in it a component. This means that the antedecent and consequent of a deductive statement are components of it, as well as all statements which occur *explicitly* in the antecedent or the consequent. A statement which is merely implied by a component of a deductive statement, without explicitly occurring in it, is thus not a component of it. In accordance with custom, and for reasons of convenience, correct statements of form '⊢...' and '*not* (⊢...)' will be regarded as deductive statements (with empty antecedents).

A component of a correct deductive statement is essential to it if, and only if, the deductive statement which results from replacing the component by its negation is no longer correct. It is thus inessential if, and only if, the deductive statement which results from replacing the component by its negation is also correct. Deductive statements, all components of which are essential, will themselves be called essential. Otherwise they will be called inessential. Our definitions allow the possibility that an essential deductive statement be logically equivalent to an inessential one. A hackneyed example is the logical equivalence between the essential deductive statement ' John is a father ⊢ John is male' and the inessential deductive statement 'John is a parent and John is male ⊢ John is male' – where we assume that any father is by definition a male parent.

Let us, in order to exemplify these notions and the genesis of the alleged deductive paradoxes, consider a deductive system, say Euclidean geometry. Assume that $e_1, ..., e_n$ are its axioms and that all of them are necessary for the deduction of a theorem t_0, say

† For an early statement of this diagnosis see Körner (1955: chs. 8 and 12). For a formal treatment see Cleave (1973/4).

Pythagoras' theorem. Thus $e_1 \wedge \ldots \wedge e_n \vdash t_0$ is an essential deductive statement. According to the logical theory L, if $e_1 \wedge \ldots \wedge e_n \vdash t_0$ then for any statement f whatever $e_1 \wedge \ldots \wedge e_n \vdash t_0 \vee f$. But this metalogical implication allows us to assert inessential deductive statements which include the so-called paradoxes. To produce them, we might substitute for f the negation of any axiom, the negation of t_0, any statement which has nothing to do with geometry, etc.

Having diagnosed the source of the alleged 'Euclidean paradoxes', it is quite simple to render them innocuous without sacrificing a single correct Euclidean statement. All one has to do is to distinguish between those correct, deductive statements of Euclidean geometry which are appropriate for one's purpose and those which are not. The simplest definition of geometrical appropriateness, which suits our purpose, is also the most radical: it is to define a correct deductive statement of Euclidean geometry as geometrically appropriate if, and only if, it is essential. The least radical definition is accepted by most geometers. For they would regard every correct deductive statement as geometrically appropriate unless it contained an inessential non-geometrical component (e.g. the deductive statement that the axioms of Euclidean geometry logically imply the disjunction of Pythagoras' theorem and the statement that Pythagoras was a Greek). Between these two extreme definitions of geometrical appropriateness there lies a variety of other definitions in terms of inessential components of different types.

In turning to the special case of the deontic paradoxes it will again be best to give an example. Let $M = m_1 \wedge \ldots \wedge m_n$ be a system of maxims, say the rules of a bridge club, and j_0 a statement describing the payment, under certain circumstances, of a sum of money by one member of the club to another. We assume further that M is adequate to our world W and that all the rules of M are needed to justify Oj_0. On the $M-W$ interpretation of standard deontic logic this means that Oj_0 is logically equivalent to $D(M) \vdash j_0$ and – because all rules of M are necessary to justify that Oj_0 – that $D(M) \vdash j_0$ is an essential, deductive statement. In other words $D(M) \vdash j_0$ is precisely analogous to our Euclidean deductive statement $e_1 \wedge \ldots \wedge e_n \vdash t_0$. In particular, if $D(M) \vdash j_0$ then $D(M) \vdash j_0 \vee f$ or, in deontic formulation, $O(j_0 \vee f)$, whatever statement may be substituted for f.

The so-called deontic paradoxes are thus special cases of the so-called deductive paradoxes. Having diagnosed their source, it is quite simple to render them innocuous. For our purpose this is most simply done by defining a deontic statement (based on some system of maxims) as inappropriate if, and only if, it is inessential. Most lawyers would accept a less radical definition. They would regard as legally inappropriate the statement that the club rules M (or rather $D(M)$) logically imply '$j_0 \vee$ the debtor is going for a walk'. But they might not object to the statement that all the club rules M (or rather $D(M)$) logically imply j_0, even if one of them (or rather its descriptive counter-part) is an inessential component of the logical implication.

By adding to our general M–W interpretation of standard deontic logic the qualification that for a theorem to be appropriate – i.e. to express with appropriate precision what is and what is not obligatory – it must not contain inessential components, we arrive at what might be called the 'qualified M–W interpretation'. It is worth emphasizing that this interpretation no longer applies to deontic forms, and hence to all their substitution-instances, but only to deontic statements. Thus, although the form $O(f \vee {\,}_7 f)$ and hence all its substitution-instances are correct in accordance with the unqualified M–W interpretation, only some of its substitution-instances are appropriate in accordance with the qualified M–W interpretation. More particularly a statement $O(f_0 \vee {\,}_7 f_0)$ is appropriate in accordance with this interpretation if, and only if, neither Of_0 nor $O{\,}_7 f_0$ (neither $D(M) \vdash f_0$ nor $D(M) \vdash {\,}_7 f_0$) are correct. For if either Of_0 or $O{\,}_7 f_0$ is correct (if either $D(M) \vdash f_0$ or $D(M) \vdash {\,}_7 f_0$) then one of the disjuncts of $O(f_0 \vee {\,}_7 f_0)$ (one of the disjuncts of $D(M) \vdash f_0 \vee {\,}_7 f_0$) is inessential.

On the loss of adequacy of a system of maxims and its restoration

A system of maxims M which up to a certain time has been adequate to the actual world, as correctly described by W, may lose this adequacy when the world is no longer correctly described by W, but by a conjunction, say W' which is inconsistent with W. The loss of adequacy may consist (1) in a loss of applicability (schematically, for every antecedent f of $M - f \text{Cons } W$, but for at least one $- {\,}_7 (f \text{Cons } W')$). It may consist (2) in a loss of practicability (schematically, for every conjunction K of maxims in $M - {\,}_7 (F \text{Cons } W) \vee (G \text{Cons } F \wedge W)$, but for at least one $K - (F \text{Cons } W') \wedge {\,}_7 (G \text{Cons } F \wedge W')$). Lastly, the loss of adequacy may consist (3) in both a loss of applicability and of practicability. It may come about through acts of man or through 'acts of God', i.e. events not involving human action. But the distinction is not always clear. Again, if a system of maxims loses its adequacy through a person's action, the action may, but need not, involve a violation of his obligations.

In order to restore the lost adequacy of a system of maxims M to the world, as described by W, one must either modify M, or the world or both. Even in the simple cases where one maxim only has become inadequate, adequacy can be restored in a great variety of ways which, however, are not always equally available. One possible way of restoring the adequacy of $f \to g!$ is the restitution in the world of the *status quo*, another is the restriction of the maxim's addressees to those who have not yet contravened it, yet another is the replacement of f by f' (if $\lnot (f \operatorname{Cons} W)$ but $(f' \operatorname{Cons} W)$) or of $g!$ by $g'!$

$$(\text{if } f \operatorname{Cons} W \land \lnot (g \operatorname{Cons} f \land W) \quad \text{but} \quad (f \operatorname{Cons} W) \land (g' \operatorname{Cons} f \land W)$$

etc. If the inadequacy has arisen because some person has violated a maxim, the original maxim is sometimes replaced by a new maxim addressed to the same person. Thus a maxim of form $f \to g!$ may be replaced by $f \land \lnot g \underset{i}{\to} h$ and this in turn by $f \land \lnot g \land \lnot h \underset{i}{\to} k$. Instead of providing for such replacements by separate steps one may introduce more general rules, for example, rules which require a person who breaks maxims of a certain kind to pay damages or which declare him to be guilty of, and punishable for, a criminal offence.

Maxims for restoring the lost adequacy of a system of maxims M to a world W by such means as the restitution of the *status quo ante* in the world, by changing the range of addressees in one or more of its maxims, by changing their descriptive antedecents, regulative consequents or both or by incorporating the violation of one or more maxims of M into new maxims as their descriptive antecedents, may be appropriately called 'maxims of readjustment' or 'secondary maxims'. A system MM of such maxims may be called a 'system of readjustment' or 'secondary system'. A secondary maxim is like a primary maxim of the general form $f \underset{i}{\to} g!$. But whereas the descriptive antecedent of a maxim of M describes a situation in the world, as described by W, and whereas its regulative consequent requires of a person that by his action he bring about a situation in the world, the descriptive antecedent of a maxim of MM describes a relation between M and W (a specific or generic inadequacy of M to W) and its regulative consequent requires of a person that by his action he bring about a different relation between the world and the system of maxims (that he remove the inadequacy by modifying the world, the system of maxims or both).

In the legal systems of the Western world the general distinction between primary and secondary systems finds expression in the distinction between substantive law and much of the law governing the procedure of the civil and criminal courts, as well as a great deal of administrative law. There, and elsewhere, it may happen that the secondary system MM loses its adequacy for restoring the adequacy of M to W. To provide for this contingency it often happens that a tertiary system of maxims MMM is adopted which under certain circumstances prescribes – or explicitly permits – changes in MM, M or both. Usually the maxims of MMM provide not only for changes needed for the restoration of the adequacy of MM to the relations between M and W or of the adequacy of M to W. They often provide for changes of M or MM which may have become desirable for other reasons. In the legal systems of the Western world the rôle of MMM is played by constitutional law.

Just as M gives rise to primary obligations of form Of, or more explicitly $D(M) \vdash f$, so $D(MM)$ and $D(MMM)$ give rise to secondary and tertiary obligations of form Of or more explicitly of form $D(MM) \vdash f$ and $D(MMM) \vdash f$. In order to indicate the difference between primary, secondary and tertiary obligations more briefly, we might express them respectively by writing $O^1 f$ for primary, $O^2 f$ for secondary, and $O^3 f$ for tertiary obligations. A secondary obligation $O^2 f$, or $D(MM) \vdash f$, is an obligation based on the secondary system of maxims MM. It is an obligation to adjust the relations between M and W and must *not* be confused with the iterated obligation $O^1 O^1 f$, which 'intuitively' means that it is obligatory that it is obligatory that f and which, in accordance with the $M-W$ interpretation, yields the ill-formed expression $D(M) \vdash (D(M) \vdash f)$. The standard deontic logic does not allow iterated obligations. From the point of view of the $M-W$ interpretation this is perfectly in order, especially as the complex relationships between MM, M, and W concerning the loss and restoration of adequacy of M to W are unlikely to find expression in the simple repetition of operators. Similar remarks apply with even greater force to tertiary obligations $O^3 f$, or, more explicitly,

$$D(MMM) \vdash f$$

which must not be confused with $O^1 O^1 O^1 f$.

CHAPTER 3

ON THE FORMAL STRUCTURE OF PROBABILISTIC THINKING

A practical thinker's interest in the future is not limited to what he believes to be factually or constructively true in it. He is also concerned with what will probably be the case and with what he can probably bring about. The purpose of this chapter is to exhibit the formal principles which govern the use of various concepts of probability and to distinguish them from each other. None of these concepts can be said – obviously or demonstrably – to represent *the* commonsense concept of probability. Yet whether this is so because there is no one such concept (as I am inclined to believe) or because the pluralistic analysis is merely a crude approximation to it, need not be decided here since the subsequent inquiry is compatible with either assumption. The chapter begins with an exposition of the measure-theoretical concept of probability of which the logical, empirical and personalist concepts can be regarded as more specific versions. In the remainder of the chapter each of them is briefly explained and examined. While their explanation is based on standard accounts it differs from them in replacing their monistic approach by a tolerant pluralism.

On the formal, measure-theoretical principles of probabilistic thinking

Let us assume that a person S who believes that his position is correctly described by a possibility tree from whose origin, associated with a finite set O_0 of atomic statements describing his present position, there issue, say, four branches ending in four nodes associated with four sets $O_1, ..., O_4$ of atomic statements. The sets are, moreover, assumed to be mutually exclusive and jointly exhaustive of the possibilities which S can expect or bring about as succeeding O_0. If he is interested merely in the factual or constructive truths which are enshrined in the tree, the logical systems L_0 and I_0 provide him with all the inferential apparatus he needs. If he is interested in what he can expect or bring about with some probability, he must enlarge L_0 or I_0 by further principles, For our purpose it will be sufficient to enlarge L_0 since the analogous enlargement of I_0 leads to no difficulties of a philosophical kind. In explaining the measure-theoretical aspects of (finite) probabilistic thinking it will be convenient to adopt an approach and terminology which do not favour any particular conception of probability. (We follow the exposition given by Kemeny, Schleifer, Snell & Thomson 1965.)

Let us call the set $U = \{O_1, O_2, O_3, O_4\}$ the universal set and its members $O_1, ..., O_4$ the possibility-sets of our example. More generally, a set U is a universal set and its members $O_1, ..., O_n$ are possibility-sets with respect to a particular situation in which a practical thinker believes himself to be if, and only if, he regards each set as representing a realizable possibility; any two sets as representing mutually exclusive alternatives; and all sets as jointly exhaustive of what he regards as realizable (by his efforts, independently of his efforts or both). The universal set of our example contains four possibility-sets and thus, if we count the empty set and the universal set as subsets, 2^4 subsets $B_1, ..., B_{16}$ among which there are, for example $\{O_1, O_2\}$ and $\{O_1, O_3, O_4\}$.

By defining the notion of the 'truth-set of a statement', one establishes a one–one correspondence between statements and the subsets of U: A subset B of U is a truth-set of a statement b if, and only if, B contains all the possibility-sets which, if realized, would make b true. For example, if b is a disjunction $f \vee g$ of two atomic statements, then its truth-set is that subset B of U which contains all the possibility-sets having either f or g as a member. If B is the truth-set of b, and C the truth-set of c, then the truth-sets of $b \vee c$ and $b \wedge c$ are respectively the union $B \cup C$ and the intersection $B \cap C$ of the truth-sets of b and c. A similar one–one relation holds between all compound and quantified statements of L_0 on the one hand, and corresponding expressions of set theory. Because to every statement b there corresponds one and only one truth-set B, it makes no difference whether we first define the probability of B and in terms of this probability the probability of b or whether we reverse the order of definition.

In looking for a method of comparing the various sets B with respect to their probability, one is looking for a numerical measure satisfying certain obvious requirements. What we desire is a numerical measure $m(B)$ of every subset B of U such that the measure of B be zero, if, and only if, B is the empty subset of U; that it be the highest possible measure if, and only if, B is the universal set U; that in all other cases the numerical value of $m(B)$, lie between 0, i.e. the value of the empty set, and the value of the universal set, which conventionally is 1; and that the measure be additive, i.e. that the measure of the union of two mutually exclusive subsets of U be the sum of their separate measures. These desiderata, which are also the axioms of finite probability theory, with L_0 as its underlying logic, can be expressed more concisely as follows:

(1) $m(B) = 0$ iff B is the empty set;

(2) $0 \leqslant m(B) \leqslant 1$;

(3) $m(B \cup C) = m(B) + m(C)$ iff B and C are mutually exclusive subsets of U.

If we define the 'probability' of a statement b, briefly $\text{Pr}\,(b)$, as the measure $m(b)$ of its truth-set, then we arrive at the following axioms:

$(1a)$ $\text{Pr}\,(b) = 0$ iff $m(B) = 0$;

$(2a)$ $0 \leqslant \text{Pr}\,(b) \leqslant 1$;

$(3a)$ $\text{Pr}\,(b \vee c) = \text{Pr}\,(b) + \text{Pr}\,(c)$ iff b and c are incompatible. The form of the axioms and much of their content remain unchanged, if we allow the set U to be infinite and replace L_0 by L.

The measure-theoretical axioms (1)–(3) govern not only the use of various concepts of probability, but also that of other concepts, for example that of a proportion of distinct things, in a certain collection of things and its subcollections. Thus if U is a collection of, say, n apples, if s_j is the number of sour apples in a subcollection B_j of U, and if $m(B_j)$ is defined as s_j/n, $m(B_j)$ clearly satisfies (1)–(3). While in measuring proportions the assignment of numerical values to $m(B)$ is unproblematic, this is not so in measuring probabilities. There the methodological problem of adequate measurement is rooted in the analytical problem of determining what it is that is to be measured.

Empirical versus logical possibilities and probabilities

The possibility-sets of our example were conceived as empirical possibility-sets representing possibilities, and their universal set $U = \{O_1, O_2, O_3, O_4\}$ was conceived as an empirically universal set exhausting what is empirically possible. From the formal point of view the possibility sets and the universal set might have also been conceived as representing and exhausting what is logically possible or what is both logically and empirically possible. According to whether probability judgments are construed as attaching weights to mutually exclusive and jointly exhaustive empirical possibilities (irrespective of their coincidence or otherwise with mutually exclusive and jointly exhaustive logical possibilities) or as attaching weights to mutually exclusive and jointly exhaustive logical possibilities (irrespective of their coincidence or otherwise with mutually exclusive and jointly exhaustive empirical possibilities), one distinguishes between the empirical and the logical conception, theory or doctrine of probability. Yet, if one considers these conceptions and theories in their elaborated versions one may well be tempted to argue that their names are misnomers.

Because of the correspondence between statements and truth-sets it will be sufficient to define the notions of logical and empirical possibilities in terms of statements. A possibility is logical if, and only if, it is described by a statement the negation of which is not valid. Schematically, a statement f describes a logical possibility with respect to L_0 if, and only if, $\neg (\vdash \neg f)$. The notion of an empirical possibility is defined not only with respect to a certain logic, say L_0, but also with respect to a body of empirical beliefs about the course of nature which the person asserting the empirical possibility holds to be true. A statement f describes an empirical possibility with respect to L_0 and a body of empirical beliefs E if, and only if, f is true or, at least, E and f are logically consistent, i.e. schematically if $f \vee \neg (E \vdash \neg f)$. Clearly, if f is empirically possible, it is also logically possible while the converse is not true. It should also be noted that the notion of empirical possibility is formally identical with the notion of ontological possibility. The difference lies in the nature of the constraining principles (see chapter 2).

By itself the distinction between empirical and logical possibilities does not suggest a probabilistic comparison between possibilities of either kind. Suggestions arise from specific and theoretically loaded examples of which the example of throwing dice is both the oldest and the best known. Let us, therefore, consider the set $U = \{O_1, ..., O_6\}$, with $O_1, ..., O_6$ respectively representing the logical and empirical possibilities of a $1, ..., 6$ being thrown. The mutually exclusive and jointly exhaustive logical possibilities do not imply anything about their measure over and above what is implied by the measure-theoretical axioms. We may, of course, assume that

$$m(O_1) = m(O_2) = ... = m(O_6) = 1/6,$$

and thus that the measures of all the 2^6 subsets of U are determined, but the ground for this assumption is – unlike the ground for discerning between six mutually exclusive and jointly exhaustive possibilities – neither a logical principle nor a logical operation. That this and similar equiprobability assumptions constitute useful or even indispensable standards of comparison makes neither the assumptions, nor their justification, nor the theory of which they form a part 'logical' in any usual sense of the word.

According to the empirical, objective or frequency theories the evidence for assigning the same or different numbers to the elements of U and hence to its subsets, is based on the empirical evidence of long-run frequencies. The difficulty here lies in the notion of a long-run frequency which in the dominant empirical theories is analysed in terms of the limit of a sequence (or series) of frequencies. Thus the judgment that, say, $m(O_5) = 1/6$ is construed as the statement to the effect that $\lim_{n \to \infty} f_n(O_5) = 1/6$, where $f_n(O_5)$ is the frequency of throwing a 6 in n throws of the dice. It has often been pointed out that statements about what happens in the infinitely long run or in an infinite population are not empirical statements and that, in particular, any finite sequence (or series) $f_1, ..., f_n$ can be so continued into infinity that $\lim_{n \to \infty} f_n$ equals any number between, and including, 0 and 1 one cares to choose. These criticisms against the frequentist version of the empirical or objective conception of probability do not, and are not meant to, imply that nature may not be governed by ultimate probabilistic laws and characterized by objective probabilities, e.g. of the quantum-theoretical sort. (For a more detailed discussion of the logical and frequentist theories see Körner 1966: ch. 9.)

Two conceptions of subjective probability

A person's statement that $m(O_5) = 1/6$ may mean (a) that a certain quantity associated with the die (or with other mind-independent features of the world), namely the objective probability that O_5 will be realized, equals 1/6; (b) that a certain quantity associated with the person's beliefs, namely his confidence or the subjective probability that O_5 will be realized, equals 1/6; (c) that both, the objective and the subjective probability equal 1/6. The objective and the subjective probability statement are logically independent, so that the truth of the subjective statement is compatible with the falsehood of the objective one and vice versa.

We shall, therefore, have to distinguish between two different notions of subjective probability: a non-exclusive notion which implies that subjective probability is a quantity associated with a person's belief and which is compatible with the applicability of a notion of objective probability in a logical, frequency or some other sense of the term; and an exclusive notion which implies that subjective probability is a quantity associated with a person's belief and that any other notion of probability is either reducible to subjective probability or else is confused or, at least, empty. It will be convenient to reserve the name 'subjective probability' for the non-exclusive, and the name 'personal probability' for the exclusive notion. The latter use conforms to that of Savage who is one of the modern founders of the personalist theory. (For a history of the theory see Kyburg & Smokler 1964.) From our present formal point of view there are no differences between the two conceptions each of which satisfies the measure-theoretical axioms.

The measurement of subjective probability as based on fair betting

Ramsey, de Finetti, and Savage have independently of each other proved the remarkable theorem that if a certain principle of fair betting is used to express the different degrees of confidence which a person attaches to the subsets of a universal set $U = \{O_1, ..., O_n\}$ then the so-expressed degrees of confidence satisfy the measure-theoretical axioms (1)–(3). The discoverers of the theorem, and the adherents of a personalist theory in general, regard the principle as an indispensable principle of practical coherence, rationality or consistency and have named it accordingly. Yet even if the applicability of the principle, henceforth to be called de Finetti's principle, should turn out to be restricted to special contexts it is worth some attention. (For a clear exposition of the principle and a proof of the theorem see e.g. Kemeny 1955.)

There are certain universal sets $U = \{O_1, ..., O_n\}$ on the realization of whose subsets a practical thinker can imagine himself to be betting different sums of money which, so he sincerely believes, correspond to the different degrees of his confidence in their realization. He may, in particular, be able to associate with every subset B of U a stake σ and a betting quotient q $(0 \leqslant q \leqslant 1)$, imagining himself to pay a sum $q.\sigma$ if B is *not* realized and to receive a sum $(1-q).\sigma$ if B is realized. In the language of the racecourse his odds are $q:(1-q)$. A set of bets associated with a set U is 'fair' if it does not guarantee a profit for the bettor and 'unfair' if it does. Thus a bettor who associates a stake of £100 and a betting quotient 1/2 with U is betting unfairly because he is sure to receive £50. Again a bettor who associates a stake of £99 and a betting quotient 1/3 with O_1 and also the same stake of £99 and the same betting quotient 1/3 with the complement of O_1 (i.e. the set $O_2 \cup O_3 \cup ... \cup O_n$) is betting unfairly because he is sure to pay £33 and to receive £66, i.e. to make a net gain of £33.

After these terminological preliminaries de Finetti's principle and theorem may be stated in a rather cautious version. Let us say that a person's assignment of stakes and betting quotients to the subsets B_j of a universal set $U = \{O_1, ..., O_n\}$ satisfies de Finetti's principle and let us call the assignment a de Finetti assignment if, and only if, (1) it assigns a stake and a betting quotient to every B; (2) the assignment is fair (i.e. does not guarantee a profit to the person making it); and (3) the person sincerely believes that he would bet in accordance with the assignment, if he wanted to prove the sincerity of his assignment and could do so only by an actual bet. The theorem asserts that if an assignment is a de Finetti assignment, then its betting quotients satisfy the calculus of probability and measure the degrees of confidence attached to the subsets by locating them on a linear interval scale. If de Finetti's principle is satisfied, then de Finetti's theorem allows us to construct a subjective probability-meter (on the analogy of a thermometer measuring absolute temperature, i.e. a scale of temperature containing an absolute zero).

The third clause of de Finetti's principle is essential to its applicability and at the same time restricts it very seriously – a fact which the proponents of the personalist conception of probability tend to overlook. For one simply may not be capable of a sincere de Finetti assignment because the seriousness of the alternative possibilities, for example the life or death of a beloved person, would make any betting on them appear reprehensible; because the triviality of the alternatives would appear incommensurable with the effort involved in the assignment and thus prevent it; because in some cases the effort involved in the assignment would be too great compared with its result; because the intellectual effort would surpass the person's powers; because his aversion to betting is insuperable; or for other reasons.

Again, some people might find it natural to estimate their subjective probabilities in terms of prizes and risks and yet be repelled by money stakes. By combining the analysis of subjective probability with an analysis of utility one can overcome this particular obstacle and replace monetary by non-monetary stakes. This refinement of de Finetti's principle is relevant to the understanding of prudent conduct and will have to be discussed (see chapter 4). Yet the refined principle with its refined third clause is subject to similar objections as the original principle with its original third clause referring to monetary stakes.

A standard calibration of subjective probabilities

Let us say that two universal sets

$$U = \{O_1, ..., O_n\} \quad \text{and} \quad U' = \{O_1', ..., O_n'\}$$

are de Finetti equivalent or, briefly, equivalent for a person if, and only if, they have the same number of possibility sets and, hence, of subsets and if the same stakes and betting quotients are associated with corresponding subsets. Each universal set belonging to a class of universal sets can thus represent all the others. It is often convenient to use ideal universal sets as representatives and to have a uniform method at hand for constructing them. Perhaps the most convenient method of this kind consists in constructing, or rather imagining, an (ideal) 'standard urn' giving rise to 'standard draws' with 'standard probabilities'. (For a clear and elementary exposition of this and related topics see Schlaifer 1969.)

A standard urn is an imaginary urn containing a certain number of balls, say, 1,000 balls numbered from '1' to '1,000', such that the person imagining it would associate the same stake σ and the same net betting quotient $q = 1/1,000$ with the drawing of any one of the 1,000 balls. This is not simply a roundabout way of saying that he regards the drawings as equiprobable, but implies that the probabilities which he regards as equal are to be understood as subjective and as subject to de Finetti's principle. A standard urn is further imagined to be a universal set $U = \{O_1', ..., O_n'\}$ in which every possibility set O_j' contains N_j balls of a distinct kind (say of distinct colour), such that the sum of these balls adds up to a thousand. It follows that the standard probability q_j associated with a possibility set O_j' equals $N_j/1,000$.

It is now easily seen how any de Finetti assignment of stakes and betting quotients and thus of subjective probabilities to a universal set $U = \{O_1, ..., O_n\}$ can be represented by a standard urn

$$U' = \{O_1', ..., O_n'\}.$$

We first imagine each possibility set S_j to correspond to one set of N_j distinct balls such that $q_j' = q_j = N_j/1{,}000$. In order that the two betting quotients q_j and q_j' be equal we must adjust the number N_j of the balls in O_j and, consequently, in the other sets of the standard urn. If, for example, the universal set to be represented by a standard urn contains 10 possibility sets we may start by considering a standard urn containing 10 sets of differently coloured balls, each containing the same number, i.e. 100 balls, corresponding to the probability $100/1{,}000 = 1/10$.

If O_1 seems more probable than $O_2, \ldots, O_n$, we must increase the number of coloured balls in O_1' and reduce the number of coloured balls in the other sets, until we feel no further need for adjustment. Quite frequently we are able to represent our possibility sets only approximately, i.e. not by fractions of form $N_j/1{,}000$, but by intervals of form $N_j \pm k/1{,}000$ (with k being an integer).

Since a standard urn has been defined as satisfying the requirement of fair betting and, therefore, de Finetti's principle the proportions $N_j/1{,}000$ are *ipso facto* subjective probabilities. We could have started our exposition of subjective probability by defining first the notion of a standard urn, secondly the notion of equivalence between a standard urn and a universal set and, lastly, the notion of a de Finetti assignment to a universal set in terms of the notions of a standard urn and of its equivalence to universal sets. (This is the approach of Schlaifer 1969.)

On the interpersonal aspects of subjective probability

A person's subjective probability judgments in terms of betting stakes and betting quotients express his personal confidence in the realization of the subsets B_j of a universal set $U = \{O_1, \ldots, O_n\}$. What prevents these judgments from becoming wildly idiosyncratic and keeps them in line with the judgments of others is his explicit or implicit acceptance of de Finetti's principle, which it is assumed, is accepted by all those who make probability judgments, and has been made part of the definition of probability. It is also, more generally, the similarity between people and their reaction to similar experiences.

However uncommon a person's tastes and attitudes to possible courses of nature and action, he must (if he is not to be guilty of logical inconsistency) select his probability – assignment to the subsets of U from the class of assignments which satisfy de Finetti's principle and, hence, the calculus of probability. The postulates of this calculus determine, among other things, how he must (if he is not to be guilty of logical inconsistency) correct his probability judgments in the light of subsequent experiences; and how, consequently, the disagreement between the probability judgments of different people diminishes in the light of subsequent common experiences. The correction of a person's probability assignment in the light of fresh experience can be explained by comparing his original probability assignment $m(B_j)$ with his conditional probability assignment $m(B_j/C)$, i.e. his assignment of a probability to B_j *given the realization of* C (where C is one of the subsets of U).

Since according to the calculus of probability

$$m(B_j/C) = m(B_j \cap C)/m(C)$$

(i.e. since the probability of B_j given C equals the probability of the set consisting of the members common to B_j and C, divided by the probability of C – assuming of course that $m(C) \neq 0$) the correction of the original assignment consists in replacing (1) every subset B_j of U by $(B_j \cap C)$ and (2) the probability $m(B_j)$ by the probability $m(B_j \cap C)/m(C)$. These two replacements represent the manner in which a person who conforms to the calculus of probability 'learns from experience'.

In order to show how as a result of such personal corrections interpersonal disagreement can be, and often is, reduced we consider the case of two persons, say, S and Q who make two widely different probability assignments to the subsets B_j of the same universal set $U = \{O_1, ..., O_n\}$, with the exception that they assign the same (or nearly the same) probabilities to subsets of a set C representing a possibility which is later realized. We assume, in other words, that S's original probability judgments are $m(B_j)$; that Q's original probability judgments are $\mu(B_j)$; that $m(B_j)$ and $\mu(B_j)$ differ widely except in C, where $m(C \cap B_j) = \mu(C \cap B_j)$ (or where the difference between them is comparatively small). We assume further that in view of the realization of C, S's corrected probability judgments are

$$m(B_j/C) = m(B_j \cap C)/m(C)$$

and Q's corrected probability judgments are

$$\mu(B_j/C) = \mu(B_j \cap C)/\mu(C).$$

Because the corrections made by S and Q involve in both cases (1) the replacement of every possibility set B_j by the set $(B_j \cap C)$ and (2) the division of the initial probabilities $m(B_j \cap C)$ and $\mu(B_j \cap C)$ by the same fraction $m(C) = \mu(C)$, it is clear that the difference between the new probabilities $m(B_j/C)$ and $\mu(B_j/C)$ is zero or much smaller than the difference between the original probabilities $m(B_j)$ and $\mu(B_j)$.

It is not difficult to point to other principles which, though neither postulates nor theorems of the calculus of probability, are yet commonly accepted and tend, therefore, to reduce interpersonal disagreement about the assessment of probabilities. One such principle of reasonable behaviour can be formulated as follows (see Schlaifer 1969: p. 207): 'If a person assessing the probability of a given event on one trial under a given set of conditions feels virtually sure that the event would occur with *relative frequency p* in a very great number of trials made under conditions indistinguishable from the given conditions, he will assign *probability p* to the event on the one trial in which he is interested.' It is worth noting that this principle – unlike the principle for replacing prior by conditional probabilities – is not a corrective principle which tends to reduce initial disagreements; but that its effect is to restrict the range of interpersonal disagreement from the very start.

On the logical status of the intersubjective principles of probabilistic thinking

The statement that a reasonable person will – in the situations in which he can sincerely imagine himself to be betting on alternative outcomes – conform to de Finetti's principle (or some other principle of probabilistic reasoning) may be understood in a number of different ways, which it is important to distinguish. It may in particular be understood (1) as a definition to the effect that 'being a reasonable person' implies 'conforming to the principle in the specified circumstances'; (2) as a normative principle to the effect that every reasonable person ought to accept the principle for the specified circumstances; (3) as an empirical proposition that as a matter of empirical fact all reasonable persons conform to the principle in the specified circumstances; (4) as a conjunction of (*a*) an empirical proposition to the effect that as a matter of empirical fact many people accept the principle as a standard of judgment and conduct in the specified circumstances, i.e. have the intention of conforming to it whether or not they succeed in doing so; and of (*b*) a definition to the effect that a person will be called 'reasonable' only if he accepts the principle as a standard of judgment and conduct for the specified circumstances and that, similarly, the person's conduct will be called 'reasonable' only if, and in so far as in these circumstances, it conforms to this standard.

The distinction between the third and the fourth sense of 'conforming to de Finetti's principle' is a special case of a more general distinction between two types of statements both of which are empirical. These are statements to the effect that during a certain period of time a person behaved in a certain manner, whatever the standard he intended to satisfy; and equally empirical statements to the effect that during a certain period of time he intended to satisfy a certain standard, whatever the manner in which he actually behaved during that period. A person's behaviour is, of course, evidence for his acceptance of a standard, i.e. his intention to satisfy it. But it is often extremely difficult to establish whether a person has accepted a strict standard which he has violated by his conduct or a less strict standard which he has satisfied by behaving as he did. In this essay the sense in which reasonable persons are said to conform to de Finetti's principle is that explained under (4).

Since even the law of excluded middle and other principles of logic are not accepted by all reasonable persons (except when reasonableness is defined by their acceptance), is it not surprising that some people reject de Finetti's principle in favour of a principle that is stronger while others reject it in favour of a weaker principle. A strengthening of de Finetti's principle consists in demanding that any assignment of betting quotients to the subsets B_j of a universal set $U = \{O_1 ..., O_n\}$ be not only 'fair' by not guaranteeing a profit to the bettor, but that it be 'strictly fair' by neither guaranteeing the absence of a loss nor the possibility of a profit to him. (For details see Kemeny 1955.)

A weakening of de Finetti's principle has been advocated by the economist W. Fellner. It implies, among other things, the abandonment of the theorem that the sum of the probabilities of a set of mutually exclusive and jointly exhaustive subsets of U equal 1; and a consequential modification of the postulates of probability theory. Yet these and other modifications do not affect the broad understanding of subjective probability as employed in many contexts of practical, especially prudential, thinking.

CHAPTER 4

ON THE FORMAL STRUCTURE
OF THINKING ABOUT PRACTICAL
PREFERENCES

A person's concern with practicabilities, whether certain or merely probable, involves him in comparing them with respect to their preferability. The purpose of this chapter is to discuss some formal aspects of such comparisons, namely the ordering, grading and measurement of preferences. The chapter begins by explaining the notion of weak preference and some notions definable in terms of it, as well as certain concepts belonging to the logic of relations and needed in characterizing various types of preferential ordering. Next, some types of preferential ordering are explained. In doing so the difference between inexact empirical preferences and their idealization by exact mathematical ones is briefly considered. There follows an explanation of grading, especially of the division of practical preferences into pro-attitudes, anti-attitudes and attitudes of indifference – a division which will be constantly used in the subsequent analyses. The chapter ends with a discussion of the measurement of preferences and its limitations.

On the notion of preference and other notions
applied in the ordering of preferences

A practical thinker who has asked himself, and answered, questions as to which mutually exclusive and jointly exhaustive practicabilities he can bring about with certainty or with some probability, will often be interested in establishing an order of preference among them. Since the number of these practicabilities is finite and since each of them is describable by a finite number of atomic statements, the logic underlying his comparisons will be finite. If all the concepts used in the comparisons are exact we may assume the logic to be L_0 or I_0; if some are inexact, L_0^* or I_0^*.

As is usual and convenient, the relation of practical preference-or-indifference (also called 'weak preference') will be taken as fundamental. It is expressed rather clumsily by 'The person S_i prefers the practical possibility described by the proposition f to the practical possibility described by the proposition g or else is indifferent between these practical possibilities', and symbolized concisely by 'fR_ig'. In these expressions the variables f and g range over propositions. The strict practical preference of a person S_i for the practical possibility described by f over the practical possibility described by g, briefly 'fP_ig' is defined by 'fR_ig and $\neg(gR_if)$'. His practical indifference between the two practical possibilities, briefly 'fI_ig', is defined by 'fR_ig and gR_if'. It is conceivable that neither fR_ig nor gR_if, i.e. that the person S_i is unable to compare the two practical possibilities. A person's inability to compare two practical possibilities must not be confused with his indifference between them. When it is clear from the context, the qualification 'practical' will frequently be omitted in referring to a person's practical preference-or-indifference, his practical preference or his practical indifference. For similar reasons one may speak of these relations as holding between propositions rather than between practical possibilities described by propositions.

Our definitions admit the possibility that different sets of ordering principles are accepted by different people or in different circumstances. Orders of preference are species of abstract types of order. The latter have been studied by mathematicians, the former by mathematically minded social scientists. As is the case with other concepts, the mathematization of the commonsense concept of preference involves clarification at the price of modification. And, as is the case with other concepts, a comparison of the commonsense concept with its modified theoretical versions sheds light on both of them. (For an excellent survey of modern theories of individual and social preference, see Sen 1970.)

Any type of order involves a set (or aggregate) of entities, say, A and a binary or two-place relation, say, ρ, by which the set is ordered. It is often enough to characterize the ordering relation and to take the ordered set for granted. Yet in many cases it is indispensable to specify both the ordering relation and the ordered set since the same ordering relation may establish different types of order in different sets. The relation 'taller than' establishes a different order among a class of men, than among a class consisting of men and ideas.

Before defining various types of order, it is advisable to define those attributes of binary relations which will be used in the definitions. *Reflexivity* (briefly $\mathfrak{R}$): A relation ρ is reflexive in A if, and only if, for every element x of $A - xpx$. *Transitivity* (briefly $\mathfrak{T}$): A relation ρ is transitive in A if, and only if, for any three elements x, y, z of $S - xpy$ and ypz together imply xpz. *Symmetry* (briefly $\mathfrak{S}$): A relation ρ is symmetric in A if, and only if, for any two elements x, y of $A - xpy$ implies ypx. *Asymmetry* (briefly $\mathfrak{As}$): A relation ρ is asymmetric in A if, and only if, for any two elements x, y of $A - xpy$ implies $\neg(ypx)$. *Antisymmetry* (briefly $\mathfrak{An}$): A relation ρ is antisymmetric in A if, and only if, for any two elements x, y of $A - xpy$ and ypx imply $x = y$ (or equivalently if, and only if, for any two elements of $A - x \neq y$ implies either $\neg(xpy)$ or $\neg(ypx)$). *Completeness* (briefly $\mathfrak{C}$): A relation ρ is complete in A if, and only if, for any two elements x, y of $A - xpy$ or ypx.

Each of the types of order which are of interest to us is characterized by a relation ρ which, within a set A, possesses a consistent combination of two or more attributes from among $\mathfrak{R}$, $\mathfrak{T}$, $\mathfrak{S}$, $\mathfrak{As}$, $\mathfrak{An}$, $\mathfrak{C}$. There is no generally agreed nomenclature for the different types of order and the same name is often given to different types. (A useful comparative dictionary of these names is found in Sen 1970.) One is, therefore, tempted to forgo any special naming and to speak simply of, say an $\mathfrak{R}$–$\mathfrak{T}$–$\mathfrak{C}$ ordering rather than a weak ordering, as such an ordering is sometimes, but not always, called. Yielding to this temptation would, however, merely increase the number of names. I shall, therefore, select one of the current names for each type of order – without claiming any special merit for the choice.

Some types of preferential ordering

The types of ordering which are most frequently employed by social scientists and which will serve as our principal examples of preferential ordering in the later discussions are the $\mathfrak{R}$–$\mathfrak{T}$–$\mathfrak{C}$ ordering, or *weak ordering*, and the $\mathfrak{As}$–$\mathfrak{T}$–$\mathfrak{C}$ ordering, or *strict ordering*. If the set A of objects to be ordered consists of athletic performances, if the ordering relation ρ is 'physically at least as exhausting as', and if we assume that any two from a finite set of performances are comparable with respect to this relation, then the set as ordered by the relation, briefly $\langle A, \rho \rangle$ satisfies the conditions $\mathfrak{R}$, $\mathfrak{T}$ and $\mathfrak{C}$. If we assume that not all members of A are comparable with respect to 'at least as exhausting as' (perhaps, because we replace 'physical' by 'physical or mental' exhaustion), then our ordering is an $\mathfrak{R}$–$\mathfrak{T}$ ordering, or a *quasi ordering*. By itself the relation 'at least as exhausting as' does not establish any *preferential* order. But for anybody who prefers being less to being more exhausted $\langle A, \rho \rangle$ is a preferential ordering.

We next exemplify the $\mathfrak{A}\mathfrak{s}$–$\mathfrak{T}$–$\mathfrak{C}$ ordering. If the set A of objects to be ordered consists again of athletic performances, if the ordering relation is 'more exhausting than', and if we assume that any two of the performances are comparable with respect to *this* relation (i.e. no two performances are equally exhausting), than the set ordered by the relation, briefly $\langle A, \rho \rangle$, satisfies the conditions $\mathfrak{A}\mathfrak{s}$, $\mathfrak{T}$ and $\mathfrak{C}$. If $\mathfrak{C}$ is not satisfied, then our ordering is merely an $\mathfrak{A}\mathfrak{s}$–$\mathfrak{T}$ ordering, or a *strict, partial ordering*.

Lastly, we consider the $\mathfrak{R}$–$\mathfrak{A}\mathfrak{n}$–$\mathfrak{T}$–$\mathfrak{C}$ type of ordering, or *linear ordering*. It differs from the $\mathfrak{R}$–$\mathfrak{T}$–$\mathfrak{C}$, or weak, ordering by the additional requirement $\mathfrak{A}\mathfrak{n}$, i.e. antisymmetry. If in our example of an $\mathfrak{R}$–$\mathfrak{T}$–$\mathfrak{C}$ order each of two performances is at least as exhausting as the other, then the performances are equally exhausting. But they are not, as required by $\mathfrak{A}\mathfrak{n}$, identical, i.e. the same performance. To give an example of linear ordering we consider the relation which holds between athletic performances when, of any two, one (wholly or partly) includes another. Clearly if of two performances either includes the other, they are not only in one or more respects equal, but are identical, i.e. the same performance. If we extend the set so as to embrace performances which are mutually exclusive the completeness requirement $\mathfrak{C}$ is no longer satisfied. The $\mathfrak{R}$–$\mathfrak{A}\mathfrak{n}$–$\mathfrak{T}$ ordering is usually called *partial ordering*. (It is particularly important in Boolean algebra and lattice theory, where the ordering relation is class-inclusion.) An athletic performance which (wholly or partly) includes another, is not, therefore, at least as highly valued as the performance which it includes. However, in the case of sets of performances where inclusion and preference are so correlated, the relation of inclusion determines a (linear or partial) preferential order.

In establishing an order of preference among his options a practical thinker's aim is frequently the determination of some kind of maximum or optimum. These notions can – like the various types of ordering – be defined in a purely formal manner, i.e. independently of the nature of the objects ordered or of any non-formal characteristics (any characteristics other than $\mathfrak{R}$, $\mathfrak{T}$, $\mathfrak{S}$, $\mathfrak{A}\mathfrak{s}$, $\mathfrak{A}\mathfrak{n}$, $\mathfrak{C}$) of the ordering relation. An element x of an ordering $\langle A, \rho \rangle$ is a maximal element if, and only if, for no element y of $A - y\rho x$. If the ordering relation is R, i.e. weak preference (preference-or-indifference) then x is a maximal element of $\langle A, \rho \rangle$ if, and only if, for no element y of $A - y$ is weakly preferred to x. An ordering $\langle A, \rho \rangle$ need not have a maximal element – e.g. if the order is cyclical. If A is infinite – a possibility which we have excluded by assuming that our underlying logic is L_0 or I_0 – and ρ is complete then there need be no maximal element in $\langle A, \rho \rangle$. Again $\langle A, \rho \rangle$ may have more than one maximal element, e.g. if A is partially ordered by ρ (if ρ satisfies the requirements $\mathfrak{R}$, $\mathfrak{An}$ and $\mathfrak{T}$).

An element x of an ordering $\langle A, \rho \rangle$ is an optimal element if, and only if, for every element y of $A - x\rho y$. If the ordering relation is R, i.e. weak preference (preference-or-indifference) then x is an optimal element of $\langle A, \rho \rangle$ if, and only if, for every element y of $x - x$ is weakly preferred to y. An optimal element is by definition a maximal element, but a maximal element need not be an optimal element. Thus a maximal element of a (finite) partial ordering need not be optimal. An ordered set, for example a weakly ordered set, may have more than one optimal element. The set of optimal elements of an ordering $\langle A, \rho \rangle$ has been called 'the choice set' of the ordering by Arrow (1951) and is symbolized by $C(A, \rho)$. In terms of this concept the economically useful and logically interesting concept of a choice function can be defined.

$C(A, \rho)$ is a choice function over A if, and only if, for every subset α of A, $C(\alpha, \rho)$ is not empty. In other words, if and only if, every set α which is included in A and ordered by ρ has at least one optimal element. It is obvious that a choice function exists for any ordered set $\langle A, R \rangle$, i.e. any $\mathfrak{R}$–$\mathfrak{T}$–$\mathfrak{C}$ or weak ordering of a set by the relation R of preference-or-indifference or weak preference (as opposed to strong preference P). It is also clear that R must be reflexive and complete in A if every subset of S is to have an optimal element. However, $\mathfrak{T}$ is not a necessary condition and can be replaced, as Sen (1970) has shown, by the weaker condition of acyclicity, briefly $\mathfrak{Ac}$. The relation R of preference-or-indifference (which holds between x and y if, and only if, xPy or xIy) is acyclical if, and only if, for any elements $x_1, ..., x_n$ of $A - x_1 P x_2, x_2 P x_3, ...,$ and $x_{n-1} P x_n$ together imply $x_1 R x_n$ (i.e. $x_1 P x_n$ or $x_1 I x_n$). Sen has moreover shown that the necessary and jointly sufficient conditions for a choice function of $\langle A, R \rangle$ to exist are $\mathfrak{R}$, $\mathfrak{Ac}$ and $\mathfrak{T}$, i.e. that R be reflexive, acyclical and complete in A.

This property of choice functions has some bearing on the contrast between the commonsense notions of a felt preference and indifference and the corresponding economic or other theoretical notions of preference and indifference. While the latter notions are usually defined or postulated as transitive, the former notions are non-transitive.

Indeed, as the felt preference between two alternatives decreases in intensity, preference and indifference merge into each other. More precisely there exist borderline cases of ordered couples, say, $(x_1; x_n)$, such that both the relation of preference and the relation of indifference are with equal correctness applicable to them. Because of the existence of such borderline cases between *felt* preference and indifference, neither of these relations is in general transitive – a shortcoming from which the corresponding theoretical notions are either free or easily freed. The situation is quite analogous to the contrast between the commonsense notions of a perceived greater and of an indistinguishable size on the one hand and the corresponding mathematical notions of being greater and of being equal in size on the other. There too the perceptual notions admit of common borderline cases with a resulting breakdown of transitivity. And there too the corresponding mathematical notions are, or are defined as, transitive. That choice functions exist not only for reflexive and complete orderings which are transitive, but also for reflexive and complete orderings which are merely acyclical, is thus particularly relevant to the analysis of felt preferences and indifferences. For such orderings are more likely to satisfy the requirement of acyclicity than the stronger requirement of transitivity.

On the grading of practicabilities and the trichotomy of practical preferences into pro-attitudes, anti-attitudes and attitudes of indifference

Often a practical thinker's decisions depend not only on the order of his preferences, but also on differences of their intensity. If his preference for f over g is small he will be more easily persuaded to choose g rather than f than if his preference for f over g is great. Again, if his preference for f over g is smaller than his preference for k over l, he will, if he must choose between f and g, forego f more easily, then he will forego k if he must choose between k and l. In so far as practical decisions depend on a comparison between the degree of intensity with which one practical alternative is preferred to another, a 'preference-meter' becomes desirable. Such a preference-meter would measure subjective degrees of preference in the same way that a Fahrenheit thermometer measures relative temperature. More technically, the desired scale of measurement would be a so-called interval scale, i.e. determined 'up to a linear transformation' (a transformation of form $\phi(x) = \alpha x + \beta$ where α and β are real numbers). It would, therefore – like any relative temperature scale – belong to a class of scales any two of which could without loss of information be linearly transformed into each other. The choice of unit, of the maximal and of the minimal point of the scale would within the limits of this condition be arbitrary.

Between the weak, or $\Re$–$\mathfrak{I}$–$\mathfrak{C}$, ordering of preferences and their measurement on an interval scale lies their grading into a finite number of grades. For our purposes the most important species of grading is the trichotomy of practical preferences into practical pro-attitudes, anti-attitudes and attitudes of indifference, and hence, of the corresponding practicabilities into good, bad and indifferent ones. Before discussing this trichotomy, it seems useful to illustrate the conditions which must be satisfied by any kind of grading with the help of a specific and familiar example. Let us choose the grading of examination results into, say, the four grades 1, 2, 3 and 4.

If an examiner is to grade correctly he must first of all, be able to establish a strict, $\mathfrak{As}$–$\mathfrak{I}$–$\mathfrak{C}$, ordering *between* the classes in the sense that 1 is strictly preferred to 2, which is strictly preferred to 3, which is strictly preferred to 4 or, more explicitly, that every result placed in a higher class is strictly preferred to every result placed in a lower class. Any apparent borderline cases between two classes must be placed into one of them. The examiner must, secondly, be able to establish a weak ordering *within* the classes to the extent that if of two results each is weakly preferred to the other (or, what comes to the same thing, if the examiner has no strong preference for one over the other) the two results are placed in the same class. (This second requirement could be weakened by merely demanding acyclicity.) The examiner must thirdly have a criterion in mind which determines the range of each class – even if it does not provide him with an interval scale.

The nature of the criterion of the range of a grade may be more or less elusive. Thus examiners in university examinations are usually assumed – at least by themselves – to have an instinctive skill in discriminating the range of a class. Their real or assumed ability expresses itself at examination meetings in statements to the effect that some candidate has shown 'clear first-class quality' while another has 'just scraped a first'. However, the criterion may be very precise, for example if the classes are determined by a rule to the effect that each class must contain a certain fixed percentage of the total number of candidates. This rule would exclude the possibility – which is not excluded by other kinds of grading – that all but one grade are empty.

In turning now to the trichotomy of a person's practical attitudes into practical pro-attitudes, practical anti-attitudes and practical attitudes of indifference, it is well to emphasize that they are directed towards mutually exclusive and jointly exhaustive practicabilities, i.e. possibilities which are (believed to be) realizable by the person's actions and are, moreover, jointly unavoidable in that one of them must be realized – whether by his actions or inaction. This means that at least one practicability has to be most preferred or best, and thus the object of a practical pro-attitude. While the class of practicabilities which are the objects of a practical pro-attitude is thus not empty, the class of practicabilities which are the objects of a practical anti-attitude and the class of practicabilities which are the objects of a practical attitude of indifference may, or may not be, empty.

Let us now assume that a person, say S, is faced with a finite number of mutually exclusive and jointly exhaustive practicabilities, say the ten practicabilities (described by) $f_1, f_2, ..., f_{10}$. In order to grade them into three classes, i.e. the class *Pro* containing the most favoured and the favoured ones, the class *Anti* containing the most disfavoured and the disfavoured ones and the class *Ind* which lies between *Pro* and *Anti*, he must, like the examiner of our example fulfil the following conditions: He must (1) be able to establish a strict, or $\mathfrak{A}$ß–$\mathfrak{X}$–$\mathfrak{C}$, ordering between the classes, i.e. between *Pro*, *Ind* and *Anti*; he must (2) be able to establish a weak ordering within these classes; and he must (3) have a criterion in mind for placing each one of the practicabilities $f_1, f_2, ..., f_{10}$ into one of the three classes. As regards this criterion we have seen that there must be at least one most preferred practicability – however repellent it may be – which must be placed into the class *Pro*. But what about the other practicabilities?

Two kinds of answers are conceivable. We may, first of all, consider a person's practical pro-, anti- and indifferent attitudes as not wholly definable in terms of his practical preferences. And we may – as in the example of our examiner – regard a person's ability to divide his practical preferences into these three grades as additional to his ability to order his preferences weakly or strongly. We may, secondly, attempt a definition of the three grades and the corresponding practical attitudes in terms of practical preferences. One method is to assume that a person S is able to choose between exerting and foregoing his power of choosing between say, $f_1, f_2, ..., f_{10}$ and to propose the following definitions: (1) S has a practical pro-attitude towards f or, briefly, $S+f$ if, and only if, f is a member of the smallest subset of practicabilities such that S would be prepared to forego his power of choosing if any one of them would be realized. (2) S has a practical anti-attitude to f or, briefly, $S-f$ if, and only if, f is a member of the smallest (possibly empty) subset of practicabilities such that S would be prepared to forego his power of choice if none of them would be realized. (3) S has a practical attitude of indifference to f or, briefly, $S \pm f$ if, and only if, f is not a member of either subset. Defining $S+f$, $S-f$ and $S \pm f$ is *ipso facto* defining the membership of the grades *Pro*, *Anti* and *Ind*.

Although this definition presupposes the possibility of an imaginative effort which is not demanded by the weak or strong ordering of preferences and which may not always be feasible, it seems capable of limited applicability as well as of further refinement and extension. Yet, however this may be, it cannot be claimed that the trichotomy of practical attitudes into pro-, anti- and indifferent attitudes and the corresponding trichotomy of practicabilities into practically good or satisfactory, bad or unsatisfactory and indifferent ones, is in all cases further analysable. Fortunately, nothing in what follows depends on the legitimacy of this claim.

On interval scales for measuring preferences by means of probabilities

Under certain special circumstances the comparison of preferences between courses of action with imagined chances, risks or, to speak concretely, lotteries may serve as a person's standard for measuring these preferences on an interval scale (after the fashion of a thermometer measuring relative temperature). The assumptions involved in such a comparison have been exhibited by F. P. Ramsey and his successors (see Kyburg & Smokler 1964). It is, *first* of all, assumed that a practical thinker who is faced with, say, n mutually exclusive and jointly exhaustive practical possibilities $f_1, ..., f_n$ is able and willing to imagine a lottery in which every ticket has a probability $0 \leqslant p \leqslant 1$ of an outcome, say, A which is weakly preferred to each f_j and at the same time the complementary probability $0 \leqslant (1-p) \leqslant 1$ of an outcome B to which every f_j is weakly preferred. We might call A the favourable and B the unfavourable outcome of the lottery and think of A as a financial gain or a holiday and of B as a financial loss or a spell in prison. It is, *secondly*, assumed that the practical thinker is able and willing to assign to each f_j a 'lottery ticket' which has a probability $\pi(f_j)$ of the favourable outcome A and the complementary probability $1 - \pi(f_j)$ of the unfavourable outcome B in *such a manner* that he would be indifferent between the certainty described by f_j and the probabilities $\pi(f_j)$ of A and $1 - \pi(f_j)$ of B. He might for example be indifferent between the certainty of attending a conference and a lottery ticket which gives him a 3/4 chance of a week in Venice and a 1/4 chance of a week in prison.

Because the practical thinker is assumed to be indifferent between f_j for certain and a lottery ticket with a probability $\pi(f_j)$ of A and $1 - \pi(f_j)$ of B – because the lottery ticket is equivalent to a certainty – the lottery ticket, or the gamble which it symbolizes, is often called 'the certainty equivalent' of the practical alternative. In stating the certainty equivalent of a practical alternative f_j one thus refers to four items, namely the favourable and unfavourable outcomes A and B, the probability $\pi(f_j)$ of A and the complementary probability $1 - \pi(f_j)$ of B. If A and B are clear from the context one may, because their probabilities are complementary, designate the certainty equivalent of f_j simply by $\pi(f_j)$. The certainty equivalent $\pi(f_j)$ must, of course, not be confused with the probability of f_j, designated by $p(f_j)$.

The assignment of certainty equivalents to the practical alternatives $f_1, ..., f_n$ is assumed to include the weak ordering of these alternatives. In other words, the *third* assumption involved in the measuring of practical preferences by comparing them with imagined chances is the practical thinker's ability and willingness not to violate the weak, or $\mathfrak{R}$–$\mathfrak{T}$–$\mathfrak{C}$, preferential ordering between the practical alternatives and the favourable and unfavourable outcome which precedes his assignment of certainty equivalents. If our three assumptions are satisfied and we designate the certainty equivalent of f_j by '$\pi(f_j)$', then the degrees of preference of the practical alternatives $f_1, ..., f_n$ are measured by their certainty equivalents on an interval scale whose minimal point is O and whose maximal point is 1 – or on any other interval scale which is derived from it by a linear transformation.

In order to protect the method of measuring preferences by certainty equivalents (i.e. lottery tickets of a certain kind) against misunderstanding, it may be worth noting explicitly that the practical possibility f – which for the purpose of being assigned a certainty equivalent must be *imagined* as certain – may or may not be certain or believed to be so. If the practical thinker believes it to be merely probable, then the imaginative effort demanded of him is considerable. It is much greater than that assumed in the attempt at analysing the trichotomy of practical preferences. Another point worth making is that our account of measuring preferences by means of certainty equivalents, and hence by probabilities, does not imply any specific theory of probability. We may, in particular, assume that the probability in question is subjective – an assumption which does not prejudge the question whether or not there are objective, mind-independent probabilities.

A person's preference for one practical alternative over all its competitors is in general not the only factor which determines his actual choice or decision to realize one alternative. Another determining factor is its probability, if it is known. Thus a person will, other things being equal, normally choose to realize f_r over f_j if in his view $\pi(f_j)$ is only slightly greater than $\pi(f_r)$, but $p(f_r)$ much greater than $p(f_j)$. Matters are even more complicated when the relevant probabilities are not known and a decision has to be made 'under uncertainty'. At the moment we are, however, merely interested in the formal principles for ordering, grading and measuring preferences.

The method of measuring practical preferences by certainty equivalents, i.e. by comparing real or imaginary certainties with imaginary gambles, is particularly suited to spheres of life which normally involve a kind of gambling, as do the routine decisions of businessmen or politicians. Yet, as has been pointed out in discussing the notion of subjective probability, there are situations in which many people would not be either willing or able to measure their preferences by means of imaginary gambles. While some decision-theorists would deny any limits to this method of measuring preferences, others are satisfied with their applicability to economic decisions to which moral considerations are not – or only negligibly – relevant. (See, for example, Fellner 1965.)

What has been said about the ordering, grading and measuring of subjective preferences does not, and was not meant to, imply an answer to the question as to whether or not they are to some extent and in some circumstances intersubjective. The question reminds one of a similar question about the intersubjectivity or otherwise of subjective perceptions. Without attempting a detailed reply to either question, it seems fairly clear that the grounds on which people assume that their perceptions sometimes more or less agree with the perceptions of others are similar to the grounds on which people assume that their preferences sometimes more or less agree with the preferences of others. They are in both cases what other people say and do. There is no more direct access to the perceptions of others than there is to their preferences. We may perceive what others perceive, but we are not aware of their perceiving. And we may prefer what others prefer, but are not aware of their preferring.

Another set of questions, which will concern us later, is the manner in which the subjective preferences of persons belonging to a social group are in fact, or ought to be, combined into a 'social decision' which the members of the group regard in fact, or ought to regard, as binding. Clearly, the actual or the morally correct way of deriving a social preference from individual preferences cannot be determined solely by reference to principles of ordering, grading or measuring individual preferences. But it is worth emphasizing that a person who expresses his preference for one way of deriving social from individual preferences over another way of doing so is in any case expressing his own individual preference.

In conclusion it should perhaps be emphasized once again that a person's practical preferences, which have been and will be our main concern, cover mutually exclusive and jointly exhaustive practic-abilities of which one must be realized by the person's actions or inactivity. His practical preferences thus differ radically from those of his preferences which cover mere logical possibilities, especially such as he compares with respect to some conception of 'intrinsic value'. To illustrate the difference, we may imagine a practical thinker faced with the choice between committing suicide, submitting to torture or betraying his friends. If he practically prefers committing suicide to submitting to torture, then he *eo ipso* (because his practic-abilities are mutually exclusive and jointly exhaustive) practically prefers committing suicide and not submitting to torture over not committing suicide and submitting to torture – thereby exemplifying an obvious principle of *practical* preference, namely

$$(fPg) \rightarrow ((f \wedge \neg g)\, P(\neg f \wedge g)).$$

It is, however, also obvious that this principle does not apply to Leibniz's God or anybody who compares logically possible states of affairs with respect to a conception of intrinsic value. (For a discussion of intrinsic preferability, see R. M. Chisholm & E. Sosa 1966.)

PART II

ASPECTS AND KINDS OF PRACTICAL EVALUATION

CHAPTER 5

ON CHOSEN INTERVENTIONS IN THE COURSE OF NATURE

The main aim of this chapter is to examine the contrast between sequences of events or states which do not involve human interventions and those which do. The chapter starts with a phenomenological description of a person's chosen intervention in the course of nature and of its concomitant segmentation into parts connected by a relation of predetermination. In terms of this relation, as it appears to the chooser, subjectively and objectively effective choices will be distinguished. Next, some objective concepts of predetermination (and effective choice) will be briefly compared and the relevance of their divergence to practical thinking and co-operation considered. The chapter concludes by emphasizing the difference between attributes applied to chosen interventions as natural occurrences, i.e. independently of their being or not being chosen, and attributes applied to chosen interventions as chosen.

On chosen interventions or non-interventions in the course of nature

If one regards the course of nature as closed to any interference, then there is no point in talking about intervening in it. Talk of this kind becomes significant if one distinguishes between the uninterrupted course of nature and the course of nature as interrupted and modified by human interventions. Most of us make this distinction and in doing so describe familiar experiences. Such an experience may, or may not, be an illusion capable of being dispelled by science, metaphysics, logic or in some other way. At the moment, however, we are concerned with the experience itself and not with any claims transcending it.

Ignoring telekinesis and similar alleged phenomena, a chosen intervention or non-intervention in the course of nature consists in bodily conduct, that is to say in moving or not moving one's body or part of it. One does not confuse in one's immediate awareness, and one must not confuse in one's thinking, a chosen bodily performance or non-performance, i.e. chosen bodily conduct, with an unchosen bodily performance or non-performance, i.e. unchosen bodily conduct. In order to emphasize the difference it will be convenient to use b as a variable ranging over constant propositions b_0, b_1, b_2 describing bodily conduct and to use sel in order to indicate that the bodily conduct described by a proposition within its scope is chosen (selected). Employing this method of schematic representation it is, for example, easy to see the relations between the following statements, in which b_0 describes a person's bodily performance of moving his little finger: sel b_0 describes a chosen performance of this movement; sel $\neg\ b_0$ describes a chosen non-performance of this movement; $\neg$ sel b_0 expresses that a performance of this movement has not been chosen (whether or not it has been performed); $\neg$ sel $\neg\ b_0$ expresses that a non-performance of this movement has not been chosen.

If a person's chosen bodily conduct (as described by) b_0 is intended as an intervention or non-intervention in the course of nature, then b_0 divides his awareness into a retrospect preceding it and one or more prospects succeeding it. A person's chosen bodily conduct, his retrospect and one of his prospects might be described by a sequence of propositions, say, r_1, r_2, r_3, sel b_0, p_1, p_2 where each r and each p describes a state of the world as it appears to the person at the time of this intervention, and where every proposition describes a state which does not precede the state described by a preceding proposition. The different states may thus overlap in time. In order to represent a continuous sequence of states we replace the commas by semi-colons, i.e. $r_1; r_2; r_3;$ sel $b_0; p_1; p_2$. This representation does not, of course, analyse the relation of continuous connection between a finite number of states (see Körner 1966: ch. 4).

To the person who consciously intervenes in the course of nature, it does not only appear that his chosen bodily conduct is placed between retrospect and prospect. It also appears to him that his choice is effective – that his bodily conduct is effectively chosen and that the prospect succeeding it is an effective option – in the sense that his chosen bodily conduct is on the one hand not wholly predetermined by the states of which he is retrospectively aware, while on the other hand it at least partly predetermines the states of which he is prospectively aware. Using pred to express the concept of subjective predetermination (exemplified by expectations that one specific or generic sequence of states is followed by another such sequence), we can characterize an apparently effective choice as satisfying the following conditions:

(1) $((r_1;r_2)\,(\mathrm{sel}\,b_0))\,\mathrm{pred}\,(p_1;p_2)$;

(2) $\lnot\,((r_1;r_2)\,\mathrm{pred}\,b_0)$;

(3) $\lnot\,((r_1;r_2)\,\mathrm{pred}\,(p_1;p_2))$.

Of these three statements – to which philosophers as different as Hume, Leibniz and Kant would make no objection – the first says that the retrospect and the chosen bodily conduct together subjectively predetermine the prospect; the second that the retrospect by itself does not subjectively predetermine the bodily conduct; the third that the retrospect by itself also does not subjectively predetermine the prospect. The statements are subjective or 'phenomenological', not objective or 'transcendent'. They describe a person's awareness, not the world beyond.

The subjective predetermination of one sequence of states by another may be either subjective (empirical) necessitation, briefly emp, or subjective probabilification, briefly prob. In the former case the intervening person expects with certainty that the predetermined sequence will follow the predetermining sequence. In the latter case he expects with some confidence, though not with certainty that the predetermined sequence will follow the predetermining sequence.

Chosen bodily conduct, subjective necessitation and subjective probabilification may be involved in repeated and interconnected interventions. The interconnection, if sufficiently articulated, can, after the fashion of contemporary decision theory, be represented by tree diagrams with two types of nodes: (1) necessitating decision nodes which mark the possibility of two or more different ways of chosen bodily conduct each of which subjectively necessitates a certain sequence of states and (2) probability nodes which mark the possibility of two or more sequences of states each of which possesses a certain subjective probability. Among the probability nodes one might further distinguish between pure probability nodes, if the probability of the sequences of states is not even partially determined by chosen bodily conduct, and probabilifying decision nodes if the probability of the sequences is partially determined by chosen bodily conduct.

On the difference between subjectively and objectively effective choices

Just as one may distinguish between having the merely subjective impression of being confronted by a material object and being in fact confronted by it, so one may also distinguish between the merely subjective impression of an effective choice and a choice which is not merely subjectively, but objectively effective. Both distinctions might be regarded as pointless – the first by a metaphysical idealist who denies the existence of material objects, the second by an anti-libertarian who denies the existence of effective choices. Yet, whether pointless or not, if one wishes to understand either distinction, one will among other considerations have to examine the grounds on which a person making it comes to regard his impression as *merely* subjective and thus as illusory. In the case of an apparent confrontation with a material object the illusion is ascribed either to making a mistake about a phenomenon or about its wider context. In the case of an apparently effective choice the illusion is ascribed to similar mistakes.

About the first kind of mistake little needs to be said. A person may, for example, have described a sequence consisting of a retrospect, his chosen bodily conduct and his prospect by $r_1; r_2;$ sel $b_0; p_1; p_2$ and later come to the conclusion that while the sequence as described satisfies the conditions (1)–(3) the sequence has been misdescribed and that if described correctly, it does not satisfy these conditions. (It goes without saying that the person may be mistaken about having been mistaken etc. etc. But let us avoid such fruitless complications.)

I now turn to the second kind of possible mistake. A choice which to a person seemed to be effective, and seems to satisfy conditions (1)–(3), may cease to seem effective to him if the context in which the choice was originally considered appears to be part of a wider context in which the conditions are no longer satisfied. The widening of context which leads to the loss of the apparent effectiveness of a choice may be diachronic or synchronic. In the diachronic case a certain restrospective sequence of states did not seem to predetermine the person's bodily conduct and the subsequent sequence of states, while a backwards prolongation of the original sequence yields a wider sequence which does seem to predetermine the person's bodily conduct and the subsequent sequence of states. In the synchronic case the original information about a certain retrospective sequence is supplemented in such a manner that although the sequence as originally described did not seem to be predetermining, the more fully described sequence does seem to predetermine both the bodily conduct and the subsequent sequence of states. The diachronic and the synchronic widening of a context of choice are not mutually exclusive, but may reinforce each other.

It is useful to represent the two cases in schematic form. To do so we assume that in the original context the apparently effective choice satisfies the three conditions, as symbolized above, in particular

(2) $\neg ((r_1; r_2) \operatorname{pred} b_0)$ and

(3) $\neg ((r_1; r_2) \operatorname{pred} (p_1; p_2))$.

The loss of apparent effectiveness by diachronic widening of the original context is expressed by replacing (2) and (3) by

(2a) $(..., r_1; r_2) \operatorname{pred} b_0$ and

(3a) $(... r_1; r_2) \operatorname{pred} (p_1; p_2)$,

where the dots preceding $r_1; r_2$ indicate a finite backward prolongation of the retrospect by adding further states to it. The loss of apparent effectiveness by synchronic widening of the original context is expressed by

(2b) $(r_1'; r_2') \operatorname{pred} b_0$ and

(3b) $(r_1'; r_2') \operatorname{pred} (p_1; p_2)$,

where $(r_1'; r_2')$ is a fuller description of the sequence of states which is less fully described by $r_1; r_2$.

Let us say that the context of a choice satisfying conditions (2) and (3) is subjectively complete if, and only if, the chooser cannot conceive of *any* diachronic widening of the context, i.e. any backward prolongation of the retrospect, or any synchronic widening of the context, i.e. any supplementary information about the retrospect which would justify the replacement of (2) and (3) by (2a) and (3a), by (2b) or (3b) or both. The context of a choice satisfying condition (2) and (3) is subjectively incomplete, if, and only if, it is not subjectively complete.

On concepts of objectively effective choice

If a person believes that he sometimes, but not always, misjudges the effectiveness of his choices he must have a concept of objective choice in mind. People differ, of course, both as regards the clarity which they have about their concept of objective choice – as measured, for example, by their ability to define and to exemplify it – as well as about its content. Yet in spite of these differences no concept of

69

effective choice will apply to a sequence (described by)

$$r_1; r_2; \text{sel } b_0; p_1; p_2$$

unless (a) the sequence is not an illusion, unless (b) its satisfying conditions (1)–(3) is not an illusion and unless (c) the conjecture that the context of the choice is complete is a true proposition (where the notion of an illusion and a true proposition are assumed to be understood).

Differences in the various concepts of objectively effective choice can be traced to differences in the various concepts applied in characterizing the course of nature, in particular in the various concepts of predetermination. Since it is not our task here to analyse these concepts, it must be sufficient to draw attention to their variety as exhibited by anthropology, the history of ideas and the philosophy of science and to taking it for granted. In doing so one must be particularly careful to avoid two confusions. The first of them, which is the less likely, but more harmful, of the two is the confusion between subjective and objective predetermination. Their difference, as has been indicated is a special case of the difference between on the one hand the mere impression of being confronted by an instance of an objective concept and on the other hand being in fact confronted by an instance of the concept. In order to express the difference between subjective and objective predetermination schematically, we might, having represented the former by pred, represent the latter by Pred. In a similar way we might contrast the subjective relations emp and prob with the corresponding objective relations Emp and Prob, using subscripts (such as emp_3 or Prob_2) where different subjective or objective relations have to be distinguished from each other.

Using these abbreviations the difference between determinism and indeterminism can be formulated concisely. A determinist and an indeterminist may both hold that neither emp nor prob are empty concepts. It is indeed difficult to imagine that anybody living in our culture would not employ both concepts. Where the determinist and the indeterminist differ, is that the former believes that the notion of objective, probabilistic predetermination, i.e. Prob, is empty and that the concept or concepts of objective predetermination which are not empty are of type Emp. Until the advent of quantum mechanics all philosophers who believed that the world is completely describable by natural science also believed that determinism was true.

This brings us to the second confusion which should be avoided. It consists in conflating the distinction between determinism and indeterminism, which depends on the emptiness or otherwise of Prob, with the distinction between anti-libertarianism and libertarianism which depends on whether the range of Pred – whether Prob or Emp – is unrestricted or admits of exceptions in the case of human interventions in the course of nature. The libertarian, who believes that there are objectively effective choices, believes *eo ipso* in a merely restricted applicability of Pred. Schematically, he believes that there are cases when

(4) $\neg\,((r_1;r_1)\,\text{Pred}\,b_0)$ and

(5) $\neg\,((r_1;r_2)\,\text{Pred}\,(p_1;p_2))$

and when no diachronic or synchronic widening of the context in which the objective predetermination is denied would justify its assertion. The transition from a context in which objective predetermination is denied to one in which it is asserted would be schematically expressed after the fashion of (2*a*) and (2*b*) and of (3*a*) and (3*b*), replacing pred by Pred in each formula.

A little taxonomy with its attendant somewhat barbaric nomenclature may be in order. Let us, as has just been suggested, call a person who believes in objectively effective choices and thus employs a restricted concept of predetermination 'libertarian', and a person who employs an unrestricted concept of predetermination 'antilibertarian'. Let us, furthermore, call a person who employs a (restricted or unrestricted) concept Prob 'probabilistic' and a person who employs a (restricted or unrestricted) concept Emp 'non-probabilistic'. We can then distinguish between non-probabilistic and probabilistic libertarians, as well as between non-probabilistic and probabilistic anti-libertarians. Since, moreover, a person may without inconsistency use both a (restricted) concept Emp and a (restricted) concept Prob and be either a libertarian or an antilibertarian, we have to distinguish between purely and impurely probabilistic (or, equivalently, non-probabilistic) libertarians or anti-libertarians. My guess would be that most people, who are not interested in, or influenced by, either science or philosophy, are impurely probabilistic libertarians. An example of pure non-probabilistic anti-libertarianism would be anybody who believes that Newtonian physics describes the world completely, an example of a pure probabilistic anti-libertarianism, anybody who believed that quantum physics, as conceived, for example, by Born is a complete description of the world. A scientific Newtonian and a Bornian who nevertheless believes in objectively effective choices would respectively be examples of a pure non-probabilistic and of a pure probabilistic libertarianism.

On the rôle of divergent concepts of choice in practical co-operation

The issue of libertarianism versus anti-libertarianism is a fundamental metaphysical problem and regarded as such by most metaphysicians, with the possible exception of the positivists. The issue of probabilism versus non-probabilism or, as Peirce called it, necessitarianism is similarly a fundamental issue in natural science and in its philosophy. Yet on the whole neither issue affects actual choosing, planning and practical thinking since on the whole a person's practical decisions would remain unaffected by his conversion from libertarianism to anti-libertarianism or vice versa or by his conversion from probabilism to necessitarianism or vice versa.

An anti-libertarian who is under the impression that he is confronted with an effective choice will normally act as if the impression were true. He will in other words choose as if he were a libertarian, so that his conversion to libertarianism would make no difference to his choice. There could, however, be exceptions to the invariance of choices under conversion if libertarianism were true – a question which is empirically undecidable. For if libertarianism were true, then an anti-libertarian might sometimes succeed in persuading himself that he cannot but avoid a certain unpleasant choice and thus provide himself with a possibility of limiting his choices by an effective excuse, which would not be available if he were a libertarian. Yet in most cases all people choose *as if* they accepted the libertarian doctrine and in these cases it makes no difference whether or not they raise the question of its truth, and if so, how they answer it.

Again, a necessitarian who chooses on the basis of evidence which he considers incomplete, chooses as if he were a probabilist who regards the necessitarian conception of complete evidence as an illusion. And the probabilist who chooses on the basis of an almost certain probability will act as if he were a necessitarian. Indeed a merely epistemic probabilism, which implies that we can never know enough to predict the course of nature with certainty, and an ontological probabilism, which implies that the laws of nature are irreducibly probabilistic, are not only logically compatible but 'practically equivalent'. Their practical equivalence extends even to science ar conceived by operationalist, instrumentalist or pragmatist philosophers. In this connection it is worth noting that Heisenberg and the other adherents of the Copenhagen interpretation of quantum mechanics regarded the transition from classical to quantum mechanics as a transition from ontological necessitarianism to epistemic probabilism. Heisenberg – who at that time was still a metaphysical positivist – even held that the disagreement between ontological necessitarians and ontological probabilists was strictly meaningless. (For a more detailed discussion of the different kinds of necessitarianism and probabilism see Körner 1971a.)

The best guarantee of efficient practical co-operation is for the collaborators to share their beliefs. The next best guarantee is for them to act as if they shared their beliefs. Because most, if not all, actions performed or envisaged by a person are not affected by his allegiance to libertarianism, anti-libertarianism, necessitarianism or anti-necessitarianism, the analysis of action can proceed by simply using the notions of subjective predetermination or of subjective and objective predetermination without prejudging their further specification.

On the physical, cognitive and evaluative attributes of chosen interventions or non-interventions in the course of nature

Having in a general way analysed the notions of subjective and objective predetermination and, in terms of them, the notions of subjectively and objectively effective choice, it will be useful to consider the kinds of attribute by whose application a chosen intervention or non-intervention can be characterized in a more specific manner. It is convenient to distinguish between physical, cognitive and evaluative attributes. The physical attributes of a chosen intervention or non-intervention specify the state of the chooser's body or a change of this state, independently of the assumption that the state or change is the implementation of a choice. The specified physical characteristics and objects thus belong to the physical world, as conceived by the chooser or another person describing the chooser's intervention by means of his categories and more specific concepts. A physical attribute of a chosen intervention is, as has been suggested earlier, of form 'x is a movement (or non-movement) of a human body which has physical properties. . . and bears physical relations. . .

to its environment'. The properties and relations cannot be completely listed; and the relations may connect any number of items.

The cognitive and evaluative attributes of a chosen intervention specify the nature of the choice which is being implemented. A cognitive attribute is of form: 'x is chosen under the impression that... is (was, will be, might now be, might have been, might later be) the case', where the variable x ranges over the chooser's apparent options. While the cognitive attributes of a chosen intervention must be distinguished from its physical attributes, a cognitive attribute may contain a reference to a physical one as in 'x is chosen under the impression that it is implemented by means of such and such a bodily movement'.

An evaluative attribute is of the form 'x is chosen with the practical attitude or attitudes... towards the apparent options... ', where x ranges over the chooser's apparent options and the practical attitudes are practical preference-or-indifference or the other practical attitudes defined in terms of it. There is no doubt that chosen interventions may, and often do, possess evaluative attributes. What is not immediately clear is whether every chosen intervention does in fact possess such an attribute. The answer would have to be affirmative if one does not distinguish between an attitude of indifference and the absence of an attitude. But the distinction is both justified and in certain cases important. If, as I shall argue, one may have an attitude towards an attitude and if there were no difference between the absence of an attitude and an attitude of indifference, every attitude would be the object of another attitude (of indifference, if no other) and thus give rise to an infinite hierarchy of attitudes. Again, in so far as an attitude of indifference between two or more options presupposes some deliberation, it is one thing to have no attitude towards them for want of deliberation and quite another to be indifferent between them as the result of deliberation. Lastly indifference, unlike the absence of an attitude may be a reason for a choice: A person who has no attitude towards two mutually exclusive and jointly exhaustive options has no reason or justification for choosing one of them, whereas a person's indifference between them is a reason or justification for choosing either.

The concept of a chosen intervention or non-intervention in the course of nature links our factual to our practical thinking. 'Bodily conduct', which implements a choice, belongs to the former; 'choices', which are implemented by bodily conduct, belong to the latter. In a loose sense of the term, actions coincide with chosen interventions or non-interventions. If, however, we ascribe actions to agents as persisting subjects of temporally separate interventions or non-interventions, then the analysis of chosen interventions or non-interventions on the course of nature is merely a preliminary to the analysis of actions and agents.

CHAPTER 6

AGENTS AND THEIR ACTIONS

The main purpose of this chapter is to consider the conditions under which different chosen interventions or non-interventions may have the same subject, and how such a subject or agent is to be conceived. The chapter starts by inquiring into the way in which the subjects of different chosen interventions or non-interventions are identified with each other and, thereby, become different aspects of one more or less persisting subject or agent. There follows a discussion of the logical relation between the concepts of being a person and of being an agent. Having clarified the concept of an agent, the concept of an action – as a chosen intervention or non-intervention ascribable to an agent by himself and by others – will be analysed.

On the concept of an agent as the persisting subject of different chosen interventions or non-interventions

According to a comparatively simple and common conception a persisting agent unites within himself the various separate subjects which at different times are the choosers of bodily conduct by one and the same human body – at least in all those cases where the body's identity from birth to death presents no difficulty. It is worth while to formulate the manner of this unification and the corresponding concept of an agent more precisely, especially as this will make the comparison with other versions of the concept more transparent.

Let us assume that $(S_1, S_2, ..., S_n)$ is a class consisting of all temporally distinct – past, present and future – choosers of bodily conduct of one and the same body whose identity is not in question. Let us further say that a temporally distinct chooser of bodily conduct is bodily represented by another if, and only if, they are both choosers of bodily conduct of the same body. The relation of bodily representation in the class $(S_1, S_2, ..., S_n)$ is clearly reflexive, symmetric and transitive. That is to say that the relation is an equivalence relation and the class an equivalence class from which is derived by abstraction the notion S of an agent of which $S_1, S_2, ..., S_n$ are temporally distinct aspects. Thus, borrowing and adapting Leibniz's example from the end of the Theodicy, if $S_1, ..., S_n$ are the temporally distinct Sextuses who during the lifetime of their common body choose its bodily conduct, then Sextus is the persisting agent, derived by abstraction from the equivalence class consisting of those Sextuses.

The concept of a persisting agent based on an equivalence class of temporally distinct choosers of bodily conduct associated with the same spatio-temporally continuous body may in a number of ways prove inadequate. There is first of all the case of organ transplants and other radically discontinuous changes of human bodies, which may lead from the impossibility of locating chosen bodily conduct in a persisting human body to the impossibility of ascribing the conduct to a persisting agent. Quite apart from this difficulty which concerns the applicability rather than the content of the concept, there are many situations in which the employment of a stronger or richer concept is required.

A stronger concept is needed when one ascribes responsibility to an agent for his past conduct. It is then not enough that his temporally distinct aspects be associated with the same body but it is in addition required that they be the bearers of sufficiently similar mental attributes. Being a responsible agent – or, if we prefer, an agent in a strong sense of the term – is incompatible with an underlying equivalence class of temporally distinct choosing subjects associated with the same body, if from a certain time onwards the choices have been pathologically abnormal.

A richer concept is needed when one judges an agent's courage, or other traits of his character, and thus has to compare what he has done with what he could have done. In such cases the equivalence class which underlies the concept of an agent must include not only actual choosing subjects, but also merely possible ones. The Sextuses mentioned in the Theodicy include not only the actual Sextus, with his temporally distinct aspects associated with his actual body, but also possible Sextuses who together with their distinct aspects belong to different possible worlds. They include, as Peirce might have put it, not only the real Sextus but also his would-be's.

If our concept of an agent implies that his distinct aspects are not only associated with the same body, but are also sufficiently similar in some respects, a further difficulty may arise. Similarity unlike identity is not transitive. Consequently in a sequence $(S_1, ..., S_n)$ of distinct choosing subjects any two neighbours might be similar, while some more distant members may not be, so that the class is not an equivalence class. On the other hand a relation, in particular similarity in a certain respect, may not be an equivalence relation within a certain class but may be an equivalence relation within one or more of its subclasses.

It would be tempting to elaborate our examples and to add some less familiar ones, especially examples in which the same persisting agent is associated with more than one human body – as in the doctrine of the transmigration of the soul. By examining a great many different examples, in particular unfamilar ones, one would draw further attention to the common form of the various versions of the concept of an agent. Yet at this point a more direct, schematic explanation seems preferable.

A schematic characterization of the notion of an agent

We start with a vast, open aggregate of ultimate elements, namely distinct (actual and possible) subjects of chosen bodily movements, say, $S_1, ..., S_n, ...$ Next, we note that for some purpose or set of purposes – the purpose of carrying on a conversation, co-operation of some other kind, explaining a sequence of interventions in the course of nature etc. – some of the elements are replaceable or representable by others, schematically $S_j \text{ Rep-}P S_r$. (The dependence on a purpose P implies a distinction between those attributes of the elements which are and those attributes which are not essential to it. Such relative essentialism, which is characteristic of much practical thinking, is no more than a moderate version of pragmatism. It is quite different from the absolute essentialism of Aristotle, which explains the nature of things by their dependence on eternal purposes. If an essentialism which presupposes unchangeable, superhuman ends is the pragmatism of God, then a pragmatism which presupposes changeable, human ends is the essentialism of man.)

Representability for a purpose is not in general an equivalence relation. The situation is analogous in the case of legal representation of one person by another, where, for example, the representability of a minor by a lawyer does not imply the converse and where the representability of one person by a second and of the second by a third does not imply the representability of the first by the third. But it is quite natural to strengthen the relation of representability for a purpose by restricting it to sets of elements for which it is an equivalence relation. The so-restricted relation of 'interrepresentability for a purpose with respect to a set of elements' may be defined as follows: S_j Interrep-P S_r with respect to the set $(S_1, ..., S_n)$ if, and only if, (1) the relation is reflexive, symmetric and transitive for all elements of the set and (2) the set is not a subset of any larger set for the elements of which the relation is also reflexive, symmetric and transitive. I shall say that the class is an 'interrepresentability class' (with respect to Interrep-P), that each member of the class is representable by every other and that each member is a 'representative aspect' of the agent S.

This general definition of the concept of an agent – in terms of sets of distinct subjects of chosen bodily conduct connected into equivalence classes by means of a relation of interrepresentability for a purpose – can be made more specific in the following two ways. The first consists in further specifying the membership conditions of the equivalence classes without reference to a common purpose, for example by requiring association with one human body, association with one human body which has been subjected to some ritual, association with one human body after it has reached a certain age etc. The second consists in further specifying the purpose of the interrepresentability, e.g. the ascription of moral or legal responsibility.

In regarding the distinct aspects of an agent S, such as Sextus, as the members of an equivalence class $(S_1, ..., S_n)$ connected by Interrep-P one neglects, of course, many of its other structural features, for example the temporal ordering of its elements, or the relation between actual and possible elements. It would, however, be out of place to go into further details here, since they would have no bearing on the following discussions. In all of them it will be sufficient to conceive of the distinct aspects of a persisting agent as associated with the same body and interrepresentable by each other for the purpose of ascribing choices to this persisting agent.

Persons as agents

The distinction between the temporally separate subjects of chosen bodily conduct on the one hand, and the persisting agent of which they are aspects on the other, is necessary for an analysis of the general

79

concept of an agent and the various versions of this concept. In most other contexts it must be taken for granted, if only to avoid pedantic repetition and cumbersomeness. Similar remarks apply to the distinction between the concepts of a person and an agent. In Western philosophy and the changing commonsense expressed and modified by it, the two concepts are closely connected without coinciding in meaning or, at times, even in extension.

Most, if not all, Western philosophers regard human beings or persons as a category (maximal kind) or species of substances – whether they conceive of a substance in the Aristotelian fashion as an independently existing particular which has characteristics but is not itself a characteristic, or whether they require in addition with Plato, that it be incapable of change and annihilation. In the case of either conception of substance, *agere est character substantiarum* to borrow a phrase of Leibniz. And in so far as persons are substances – whether a category or a mere species – their being active is one of their constitutive attributes. In so far as they are human, their being active consists in their being persisting agents each of which, in the manner explained, unites within himself a set of distinct subjects of chosen bodily conduct satisfying an equivalence relation of interrepresentability for a purpose, as well as conforming to other structural requirements.

In other respects the various concepts of a person which are conceivable, and have in fact been employed, may differ very widely in content. Thus apart from human beings, Homeric gods or angels may be conceived as persons. Again, for some species of persons activity may be considered as disembodied, while for others it may be conceived as being both either embodied or disembodied. Lastly, even if 'being a person' is defined in terms of 'being an agent' this concept in turn has to be defined in terms of 'physical body' and 'predetermination' each of which can be, and has been, conceived in a variety of widely different ways. Our enquiry into the structure of practical thinking requires awareness of these differences, rather than their detailed discussion. On the other hand, the more general distinction between separate subjects of chosen conduct, agents and persons is relevant to much that follows. But it will often not be necessary to spell it out and harmless to speak of persons when it would be more precise to speak of agents or temporally separate subjects of chosen conduct.

On the ascription of actions by their agents to themselves

The term 'action' has many meanings which, even if this were possible, it is not necessary to list here. Thus in one sense actions are simply chosen interventions or non-interventions in the course of physical nature, while in another they need not even be chosen. In what follows actions will be conceived not only as chosen interventions or non-interventions in the course of physical nature, but also as chosen interventions or non-interventions in the course of social life. And in this social sense, which involves their being subject to prudential, legal and moral evaluation, the structure of an action is much more complex – both as regards its ascription to an agent and as regards the demarcation of its content. In either of these respects account must be taken of the agent's judgment, of the judgment of others, be they authorized or unauthorized judges, and of the extent to which these judgments agree with each other.

The rôle of the personal or internal and the external perspective, as well as of their concurrence in ascribing an action to an agent and in demarcating its content are clearly characterized in those parts of the law which, forsaking fiction and presumption, are intended to explain or to embody the ordinary view of the nature of action, as it is held by ordinary people in their ordinary social intercourse. Yet it goes without saying that a philosopher's decision to use 'action' in this general fashion does not free him from the task of protecting the notion from ambiguity or misunderstanding. Nor does it make the attempt at a deeper analysis superfluous.

Let us, then, turn to the ascription of an action to an agent and begin by examining its personal perspective, i.e. the ascription of an action by an agent to himself. We assume that the agent is S, say the Sextus of our example, that he employs an interrepresentability relation Interrep-P and that the corresponding interrepresentability class is $(S_1, ..., S_{n-1})$. We further assume that S (the persisting agent whose representative aspects are the distinct subjects $S_1, ..., S_{n-1}$) is considering a chosen intervention or non-intervention in the course of nature whose subject S_n (though associated with the same body as $S_1, ..., S_{n-1}$ and, hence, S) is not a member of the representability class $(S_1, ..., S_{n-1})$. On the assumptions mentioned, S ascribes the chosen intervention or non-intervention, whose subject is S_n, to himself if, and only if, he judges the extension of the representability

81

class $(S_1, ..., S_{n-1})$ by S_n to $(S_1, ..., S_{n-1}, S_n)$ to be correct (i.e. to satisfy the conditions (1) and (2) on p. 79).

It is difficult to think of ordinary situations in which S during the actual occurrence of the chosen intervention or non-intervention would not ascribe it to himself as *his* action. But S might judge himself to be obsessed by the devil or to be in a similarly extraordinary situation of the kind in which psychiatrists and anthropologists are particularly interested. It is equally quite easy to think of situations in which after or before the occurrence of a chosen intervention or non-intervention he would not ascribe it to himself – for example because '*he* (S_n) must have been mad' or because he (S) could never be 'as foolish or as wicked'. Between refusing to ascribe a chosen intervention or non-intervention to oneself and judging it to be 'rather out of character' lies a continuum of cases to which the art of a Proust or Kafka might do better justice than a phenomenological taxonomy.

In order to understand and evaluate a person's actions, it is sometimes important to distinguish among the actions which he ascribes to himself, those which he judges to be self-destructive, those which he judges to be self-preserving and those which he judges to be self-suspending. All these cases are cases of self-ascription. In other words, in all of them S judges that the interrepresentability class $(S_1, ..., S_{n-1})$ is correctly extended to $(S_1, ..., S_n)$ by S_n, i.e. the subject of the chosen intervention or non-intervention, which is thus judged to be an action of S.

He judges a self-ascribed action to be self-destructive if, and only if, in addition to ascribing the action to himself, he believes it physically impossible that there is any S_r (a subject of a chosen intervention or non-intervention not yet contained in the interrepresentability class) by which $(S_1, ..., S_n)$ can be further extended (without violating conditions (1) and (2) on p. 79). The judgment that an action would be self-destructive depends among other things on one's relation of interrepresentability and in particular on the purpose by which it is partially defined. Examples of actions judged self-destructive by their agent would not only be physical suicide, but also various kinds of mental suicide, such as a complete change of personality induced by certain drugs.

S judges a self-ascribed action to be self-suspending if, and only if, in addition to ascribing the action to himself, he believes it physically impossible that some, but not all, 'later subjects', say $S_{n+1}, ..., S_{n+r}$ (i.e. subjects of chosen interventions or non-interventions associated with the body of S and later than those whose subjects are members of $(S_1, , \ldots S_n))$ can be added to the interrepresentability class (without violating conditions (1) and (2) on p. 79). An example of a self-suspending action would be getting drunk or drugged to such an extent that one would expect one's subsequent 'actions' to have been due to the influence of drink or drugs rather than to oneself.

Lastly S judges a self-ascribed action to be self-preserving if, and only if, he judges it to be neither self-destructive nor self-suspending. Depending on one's interrepresentability relation and in particular the purpose for which it is being used, one's self-preserving actions may differ widely from 'conservatively' extending $(S_1, \ldots, S_n)$ by an S_{n+1} which is hardly distinguishable from the other members of the class to 'creatively' extending it by an S_{n+1} which is almost inelegible for membership. In so far as a person regards his actions as self-preserving – however much creative of a changed self or out of character – he will normally be willing to shoulder responsibility for them, even if others are not inclined to burden him with it.

It is tempting to elaborate the distinctions between the different ways in which a person may choose and judge his actions and, thereby, in a perfectly intelligible sense choose himself. In doing so one would naturally make contact with Merleau-Ponty and other existentialist philosophers who employed similar notions of choosing oneself. It would also be tempting to divide, say, the interrepresentability class of Sextus $(S_1, \ldots, S_n)$, in accordance with various strengthened inter-representability relations, into subclasses – for example, one corresponding to the young Sextus, another to the adolescent Sextus, a third to the mature Sextus. By thus allowing for the growth of Sextus's personality, one might treat the changing class of his representative aspects as 'an open system' in the sense of the biological theory of open systems proposed by Bertalanffy and others. Both temptations must be resisted as not really serving our present purposes.

On the demarcation of actions by their agents

The action which an agent S, say Sextus, ascribes to himself by adding a new member S_n to the interrepresentability class $(S_1, \ldots, S_{n-1})$ is, of course, the chosen intervention or non-intervention in the course of nature of which S_n is the subject. It may, as before, be schematically expressed by

$$\ldots, r_1(\text{sel } b_0) \text{ pred } p_1, \ldots$$

and includes some but not all circumstances of his chosen bodily conduct. If it included them all, it would include the whole world. In accordance with our earlier distinction between physical, cognitive and evaluative attributes of a chosen intervention or non-intervention we may distinguish between the agent's physical, cognitive and evaluative demarcation of his action.

The physical demarcation includes all those attributes of which S believes (1) that they apply to his bodily conduct, independently of its being or not being chosen and (2) that their absence would imply the bodily movement's being of a different type from the type he believes it to be (e.g. the motion of a hand by which a poison is being released into a glass of wine). The cognitive demarcation of his action includes all those attributes of which S believes (1) that they apply to his chosen intervention or non-intervention *qua* chosen and (2) that their absence would imply his action's being of a different type from the type he believes it to be (e.g. the poisoning of an old man who is incurably ill). Lastly the evaluative demarcation of his action includes all those attributes of which S believes (1) that they apply to his chosen intervention or non-intervention *qua* chosen and (2) that their absence would imply his having a different practical attitude towards the action from that which he in fact has (e.g. the old man's incurable illness whose absence would imply S's no longer being in favour of poisoning him).

The triviality that the same bodily movement could be involved in an unlimited variety of different actions must not be inflated into a deeply perplexing question. It makes, of course, sense to ask whether when the poison moved from S's hand into the old man's wine glass, S was acting at all and, if so, whether his action consisted in putting the poison into the wine, in putting the poison into the wine and thereby poisoning the old man, in putting the poison into the wine, thereby poisoning and killing the old man and thereby ridding him of his incurable disease, etc. At the moment we are concerned with the agent's answer. And he will – making allowances for confusion, self-deception and other human shortcomings – be able to demarcate his action by indicating the physical, cognitive and evaluative attributes which he regards as essential to his action, i.e. those attributes in the absence of which he would not have regarded the action as being of the type of which he believes it to be.

It should, moreover, be remembered that it is not only the per-ceptual core of actions which admits of an unlimited variety of interpretations but that the same is true of perceptions in general. It makes sense to ask whether or not what appears to be a chair is in fact a chair, and if so, whether it is a ceremonial chair, whether in that case it gives its occupants a feeling of security, etc. And if we are concerned with a particular percipient's answers, he will – making again the necessary allowances – be able to demarcate his perception by indicating the attributes he regards as essential to the perceived object, i.e. those attributes in the absence of which he would not have regarded the perceived object as being of the type of which he believes it to be.

On the external perspective of an action and the concurrence of its internal and external perspectives

An external perspective of an action differs from the internal one in being made not by the person observing and judging the chosen bodily conduct associated with his own body, but by somebody else. Apart from this fundamental difference, an external perspective is like the internal perspective in that it involves the ascription of a chosen intervention or non-intervention to a persisting agent as well as its physical, cognitive and evaluative demarcation. While the external and the internal perspective of an action may be very different from each other, there must be some minimal agreement between them, since otherwise it would make no sense to speak of them as different perspectives of the same action, of apparently the same action, or even of the same apparent action. It is in harmony with both commonsense and the law that S, say Sextus, and his judge J, say the priest of Jupiter at Dodona, agree on the bodily conduct in question.

There is no need to characterize J's ascription of an action to S and J's demarcation of the so-ascribed action. One would simply have to repeat what has been said about the ascription of a chosen intervention or non-intervention by S to S and the demarcation by S of what has been so ascribed to S – with the obvious difference of substituting J for S as the person who makes the ascription and the demarcation. On the other hand, it might be unwise not to make at least a few remarks about the concurrence or lack of it between an action's internal and its external perspectives. For although the need to distinguish between the internal and the external ascription and demarcation – physical, cognitive and evaluative – cannot be overlooked in the case of speaking or writing and other special kinds of conduct, it is sometimes forgotten that it implies to all actions of man *qua* social animal.

As regards the concurrence of internal and external ascription of an action to S the widest divergence between S and J consists in one of them ascribing an apparent action to S while the other believes that the bodily conduct observed in S's body was not chosen at all. English criminal law recognizes the possibility of wholly unchosen conduct, e.g. in the case of epileptic seizures, under the name of automatism. (See e.g. Williams 1961: §§ 156ff.) A less wide divergence exists, if S and J agree that there is a chooser S_n of the bodily conduct observed in S's body, but only one of them judges that the choice is S's in the sense that adding S_n to the interrepresentability class $(S_1, ..., S_{n-1})$ will yield an extended interrepresentability class $(S_1, ..., S_n)$ (defined under the same equivalence relation Interrep-P).

The nature of this difference is often expressed by saying that the point at issue between S and J is whether or not the action is so much 'out of character' that it cannot be ascribed to S. Since S's character is determined by his past cognitive judgments and his past preferences, one may distinguish between whether the action is cognitively, evaluatively, or both cognitively and evaluatively out of character. English criminal law (see Williams 1961: §§ 156ff.) acknowledges the legitimacy of these questions and gives guidance to its judges in certain simple situations. The M'Naghten rules, in particular, imply that S_n should not be regarded as a representative (member of the interrepresentability class) of S if S is cognitively and evaluatively normal, whereas S_n is not because, for example, S_n is under severe delusions or because S_n 'knowing the nature and quality of his act' did not know 'that it was wrong' in an (evaluative) sense of the term, whose legal interpretation is by no means constant. Outside the sphere of law the meaning of cognitive and evaluative normality varies even more. The former depends among other things, on a society's dominant theoretical principles, the latter on its dominant moral principles (see chapter 14).

If S and J agree that the action of S_n is to be ascribed to S as 'not being wholly out of character' they may, of course, still disagree about its physical, cognitive or evaluative demarcation, i.e. about the attributes which they regard as essential to the classification of the action *qua* physical occurrence; to its classification *qua* intervention or non-intervention in the course of nature chosen under certain impressions about it; and lastly to its classification as chosen not only under certain impressions about the course of nature but also with a certain practical attitude towards the chosen intervention or non-intervention in it.

In order to illustrate these three types of disagreement between S and J we assume, as before, that S believes that he has put poison into the wine of an old man who suffered from an incurable disease and that he classified his action as a mercy killing. We further assume that J is an English criminal judge and consider some cases in which J's and S's physical, cognitive and evaluative demarcation of S's action differ from each other. As regards a possible divergence in their physical demarcation of S's action, J may believe or even know that, quite independently of S's choice, the old man had died a day before S put the poison in his wine and that consequently S's action could not even be classified as an attempt at killing. In technical legal language J would hold that there was no *actus reus*. As regards a possible divergence in S's and J's cognitive demarcation of S's action, J may believe or even know – that while the substance which S put into the old man's wine was poisonous, there was not enough of it to kill the old man, who was in any case prevented from drinking the wine. J would consequently classify S's action as an attempted killing. Lastly, as regards a possible divergence in their evaluative demarcation of S's action, J may believe that S would not have changed his attitude towards killing the old man had he learned that he was not ill at all. J would consequently not classify S's notion as a mercy killing but, depending on the circumstances, as, say, a killing for gain.

What now is the correct description of an action whose external and internal perspectives differ from each other and what is its correct description, if one wishes to take account of more than one different external perspective? The answer is, it would seem, not in doubt. The correct description is that which contains in the greatest possible detail each of the different demarcations of the action – by the agent himself and by everybody who observed his bodily conduct at the time of the action. But as a rule there will be a sufficient concurrence between the internal and the various external perspectives to allow for a common classification of an action – as the opening or closing of a door, the buying of theatre tickets, the making and breaking of promises, etc. Indeed our curiosity about a person's actions is often fully, and truthfully, satisfied when a whole course of his actions is (internally and externally) classified as going to school, taking a holiday, trying to make a career in politics, etc.

CHAPTER 7

PRACTICAL ATTITUDES: THEIR
OBJECTS AND LEVELS

Among the tasks of the formal, and in some ways preparatory, part of this essay was the presentation in outline of the so-called logic of practical preference or, more precisely, a theory of the ordering, grading and measuring of practical attitudes. While presupposing this 'logic', the present chapter goes beyond it. Its aim is to advance the analysis of practical attitudes by exhibiting some characteristic relations between practical attitudes and beliefs and by examining the objects of practical attitudes, especially practicabilities which themselves involve practical attitudes.

The chapter begins by considering practical attitudes in their dependence on practical beliefs and by briefly commenting on the alleged contrast between the irremediable subjectivity of practical attitudes and the possible objectivity of practical and other beliefs. Next, attention is drawn to the frequently realized possibility of practical attitudes being themselves the objects of practical attitudes. By recognizing this stratification of attitudes one is led to a clear characterization and distinction of the ways in which practical attitudes may conflict with each other. The chapter ends by considering the relation of practical implication between attitudes.

The objects of practical attitudes as dependent on practical beliefs

It is quite common, and makes perfectly good sense, that a person should prefer an unrealized situation or sequence of situations (described by a proposition) f_1 to an equally unrealized situation or sequence of situations (described by a proposition) f_2 – even if he believes that he has no influence whatever on the realization of either. Yet his preference for f_1 over f_2 or, more generally, over $f_2, ..., f_n$ will be practical only if he believes that he can effectively choose to realize each of these alternatives by one or more actions. (See chapter 4, p. 51.) If one action suffices for the realization of each

88

alternative f_r we can, as before express its being effectively choosable by:

(1) $f_r = ..., r_0, \text{sel} (b_r) \, pred \, p_r,$

(2) $7 \, (..., r_0 \, pred \, b_r),$

(3) $7 \, (..., r_0 \, pred \, p_r),$

where $f_1, ..., f_n$ share the same retrospect, but differ in their chosen bodily conduct and the subjectively predetermined prospect.

What has just been said about preferential ordering applies also to the grading of preferences. It makes, for example, good sense for a person to have a pro-attitude towards f_1, whether or not be believes himself to have any effective choice in the matter. But his pro-attitude is practical if, and only if, he believes that he can effectively choose to realize each among the situations or sequences of situations $f_1, f_2, ..., f_n$ and if he believes in addition that they are mutually exclusive and jointly exhaustive of what he believes to be effectively choosable for him. The same practical beliefs, namely that $f_1, f_2, ..., f_n$ are effectively choosable, mutually exclusive and jointly exhaustive of all choosable alternative are presupposed by a person's practical anti-attitude towards f_1 and by his practical attitude of indifference towards f_1.

Actions are the fundamental practicabilities, as one might call the possible objects of practical attitudes. Two other kinds of practicability, which are definable in terms of actions, are on the one hand courses of action, on the other abstract practicabilities. A course of action contains at least two actions and differs thus from a simple action by being a sequence of situations containing at least two different occurrences of chosen bodily conduct, each of which (subjectively) predetermines a different prospect. As to the demarcation of a course of action, one must naturally take account of the internal and external perspectives of the component actions, as well as of their concurrence. While it is often convenient not to distinguish between actions and courses of action, it is occasionally useful to distinguish between different kinds of courses of action, for example, those in which the same sort of chosen bodily conduct is repeated at regular intervals, or those in which all the prospects, although predetermined by different occurrences of chosen bodily conduct, are in certain important respects similar. These and similar refinements, however, need not be considered here.

An abstract practicability is any feature of a situation or sequence of situations – other than being an action or course or actions – of which the performance of an (effectively choosable) action or course of actions is in the agent's belief a necessary and sufficient condition. The variety of abstract practicabilities is enormous. Examples are 'becoming a teacher', 'getting tired', 'being considered stupid', 'continuing to be honest', 'getting oneself killed', becoming a better man', 'changing one's style of life', etc.

Having a practical preference for one practicability over another obviously presupposes the belief that they are in fact practicabilities, but not that they are practicabilities of the same type. One may well practically prefer an action to an abstract practicability, for example opening a locked door to not getting into trouble. It is similarly not uncommon to have a pro-attitude towards a practicability which consists in not preferring to it any member of a set of mutually exclusive and jointly exhaustive practicabilities of different types. One may, for example, have a practical pro-attitude towards spending a quiet weekend – considering all those courses of action which are open to one, which are exclusive of spending a quiet weekend and of each other and which together with spending a quiet weekend are jointly exhaustive of what is practicable during that weekend.

On an alleged contrast between the irremediable subjectivity of practical attitudes and the possible objectivity of practical beliefs

Before examining the systematic connection of a person's practical attitudes with each other and with other attitudes and before contrasting the peculiarities of these relations with the relations which hold between beliefs, it will be useful to dispel the spurious impression of a certain allegedly fundamental difference between practical attitudes and practical beliefs. The difference is supposed to consist in an irremediable subjectivity of practical attitudes and a possible objectivity of practical beliefs, as a consequence of which the former – in contrast to the latter – are incapable of being either correct or incorrect. But there are, at least, two reasons why practical attitudes are capable of being incorrect. The first is simply that since a person's possessing a practical attitude logically implies his possessing a practical belief and since a practical belief may be correct or incorrect, it makes sense to judge a practical attitude, based on an incorrect belief, as being incorrect. Thus my practical preference for having my cake and eating it over either having it or else over eating it is incorrect; and so is my practical preference for eternal youth over getting older or dying.

The second reason which will be explained in greater detail, lies not so much in the systematic connection of practical attitudes with practical beliefs, as in the systematic connection of practical attitudes with each other. Practical and other beliefs as well as practical and other attitudes are not held in isolation from each other, but in systems whose organization may be correct or incorrect by standards which the person who holds the beliefs or attitudes has explicitly or implicitly accepted. Frequently these standards are not peculiar to him, but are interpersonal and anchored in social institutions. In the case of a person's beliefs one can distinguish between his separate beliefs about what *seems* to him to be the case, which by themselves are not capable of incorrectness; the attempted organization of his beliefs into logically consistent systems, which has the consequence that of two mutually inconsistent beliefs at least one must be incorrect; and the attempted organization of his beliefs into a system in such a manner that all of them are required to be consistent with certain overriding theoretical principles such as the principle of causality, which has the consequence that a belief in uncaused events is incorrect.

In the case of a person's practical and other attitudes, one can similarly distinguish between his separate practical attitudes, such as his practical preference for eating his cake over having it, which by themselves are not capable of incorrectness; the attempted organization of his practical attitudes into 'practically consistent' systems, which has the consequence that corresponding to each required kind of practical consistency there arises a possibility of practical inconsistency between practical attitudes; and the attempted organization of his practical (and other) attitudes into a system in such a manner that all of them are required to be consistent with certain overriding practical principles, such as the principle of loving one's neighbour, which has the consequence that a hateful act against one's neighbour is practically incorrect. Just as the analysis of the logical consistency of our beliefs with overriding factual principles presupposes an understanding of logical consistency, so the analysis of the 'practical consistency' of our practical attitudes with overriding practical principles presupposes an understanding of practical consistency. An analysis of the various types of this relationship between attitudes is badly needed since, in spite of its importance, it has been largely ignored by moral philosophers and others concerned with the structure of practical and evaluative thinking.

On practical attitudes as objects of practical and other attitudes

In looking for the kind of conflict between practical attitudes which would correspond to logical inconsistency between beliefs, several plausible candidates seem to offer themselves. Since, as will become clear, one source of this competition lies in the manner in which practical attitudes may themselves become objects of practical or other attitudes, it is necessary to examine the relations between the so stratified attitudes. The fundamental fact is (*a*) that the character of a person's practical attitude of first (or nth) level towards some practicability does not determine whether the person has, or has not, an attitude of second (or $(n+1)$th) level towards this first (or nth) level attitude and (*b*) that if the person has such an attitude of second (or $(n+1)$th) level its character is not determined by the practical attitude of first (or nth) level which is the object of the higher level attitude.

In order to make this clear it seems advisable to use a transparent symbolism for the expression of both the character and the level of practical attitudes and to choose examples which are unlikely to engage anybody's emotions very strongly. The symbolism, explained earlier (in chapter 4), for the representation of first level practical attitudes is readily adjusted to the representation of practical attitudes of higher level. Let us, then, assume (1) that f and g are members of a set of (propositions which describe a set of) mutually exclusive and jointly exhaustive practicabilities which a person S_0 believes to be realizable by himself and (2) that none of these practicabilities involves the presence or absence of a practical attitude. Any practical attitude of S_0 towards f or g is thus a practical attitude of first level. Examples are: (fR_0g), i.e. S_0 weakly prefers f to g; (gP_0f), i.e. S_0 strongly prefers g to f; S_0+f, i.e. S_0 has a practical pro-attitude towards f.

If, as will be argued, a person may have practical attitudes of second level, i.e. practical attitudes towards his practical attitudes, the method of symbolic representation can remain the same. For example $(fR_0g)P_0(gR_0f)$ means that S_0 strongly prefers his weak preference for f over g to his weak preference for g over f; and $S_0-[S_0+f]$ that S_0 has a practical anti-attitude towards his having a practical pro-attitude towards f. It will be sufficient to consider only practical pro-attitudes, anti-attitudes or attitudes of indifference of first or higher level, since these will henceforth be our main concern and since what will be said about them is easily extended to other kinds of preferential grading, ordering and measuring.

Consider, then, the situation described by the statement $(S_0 * f)$ to the effect that S_0 has a certain first level practical attitude towards f (where $*$ stands for $+$, $-$ or $\pm$). We can distinguish the following possible second level practical attitudes: (1) S_0 has no second level practical attitude towards his first level attitude. The first level attitude is undominated. (2) S_0 has a practical pro-attitude towards his first level attitude. The first level attitude is positively dominated, i.e. $S_0 + [S_0 * f]$. (3) S_0 has a practical anti-attitude towards his first level attitude. The first level attitude is negatively dominated, i.e. $S_0 - [S_0 * f]$. (4) S_0 has a practical attitude of indifference towards his first level attitude. The first level attitude is indifferently dominated, i.e. $S_0 \pm [S_0 * f]$. Practical attitudes of third and higher level are represented on the same lines.

We are now ready to verify the fundamental fact about the relation between a person's first level and his second and higher level practical attitudes. This can be done only by means of examples combined with an appeal to introspection or, at least, imaginative empathy. It should thus not be too difficult to feel empathy with a person S_0 who teaches at a University and who dislikes sitting on committees, i.e. who has a first level attitude $S_0 - c$. It should further be easy to conceive of this person as an intellectual snob who likes his dislike for sitting on committees, i.e. who has a second level attitude $S_0 + [S_0 - c]$. Lastly, for good measure, it should be possible to imagine that S_0 has a fairly well developed social sense combined with the conviction of the importance of committee work and consequently to imagine that $S_0 - [S_0 + [S_0 - c]]$, i.e. that S_0 dislikes his liking his dislike for sitting on committees. Now in order to establish (1) that S_0's first level practical attitude does not determine whether or not he has a second level practical attitude towards it, one must either be able to vary our example by imagining that S_0 has no attitude towards his dislike of committees or produce another example of a first level practical attitude which is not the object of an attitude of second level. And in order to establish (2) that S_0's first level practical attitude does not determine the character of his second level attitude, if he has such an attitude, one must again be able to vary our example by imagining that S_0 dislikes or is indifferent towards his first level anti-attitude or to produce another example of a first level anti-attitude which is the object of a second level anti-attitude or attitude of indifference.

To insist that introspection and empathy provide the necessary clear illustrations of the range of higher level attitudes directed towards attitudes of lower level, is not to imply that the character of our attitudes on every level is always clear to us. There may be uncertainty about some of our attitudes, just as there may be uncertainty about some of our beliefs – another similarity between attitudes and beliefs. As against this it is instructive to note an important dissimilarity between them, namely the difference between clearly held attitudes towards clearly held attitudes and clearly held beliefs about clearly held beliefs. The latter relation, unlike the former, is a clear one-to-one correspondence: If S_0 believes with complete certainty that f then he also believes with complete certainty that he believes that f. Whether one construes the statement of this one-to-one correspondence as an empirical generalization or a phenomenological truth is of little consequence. (The same applies also to the question whether the statement should not be given the additional force of being made true by suitable definitions of its terms.)

While one clearly has attitudes towards one's practical attitudes, it might be doubtful whether these higher attitudes are themselves ever practical – in particular when the higher and the lower attitude are in discordance with each other. Can a person's second level anti-attitude towards his first level pro-attitude towards smoking be regarded as practical at a time when his first level pro-attitude is such that he cannot refuse a cigarette whenever he is offered one? Since a person's attitude is practical if, and only if, he is capable of implementing it and has chosen to do so, the answer depends on whether he is capable of breaking himself of his habit and whether he is taking serious steps gradually to cut down his smoking or showing other evidence of having chosen to implement his second order preference. Thus a person who is undergoing aversion therapy against smoking should, it seems, be credited with a practical anti-attitude towards his practical pro-attitude towards smoking. Many of our resolutions and our beliefs in our ability to become morally better persons imply our conviction that at least some of our higher level attitudes are practical. It seems that as we ascend to the third and higher levels the question of whether an attitude is practical becomes more difficult to answer with confidence.

In considering $S_0 + [S_0 - c]$, i.e. S_0's second level pro-attitude towards his first level practical anti-attitude toward his sitting on committees, and in considering higher level attitudes in general, it has been assumed that the subject of the lower and the higher attitude is the same. This reflectiveness is preserved if the higher attitude is directed towards a lower attitude held by a class of people, provided only that this class includes the subject of the higher attitude. In other words not only $S_0 + [S_0 - c]$ but also $S_0 + [X - c]$ is a second level (reflective) attitude if S_0 is included in the range of X. An attitude $S_0 + [S_1 - c]$, where S_0 and S_1 are different subjects, or an attitude $S_0 + [X - c]$ where S_0 is not included in the range of X, is no longer reflective. If, as seems convenient, we make reflectiveness a condition of a higher level attitude, then all non-reflective attitudes – even if directed towards (other people's) attitudes are of first level.

On the opposition between practical attitudes of the same level and some other relations defined in terms of it

The opposition of preferential attitudes of the same level may be regarded as a relation which is clearly understood and not in need of definition. It is quite clear what is meant by saying that, if f and g describe two situations then any two members selected from the triplet 'strong preference for f over g', 'strong preference for g over f' and 'indifference between f and g' are opposed; and that the same holds for any two members of the triplet 'pro-attitude towards f', 'anti-attitude towards f' and 'indifferent attitude towards f' (as defined on p. 57). If the preferential attitudes are not practical then their opposition does not seem to be further analysable. In particular, to say that two such attitudes are opposed to each other if, and only if, they cannot be simultaneously held by one and the same person, is simply false: people do hold opposed attitudes not only, as in the case of incompatible beliefs, without being aware of their opposition but also with the full knowledge of their opposition. The so-called 'ambivalence' of attitudes is not an invention of psychology.

In the case of practical attitudes their opposition is definable in terms of their joint realizability: two practical attitudes of a person are opposed if, and only if, they (i.e. their objects) are separately, but not jointly realizable by his action. According to the nature of the impossibility of realization one can distinguish between logical, empirical and practical opposition. The opposition is logical, if the joint realization of the attitudes is incompatible with the principles of logic; empirical, if the joint realization is incompatible with the laws of nature, but not the principles of logic; practical, if the joint realization though compatible with the laws of nature, cannot be brought about by the person's action. An example of a logical opposition is a person's practical pro-attitude to smoking (realized by his smoking) and his practical anti-attitude to smoking (realized by his not smoking). Instead of speaking of the 'opposition between practical attitudes', it will often be possible, without causing misunderstanding, to speak briefly of 'practical opposition' in a wide sense, which covers all the types of opposition between them.

Another important relation between practical attitudes is their practical complementarity: two practical attitudes of a person are practically complementary if, and only if, they are practically opposed and if whichever course of action the person adopts it is necessary that one of them will be realized by it. Two practical attitudes of a person are empirically complementary if, and only if, it is incompatible with the course of nature, but not logically impossible, that one of them should not be realized. And two practical attitudes of a person are logically complementary if, and only if, it is logically impossible that one of them should not be realized. The complementarity and opposition of attitudes are related in the same way as the contradictoriness and incompatibility of beliefs. The first of each pair implies, but is not implied by, the second.

On the discordance and incongruence between attitudes

Opposition is not the only kind of conflict between attitudes. Another is discordance which is a relation between an attitude directed towards another attitude and the attitude towards which it is directed. It consists of the lower attitude's being negatively dominated by the higher, i.e. in a person's having a practical anti-attitude towards a situation which itself includes his having a practical attitude. Although as kinds of conflict between attitudes both discordance and opposition bear a certain analogy to logical inconsistency between beliefs, it is important to notice one feature which logical inconsistency between beliefs shares with the opposition of attitudes but does not share with their discordance. Having opposed practical attitudes – such as being in favour of some practicability and also being in its disfavour or of strongly preferring f over g and also g over f – is, like holding inconsistent beliefs, always mistaken and is always regarded as a human shortcoming. Because every practical attitude involves a belief in the practicability of its object, having opposed practical attitudes implies having logically inconsistent beliefs and thus making an intellectual mistake. On the other hand, having discordant attitudes – such as having an anti-attitude towards one's preference for smoking over non-smoking or towards one's enjoyment of the infliction of needless pain – may sometimes be regarded as being far from mistaken or from being a human shortcoming. Indeed, some of our practical anti-attitudes towards some of our practical pro-attitudes may make us feel more hopeful for ourselves and mankind.

Psychologically the discordance between a higher and a lower attitude is often felt as a tendency towards weakening the latter, just as a concordance is often felt as its strengthening. Under certain conditions, whose precise formulation presupposes a fuller inquiry into the structure of a person's system of practical and other attitudes, the discordance between a higher and a lower attitude is felt as a conflict between duty and inclination. Indeed, the distinction between higher and lower attitudes in the sense implied by the stratification of attitudes will turn out to be relevant to the ethical distinction between morally higher and lower attitudes.

So far we have considered only relations between attitudes of first and second or other immediately adjoining levels. But there is no difficulty in covering other possibilities which are of interest. This could be done by distinguishing between immediately dominated, mediately dominated and undominated attitudes. An attitude, say B, is immediately dominated by another attitude, say A, if, and only if, A is directed towards B. An attitude B is mediately dominated by an attitude A if, and only if, A is directed towards A_1 which is directed towards A_2... which is directed towards A_n which is directed towards B, provided that A and B are separated by at least one attitude. An attitude B is undominated if, and only if, it is neither immediately nor mediately dominated by another. The mediate, like the immediate domination, may, depending on the character of the highest attitude, be positive, negative or indifferent. According to the simplest definition an undominated negative attitude would be discordant with all the lower attitudes which are immediately or mediately dominated by it.

We now turn to a third kind of conflict between practical attitudes which, though different from opposition and discordance, presupposes both of them. Second level attitudes may conflict not only by being opposed to each other, but also by being directed towards an 'unfitting' combination of first level attitudes. More precisely two unopposed attitudes of second level (of nth level with $n \geqslant 2$) are incongruent – as I shall say to distinguish this kind of conflict from opposition and discordance – if, and only if, (1) each of them positively dominates a first $((n-1)$th) level practical attitude and the dominated attitudes are opposed to each other or (2) if each of them negatively dominates a first $((n-1)$th) level practical attitude and the dominated attitudes are complementary to each other. The incongruence is again logical, empirical or practical according to whether the opposition or complementarity of the dominated attitudes is logical empirical or practical. An example of two logically incongruent attitudes are a pro-attitude towards a pro-attitude towards committing suicide on a certain day and a pro-attitude towards a pro-attitude towards starting a month's vacation on that day (because the two positively dominated attitudes are logically opposed). Another example of two logically incongruent attitudes are an anti-attitude towards an anti-attitude towards committing suicide on a certain day and an anti-attitude towards an anti-attitude towards not committing suicide on that day (because the two negatively dominated attitudes are logically complementary). Examples of empirically and practically incongruent attitudes are also easily given although there is less agreement between different people as to which attitudes are empirically opposed (or complementary) and still less agreement as to which are practically opposed (or complementary).

Practical implication and practical constraints of higher level

The analysis of practical inconsistency leads to a definition of practical implication and of constraints by practical attitudes of higher level which invite comparison with the corresponding cognitive notions of logical implication and of ontological constraints. Of the three species of practical inconsistency – opposition, discordance and incongruence – opposition is least removed from its cognitive counterpart. For to state that two practical attitudes are logically opposed is simply to state that the propositions describing their joint realization are logically inconsistent; and to state that they are empirically or practically opposed is to state that the proposition describing their joint realization is logically inconsistent with certain non-logical propositions. With the notion of discordance – and therefore of incongruence which presupposes the opposition and discordance of practical attitudes – a non-logical feature, based on the stratification of practical attitudes, enters the notion of practical inconsistency in the wide sense of the term. Indeed, that the character of a second level practical attitude which is directed towards a first level practical attitude is not logically dependent on the character of the first level practical attitude, radically distinguishes practical inconsistency from logical inconsistency and logical implication.

It is nevertheless possible to exhibit a relation of practical implication, to characterize its function in practical reasoning and to indicate how a formal system of practical implication might be developed. The fundamental notion is the concept of practical possibility applied to statements which ascribe a practical attitude to a person. More particularly, if '$S * f$' is such a statement, then $\Diamond (S * f)$ – i.e. $(S * f)$ is practically possible – if, and only if, the practical attitude $*f$ ascribed to S cannot be decomposed into component attitudes two of which are practically inconsistent with each other. (Example: $\Diamond (S$ has a practical pro-attitude towards smoking and dancing whether at the same time or at different times).) Consequently $7 \Diamond (S * f)$ – i.e. $(S * f)$ is practically impossible – if, and only if, the practical attitude $*f$ ascribed to S can be decomposed into component attitudes two of which are practically inconsistent with each other. (Example: $7 \Diamond (S$ has a pro-attitude towards smoking and not smoking).) Lastly, $7 \Diamond 7 (S * f)$ or $\square (S * f)$ – i.e. $(S * f)$ is practically necessary – if, and only if, the practical attitude $*f$ ascribed to S is such that his not having it would involve his having a practically impossible attitude. (Example: $\square (S$ has an anti-attitude towards smoking and not smoking at the same time).) Using a, b, c, etc. as variables ranging over statements ascribing a, possibly compound, practical attitude to a person S, the definition of practical necessity can be written as

(1) $\square a \overset{=}{_\text{D}} 7 \Diamond 7 a$

and practical implication can be defined by

(2) $a \text{-}{\prec} \cdot b \overset{=}{_\text{D}} 7 \Diamond (a \wedge 7 b)$

Just as a person's thinking about matters of fact may be subject to cognitively dominating principles, so his evaluative thinking may be subject to practical principles of higher level. Assuming that a person has accepted a set of higher level practical principles, be they moral, prudential or of some other kind, we can, on the analogy of ontological necessity and possibility *with respect to* a set of cognitive principles, define a notion of practical necessity and possibility or coherence with respect to a set of practical principles. If P is a set of such practical principles (to be analysed in chapter 9) and if we assume a notion of practical acceptability we may define the practical necessity of a practical attitude with respect to P as its being not only practically acceptable but as also being practically implied by P. Schematically

(3) $\square_P a = \mathrm{Acc}\,(a) \wedge P \mathrel{-\!\!\!\diagdown}\cdot a$

And we may define the practical possibility or coherence of a practical attitude with respect to P by

(4) $\diamondsuit_P a \stackrel{=}{_D} \mathrm{Acc}\,(a) \vee {}_7 (P \mathrel{-\!\!\!\diagdown}\cdot {}_7 a)$

The analogy between these practical notions and the corresponding cognitive notions of ontological necessity and coherence must not obscure their differences. Thus, to give an obvious example, the statement that S has a second level anti-attitude towards his first level pro-attitude towards smoking means that the two attitudes are practically inconsistent or, more precisely, discordant. Hence the statement that S has a practical anti-attitude towards his practical pro-attitude towards smoking *practically* implies that he does not have a practical pro-attitude towards smoking. But the antedecent of this practical implication does not logically imply its consequent and is neither logically inconsistent nor ontologically incoherent with its negation.

While the construction of a formal system of practical implication seems both unnecessary for our purpose and premature, the following remarks seem in order. First, both formal and informal reasoning would get into difficulties by ignoring that all the statements which occur in practical implications are statements ascribing specific practical attitudes to one person or negations of such statements. Second, any attempt at an axiomatic treatment of practical implications will be confronted with apparent paradoxes due to inessential components. These apparent paradoxes can be dealt with in the same way as the analogous so-called 'paradoxes' of deontic and logical implication (see chapter 2). Lastly, one would have to distinguish clearly and explicitly between a weak negation of a which merely denies the presence of an attitude and a strong negation of a which in addition asserts the presence of a practically incompatible attitude.

CHAPTER 8

ON SOME COMMON CHARACTERIZATIONS OF ACTIONS AND AGENTS

The main task of the preceding three chapters was to analyse the (italicized) key concepts in statements to the effect that *an agent* (as opposed to a member of the equivalence class of his 'could-be's' and his other aspects) by his *chosen bodily conduct* (a chosen bodily performance or non-performance) *subjectively predetermines* (causally, probabilistically or in some other way which he regards as *effective*) the realization of a *practicability* (a possible action, course of action or abstract practicability), holding certain beliefs about the *retrospect* and *prospect* of his bodily conduct (without which beliefs its cognitive demarcation would be different) and having certain *practical attitudes* (without which the evaluative demarcation of his action would be different), namely a *practical attitude of first level* (towards a set of apparent practicabilities) which is either *undominated* or (positively, negatively or indifferently) *dominated* by a *reflective* attitude of *second level* (with the further possibility of reflective attitudes of a finite number of higher levels). Before putting these key concepts to further work, it seems advisable and useful to relate them to some of the vaguer and more flexible concepts – feeling, will, motive, purpose, reasons, interest, character and others – which are sometimes used in the description of the structure and substance of chosen conduct. In comparing the two groups of concepts one may hope to clarify and sharpen the meanings of both.

The place of practical attitudes in some psychological classifications

Our definition of the various practical attitudes in terms of preference relations between possibilities which are believed to be mutually exclusive, jointly exhaustive and realizable by chosen bodily conduct, cuts across the usual classifications of mental phenomena and mental faculties. Since nothing in this enquiry depends on assumptions about an unconscious mental life, it will be sufficient to consider briefly a familiar classification of conscious mental phenomena, which goes back at least to Descartes, and a familiar classification of mental faculties, which goes back at least to Kant.

The Cartesian classification of mental phenomena, as refined by Brentano, distinguishes between presentations in which one is aware of an object which may or may not exist outside one's awareness; judgments in which one judges that an object of one's awareness exists also outside it; and emotions in which a pro- or anti-attitude is directed towards an object of one's awareness which is judged to exist. Leaving aside the general question of the suitability and completeness of this classification – whether for example it does justice to emotions which, like depression, can be without an object – it allows us to characterize a practical attitude fairly well as consisting of the presentation of an object (which may or may not exist outside one's awareness), i.e. a practicability, of the judgment that it exists in the sense of being realizable by chosen bodily conduct and of an emotion, namely a pro- or anti-attitude or an attitude of indifference directed towards the object.

Although Descartes and Brentano distinguish between simple and reflective awareness, i.e. a person's awareness of an object and a person's awareness of his awareness of this object, they do not make the analogous distinction between simple or first level attitudes and reflective attitudes or attitudes of higher level. This distinction enables one to gain a clearer insight into the complex structure of a person's system of practical attitudes as manifested, for example, by the different ways in which practical attitudes may conflict with each other. On the other hand Descartes and Brentano do make a distinction between two types of emotions, namely those which are and those which are not self-evidently correct.

Making the later distinction is, from the point of view of this inquiry, no less mistaken than failing to acknowledge the stratification of practical attitudes. It is of some interest briefly to trace a possible connection between these characteristic features of the Descartes–Brentano doctrine. If a person's system of attitudes is acknowledged to be stratified and thus to have a fairly complex structure, one may seek – as will be done here – for an explanation of the difference between moral attitudes (such as an anti-attitude to killing for gain) and morally irrelevant attitudes (such as an anti-attitude towards eating cheese) in terms of the different place which these attitudes occupy in the person's system of attitudes. If on the other hand a person's system of attitudes is conceived as a uniform collection, without any hierarchical or other structure, then the alleged self-evidence of moral attitudes might appear the only way of philosophically justifying the difference between moral and other practical attitudes.

Both these shortcomings are avoided by the Kantian classification of mental faculties. Kant distinguishes between a faculty of sensory and intellectual cognition, a faculty of feeling pleasure and displeasure and lastly, a faculty of lower and upper desire (*Begehrungsvermögen*). This last faculty is the faculty of practical attitudes (towards the realization of options through action); and its division into a lower and an upper level implies a stratification of practical attitudes – even if in some important respects it differs from ours. According to Kant the lower faculty of desire manifests itself in practical attitudes towards specific practical options or in practical attitudes expressed by general rules or maxims. The higher faculty of desire is directed towards practical attitudes expressed by maxims and manifests itself in a purely formal principle, the categorical imperative, whose applicability to a maxim is considered a necessary and sufficient condition of morality. While this assumption – quite apart from its intricate connection with Kant's doctrine of natural necessity and noumenal freedom – will not be borne out by our enquiry, it must be emphasized that he clearly recognized the stratification of practical attitudes and its importance for an understanding of their function. It might be argued that the Aristotelian concept of will (βούλησις) as opposed to desire (ἐπιθυμία) anticipates some aspects of the Kantian distinction and that the Freudian concept of the super-ego, as opposed to the ego and to the id, is a naturalistic descendant of it. Although economists have on the whole ignored the stratification of practical attitudes, they have recently started to give it some attention. (See e.g. Sen 1974. A brief discussion of the stratification of practical attitudes and its relevance to the analysis of morality is found in Körner 1955: ch. 18.)

Motives and ends

In ordinary life one is usually satisfied if an enquiry after the motive for a person's action is answered by indicating the purpose or end of his action; and conversely, if an enquiry after, the purpose of his action is answered by indicating his motives. This is why in the explanation of actions 'motive' and 'end' tend to be used interchangeably unless one's awareness of etymology or of a special terminology acts as a brake. Etymology, in particular, subsumes the notion of a motive, which moves a person to act in a certain way, to that of an Aristotelian efficient cause, whose actual occurrence precedes the person's bodily conduct; and the notion of an end to that of an Aristotelian final cause, whose actual occurrence succeeds it. Yet not only a motive, which is actually present before or during the chosen bodily conduct, but also an end which before or during the chosen bodily conduct is only 'potentially' present, can be (and has been) conceived as predetermining the sequence of events which succeeds the chosen bodily conduct. Such teleological predetermination is understood as a necessary transition from potentially to actually present ends – whether or not the ends are conscious human ends.

Teleological explanation, i.e. explanation by teleological predetermination, still persists to a small extent in biology. Even there, however, some of the more recalcitrant types of teleological predetermination of actual by potential situations have by now been replaced by new types of causal predetermination of actual by preceding actual situations. These replacements have come about mainly as the result of new theoretical developments, in particular the thermodynamics of open systems, cybernetics and general system theory (see e.g. Bertalanffy 1968).

If one rejects the assumption of teleological predetermination, then a person's conscious end or purpose when choosing an action and implementing his choice is part of his conscious motive, i.e. among the beliefs and practical attitudes which, as it seems to him, move him to choose and act as he in fact chooses and acts. Hence, if for want of a suitable terminology, one wished to replace the almost interchangeable ordinary use of motive and end, in describing and explaining actions, by a distinction which would do justice to contemporary common sense, it would seem advisable first to define the concept of a motive and in terms of it the concept of an end. Although these definitions will not be needed in what follows, a few remarks on them are in place here.

A definition of a person's conscious motive for an action, which would be in harmony with common sense, would consist in identifying his motive with his evaluative demarcation of the action. In other words, a person's conscious motive for an action is his belief that the action has certain characteristics in the absence of which he would have a practical preference for one of its practicable alternatives.

Simply to state a preference for an action is on this definition not to state the motive for it – although even this use of the term could be lexicographically defended.

If, rejecting teleological predetermination, one regards the end of an action as part of its motive, then common sense, common usage and etymology suggest that the conscious end of an action be identified with the evaluative demarcation not of the whole action, i.e. the retrospect, the chosen bodily conduct and its prospect, but only the prospect of the action. In other words, the conscious end of a person's action is his belief that its prospect has certain characteristics in the absence of which he would prefer one of the alternatives of the action.

The proposed characterizations of the motive and the end for an action could be easily extended to abstract practicabilities and courses of action. In the latter case one can isolate a sequence of ends which corresponds to the sequence of actions in the course of action to which they belong. An earlier end is a person's means to a later end in the sequence in so far as he believes that a change in the evaluative demarcation of the later end would lead to a change in the evaluative demarcation of the earlier end. All these definitions can do with a great deal of refinement and admit of alternatives which could be plausibly defended on lexicographical grounds. Yet, it seems, that all of them could without much difficulty be expressed in our terminology and sharpened by means of it.

Reasons for practical choices

The motive for an action need not be simple, but may consist of subsidiary motives or reasons. While one might plausibly define a reason for an action as a component of the motive for it, one can also find lexicographical support for the following wider definition: Assume that a person, say S, is considering the choice of an action, say $f = r \operatorname{sel}(b) \operatorname{pred} p$. Then S's pro-attitude towards a situation (described by) q, i.e. $S + q$ is a reason *for* his choosing f if, and only if, S believes (1) that the action f logically implies the situation, i.e. $f \vdash q$ or (2) that the retrospect and the bodily conduct of the action predetermine q, i.e. $r \operatorname{sel}(b) \operatorname{pred} p \wedge q$. Similarly, S's anti-attitude towards q, i.e. $S - q$, is a reason *against* his choosing f if, and only if, S believes (1) that $f \vdash \lnot q$ or (2) that $r \operatorname{sel}(b) \operatorname{pred} p \wedge \lnot q$. The first type of reason for or against an action is ostensibly logical, the second ostensibly empirical – the meaning of predetermination being necessitarian, probabilistic, or of some still other variety.

Whereas the motive, as here defined, coincides with the evaluative demarcation of a chosen action, a reason is related to a merely contemplated action, which may be or may not be chosen. And even if the contemplated action is chosen, a reason for it need not be part of the motive for it. It may be a merely supporting reason whose apparent absence would make no difference to the choice. Again, a person may have a reason against the action which he in fact chooses.

In order briefly to exemplify some of these distinctions one might return to the case of a person, say S, who has chosen to kill an old man by poison, and assume that the motive, i.e. the evaluative demarcation of his action, was to deliver the old man from an incurable disease. If S is in favour of sending the old man's soul to Hades and if he believes that a man's death logically implies the transition of his soul to Hades, then his being in favour of sending the old man's soul to Hades is an ostensibly logical reason for killing him. If S is in favour of inheriting the old man's golden watch and believes that the retrospect, which includes a will made by the old man, makes it probable that he will inherit it after the old man's death, then his being in favour of inheriting the old man's watch is an empirical reason for killing him – even though it is not part of the motive for killing him. If S is against causing the old man pain and if he believes that the retrospect and his chosen bodily conduct makes it probable that the old man will die painfully, then his being against causing the old man pain is an empirical reason against killing him.

It should be noticed that a reason for or against an action, as defined here, may be moral or immoral. And it must be emphasized that just as our distinction between motive and purpose has some support in commonsense and common language without being the only such distinction, so our distinction between *the* motive of an action and a reason for, or against it, is not the only distinction which can claim such support.

Practical interests

In the most general sense of the phrase, 'to be interested in something' is to have some attitude towards it which need not even be practical. Here we shall be concerned only with practical interests in a narrow of sense the term, the importance of which consists in taking account of those of a person's practical attitudes which he holds as a social being. I shall say – without conflicting with commonsense and common usage – that a person S has a practical interest in the establishment and continuation of a situation (described by) f if, and only if, (1) he has a practical pro-attitude towards the establishment of f, if f has not yet been established, and towards its continuation if f has been established and (2) the establishment or continuation of f depends to some extent on the conduct of other people.

Practical interests, as here defined, connect different personal systems of practical attitudes with each other into systems of personal systems or social systems of practical attitudes. This, of course, is so because conduct which serves the realization of one person's practical attitudes may *ipso facto* serve or hinder the realization of the practical attitudes of others. This relationship may, even in the case of two persons, be fairly complex. For if they have the same practical interest, i.e. have a pro-attitude towards the bringing about and continuation of the same situation, this identity of interest need not imply their co-operation, since they may not be aware of the identity or disagree about the type of conduct leading to what is in their interest. Again, two persons whose interests conflict in such a manner that their joint realization is impossible may because of partly or wholly mistaken beliefs, co-operate in bringing about and preserving a situation which is in the interest of only one of them or of neither. With an increase in the number of persons whose interests affect each other through their conduct, in the variety of these interests and in the variety of beliefs about the possibilities of intervening in the course of nature, the social system of practical attitudes soon becomes too complex for accurate description and for predictions based on it.

This complexity is one of the reasons why many thoughtful persons have felt tempted to base the prediction of the course of social phenomena not on the analysis of social systems of interests, but on divine providence, a rational and rationally reconstructible historical process or some other view which implies that the course of history is no more determined by man's practical attitudes, than is the free fall of a stone by its colour. By itself the complexity of social systems of practical attitudes is not the only conceivable reason why up to the present the attempts at creating a 'social physics' have fallen far short of Comte's hopes. Yet unless the impossibility of a social science is demonstrated beyond doubt – a demonstration which would imply the spuriousness even of economics – the complexity of social systems of attitudes seems at least a plausible excuse for the slow growth of the social sciences.

The history of the natural and of the social sciences seems to indicate that if social systems of interests are to become the subject matter of a scientific theory, their complexity has to be simplified in the same fashion as the complexity of natural systems had to be simplified in order to make them the subject matter of the natural sciences. One possible approach in this direction is to separate human conduct from the human attitudes and interests it appears to realize and to search for a suitable vocabulary describing (in a more or less idealizing manner) types of human conduct and laws connecting them. Attempts in this direction have been made by Max Weber and, more radically, by some contemporary behavioural and behaviourist scientists.

Whereas simplification of social phenomena by totally or partially neglecting attitudes and interests in favour of the conduct associated with them is a controversial theoretical procedure, it is a well-established practical procedure for the mutual adjustment of the different and often divergent interests of different reasons and social groups. Legal and other social codes of conduct consist of regulative maxims whose regulative consequents describe conduct which is required if the conditions expressed by their descriptive antecedents are satisfied (see chapter 2). These conditions either make no reference to practical attitudes or refer to practical attitudes whose presence or absence either clearly follows or is deemed to follow from certain well-defined characteristics of conduct (such as oaths and other utterances of prescribed form made by an agent or a witness).

A comparison of the kinds of conduct associated with a person's practical interests and the kind of conduct required by the maxims of a code of conduct, in particular a legal code, leads to various classifications of practical interests from the point of view of a code of conduct. Among them are the dichotomies of all practical interests into those which are or are not legitimate; into those which are or are not protected; and into those which do or do not constitute rights. A person's practical interest in the creation or continuance of a situation is legitimate if, and only if, at least some kind of conduct leading to the realization of the interest is not forbidden. It is protected if, and only if, other people are required to conduct themselves in such a manner that the realization of the interest by the interested person is not made impossible. It constitutes a right if, and only if, the interested person is permitted effectively to call upon the authority which implements

108

the code to protect his interest. A code of conduct expresses practical attitudes held by the original proposers of the code as interpreted by those charged with interpreting and implementing it. The objects of these practical attitudes are not so much the separate practical interests of those whose conduct is regulated by the code, as the manner of their adjustment to each other.

The various ways in which the practical interest of different people may be so adjusted depend on the nature of the practical interests, in particular on the extent of their joint realizability. Some practical interests, such as the exclusive use of a library by one person, are not jointly realizable. Some of these can by suitable restrictions be turned into practical interests which are jointly realizable. The restrictions may consist in a quantitative adjustment, e.g. by allowing each library user to borrow a certain fixed number of books for a certain period of time; or in a non-quantitative adjustment, e.g. by allowing certain library users to use the library at all times of day and the remaining library users only by special permission of an official who is required to use his discretion in giving it.

Although practical interests differ from legal rights, they are sufficiently similar for the various classifications of legal rights to be easily changed into corresponding classifications of practical interests. For example, to the distinction, made in Roman law, between *jura in rem* and *jura in personam* there would correspond a distinction between practical interests in *rem*, such as the ownership of a house, and practical interests in *personam*, such as the receiving of piano lessons by a competent teacher. The usefulness of classifications of practical interests derived in this manner from classifications of legal rights is, of course, based on the rôle played by legal rights in the protection and adjustment of practical interests.

Personality and character

In speaking of a person's personality or character one usually refers to the intellectual dispositions and practical attitudes which he normally manifests in his life and which one regards as distinctive of him or of a class of people to which he belongs. In trying to distinguish between a man's personality and his character one would, it seems, tend to use the latter term to cover the practical attitudes which he manifests as a member of a class or type. Classifying a person's character may involve making a moral judgment, e.g. when he is described as a morally good character or type, or it may have no moral connotations, e.g. when he is described as a military character or a scholarly type.

To be, or to have, a certain character in this sense of the term is, first of all, normally to have and to implement certain first level practical preferences for some practicabilities over others. Thus a scholarly character will normally prefer a course of action which increases his knowledge in his chosen field of scholarship to one which does not do this. And a military character will in times of war normally prefer a course of action which will enable him to fight the enemy in battle. The distinction between normal and abnormal conditions – e.g. a serious illness in the cases of the scholar or military man – is not sharp, but can be sharpened without difficulty.

It is perhaps somewhat less obvious that to be, or to have, a certain character is, secondly, to have certain higher level attitudes towards one's lower level attitudes, namely pro-attitudes to those of one's first-level attitudes which are 'in character' and anti-attitudes towards those first level attitudes which tend to weaken the first level attitudes which are in character. Thus a scholar who has a practical preference for carefully checking the facts which are relevant to this scholarly work over not doing so, will have a practical pro-attitude towards this first-level preference. On the other hand, a scholar who has a practical pro-attitude towards a weekly drinking bout which is likely to impair his scholarship, will have a practical anti-attitude towards this pro-attitude.

A third point about being or having a scholarly, military or other character concerns the relation between his first and higher level characteristics on one hand and his moral convictions on the other. It is that a person who would otherwise be regarded by himself and by others to be acting out of character, is not so regarded in cases in which acting in character would conflict with his moral conviction. Thus a scholar who is faced with the alternative of making use of his only opportunity to check a crucial reference and of helping a sick man to reach hospital in time would be acting in character, if he chose to check the reference, but he would not be acting out of character if he followed his moral convictions rather than the demands of scholarship.

There are also uses of the term, in which to be, or to have, a certain character implies having certain moral strengths or weaknesses. A Marxist's conception of the bourgeois, as a type of person, implies immoral acquisitiveness, at least from the point of view of the

Marxist's morality. And a liberal's conception of the loyal party member (of the communist party) implies immoral submission to the commands of authority, at least from the point of view of the liberal's morality. Lastly, one sometimes uses the term in the same sense as the term 'moral character'.

In speaking of a person's character in the sense of his moral character one expresses moral judgments on the practical attitudes which he manifests in his life. A perfectly moral or virtuous character is a person who whenever the choice arises between an action which is and an action which is not moral, will choose the former. A perfectly immoral or wicked character is a person who faced with these possibilities will make the opposite choice. And there are, of course, virtuous and wicked characters which sufficiently resemble the perfectly virtuous and wicked characters to be called 'virtuous' or 'wicked' (on the whole). One also distinguishes between more specific moral characters according to whether one judges the practical attitudes which they manifest towards certain classes of options to be moral or not. To be a philanthropist is to be in a certain respect virtuous, to be a bigot is to be in a certain respect wicked, to be a bigoted philanthropist is to be a mixture of the two. More complex moral characters of specific types are derived if one uses the characterization of a real or imaginary individual as the characterization of the type to which the individual belongs. In this sense one speaks, for example, of Tartuffes or Micawbers.

Although what has been said about the non-moral and moral senses of the term 'character' could be easily elaborated, it might well be objected that, even as it stands, it seems boringly obvious. This impression rests, among other things, on the correct assumption that the notions of moral attitude and of a moral judgment are quite familiar. Since, however, what is quite familiar need not coincide with what is well analysed, it should be noted that the notions of a moral attitude, a moral judgment, a morality and their cognates have (unlike the other key notions mentioned at the beginning of this chapter) so far not been analysed in this enquiry. To this analysis we must now turn.

CHAPTER 9

PRINCIPLES OF PRACTICAL
EVALUATION

The main aim of this chapter is to exhibit the general structure of
principles governing the evaluation of practical attitudes, or, more
briefly, of (practically) evaluative principles. The analysis, which is
meant to lay the foundations for an enquiry into the nature of morality
and of the relation between moral and other values and obligations,
starts with a brief characterization of cognitive principles, and an
equally brief comparison of cognitive with evaluative principles. Next
an important species of practically evaluative principles, namely strict
evaluative principles will be analysed. These will then be distinguished
from competing evaluative principles – a principle being competing
if it competes with at least one other principle for application. There
follows an analysis of the structure of a supreme principle of practical
evaluation or principle of practical rationality. The chapter ends by
discussing the extent to which a person's practical attitudes are
rational, irrational or non-rational by his and by another's standards.

Some remarks on the structure of cognitive principles

Both theoretical and evaluative principles are standards governing
aspects of men's conscious life. Both are general in the sense of covering
(applying to or being directed towards) a variety of circumstances
rather than merely a single, concrete situation; and in the sense of
being considered by their acceptors as standards not only for themselves but also for others, possibly everybody. The first sense of
generality might appropriately be called 'circumstantial', the
second 'personal'. Another characteristic feature common to theoretical and practically evaluative principles, is that a person may
accept two or more such principles, provided that their joint application does not lead to absurdity. As it stands, this characterization of
the common features of theoretical and evaluation principles may well
appear altogether too metaphorical. It will, however, gain in precision

112

by being specified for cognitive principles on the one hand and for evaluative principles on the other.

Like every cognitive standard, a cognitive principle expresses a belief which dominates or governs other beliefs. Thus, to use an earlier example, the principle of causality expresses the belief that every event has a cause and dominates all beliefs about events, in the sense that whoever accepts the principle, thereby rejects as inadequate any belief which he considers logically inconsistent with it, for example the belief that an uncaused miracle has occurred (see p. 26). The circumstantial generality of the principle consists in its application to everything that is characterized as an event. As to its personal generality, it consists in its acceptor's pro-attitude towards the acceptance of the principle by others as well as by himself. His pro-attitude may even be practical, e.g. if he is prepared to induce the acceptance of the principle in others by arguments.

A person may accept two or more cognitive principles for application in the same kind of circumstances, for example the principle of causality and the principle of the conservation of energy. The obvious condition that the joint acceptance of the two principles should not lead to absurdity, means simply that it should not lead to logical inconsistency. Thus logical inconsistency plays a crucial role in characterizing cognitive principles: it is needed to explain the manner in which theoretical principles dominate their subordinate beliefs, as well as the condition of the joint application and acceptance of cognitive principles expressing co-ordinate beliefs.

Another point which emerges from this very brief consideration of cognitive principles is the rôle played in it by practical attitudes. They were explicitly mentioned in explaining the personal generality of cognitive principles. But they are also involved in accepting a cognitive principle (in practical preference to rejecting it) and rejecting beliefs which are logically inconsistent with a cognitive principle (in practical preference to rejecting the principle). Since the so-involved practical attitudes may be subject to evaluative principles, one must not rule out the possibility that the acceptance of cognitive principles may depend not only on practical attitudes but also on practical principles or that the acceptance of cognitive and practical principles may be interdependent. The distinction between theoretical and practically evaluative principles and their separate analysis, which concern us here, must not be taken to imply a denial of their interdependence, which will concern us later (chapter 16).

Strict evaluative principles

Practically evaluative principles or, more precisely, evaluative principles governing practical attitudes, must be distinguished from regulative principles, maxims or regulations. Both are standards of conduct. But whereas practically evaluative principles govern conduct, as it were indirectly, through governing practical preferences, regulative principles govern it directly by describing in their descriptive antecedents conditions, which may or may not involve practical attitudes, and by prescribing in their regulative consequents a certain kind of conduct in the conditions described (see chapter 2). Practically evaluative and regulative principles, such as the regulative principles of legal systems, are related in many ways. But it seems sound strategy not to examine these relations until the analysis of practical principles has been sufficiently advanced. Another strategic measure, which commends itself, is to start the analysis with the possibly restrictive assumption that all practically evaluative principles are strict, that is to say, do not compete for application with other principles. However, once strict evaluative principles have been characterized, one must consider the problem whether and, if so, why there are practical principles which are not strict, and how in the light of these considerations the analysis of practically evaluative principles in general is affected.

If a person, say, S has a practical attitude towards a practicability, say, one described by f, briefly if $S * f$ (where $*$ stands indifferently for $+$, $-$ or $\pm$), it does not follow that he holds an evaluative principle. In particular, $S * f$ itself does not ascribe an evaluative principle to S. It merely expresses that S has a practical attitude towards f – not even that he prefers his having the practical attitude to his not having it. If S has such a second level practical attitude towards his first level attitude, that is to say if $S * (S * f)$, it still does not follow that S has an evaluative principle. In particular, $S * (S * f)$ itself does not ascribe an evaluative principle to S, even if by asserting that he has a practical attitude towards a practical attitude, it comes nearer to ascribing an evaluative principle to him than does $S * f$ by itself.

One reason why $S * (S * f)$ falls short of ascribing an evaluative principle to S is its lack of generality, both personal and circumstantial. Yet S may have the attitude because it is an instance of an attitude which is personally and circumstantially general: he may have a certain, second level practical attitude directed towards a state of affairs in which every member of a certain class U, including himself, has a certain practical attitude towards any situation with certain characteristics, say, $X_1, ..., X_n$. This personally and circumstantially general practical attitude, an instance of which is described by $S * (S * f)$, may be expressed by $S * (U * X_1 \wedge ... \wedge X_n)$.

Now, this statement might well, because of the twofold generality of the second level practical attitude to which it refers, be regarded as asserting that S holds an evaluative principle. What seems to speak against this is the possibility of S's having a third level anti-attitude towards the second level attitude. He may, for example, be a member of an eating and drinking club and have a second level practical pro-attitude towards a generic situation in which all members of the club have a first level pro-attitude towards gluttony and may do his best to induce it in those who do not yet have it. But he may at the same time have 'a bad conscience' about his second level attitude or manifest a third level practical anti-attitude towards it in other ways. Indeed the strongest reason for requiring that a practically evaluative principle of second level, for example a prudential principle, be at least negatively undominated (i.e. undominated, positively dominated or indifferently dominated) by a practically evaluative attitude of third level is the tendency to withhold the name of a practically evaluative principle from a practical attitude which is the subject of a moral anti-attitude – whatever the precise analysis of such attitudes may be.

While we have so far considered only second level attitudes which are negatively undominated by undominated attitudes of third level and while there is no reason to go beyond the third level, the possibility should be kept in mind. It is provided for by defining a practical attitude of nth level ($n \geqslant 2$) as negatively undominated if, and only if, (1) it is either undominated or else positively or indifferently dominated by a practical attitude of $(n+1)$th level and if (2) in the latter case the $(n+1)$th level practical attitude is either undominated or else positively or indifferently dominated by a practical attitude of $(n+2)$th level and (3) ... – until in this ascent to higher ever levels an undominated practical attitude of some (necessarily) finite level is reached.

By stipulating, as is hereby done, that the absence of negative domination be a defining characteristic of a practically evaluative principle, no important question is being prejudged. What matters is the distinction between negatively dominated and negatively undominated practical attitudes, expressed by statements of form $S*(U*X_1 \wedge \ldots \wedge X_n)$, rather than the decision to confer the name of a principle on the latter only. If this decision is made, then a practically evaluative principle may be defined as a personally and circumstantially general practical attitude which is negatively undominated. In accordance with this definition a practically evaluative principle (of second level) can be ascribed to a person by the following schematic statements:

$$(1) \quad S*(U*X_1 \wedge \ldots \wedge X_n)$$

and

$$(2) \quad \neg\,(S-(S*(U*X_1 \wedge \ldots \wedge X_n)))$$

– with the tacit understanding that no exceptions are possible, i.e. there are no situations possessing the characteristics $X_1 \wedge \ldots \wedge X_n$ of which the two statements are not true.

In accepting two or more cognitive principles or two or more evaluative principles one normally assumes that their joint acceptance does not lead to absurdity. In the case of cognitive principles the absurdity is, as has been said before, logical inconsistency. In the case of evaluative principles it is either opposition or incongruence – the possibility of discordance or negative domination being excluded by definition. Obviously, a person may be just as mistaken about whether two practically evaluative principles are opposed to, or incongruent with, each other as he may about the logical inconsistency or consistency of two cognitive principles. In either instance argument or reflection may remove the mistake.

On competing evaluative principles

Let us consider two evaluative principles, say $S+(U+X_1 \wedge \ldots \wedge X_n)$ and $S+(U+Y_1 \wedge \ldots \wedge Y_n)$ of which the first expresses S's negatively undominated pro-attitude towards a generic situation in which everybody including himself has a pro-attitude towards keeping a promise in circumstances exemplifying the conjunction of characteristics $X_1 \wedge \ldots \wedge X_n$; and of which the second expresses S's negatively undominated pro-attitude towards a generic situation in which everybody including himself has a pro-attitude towards helping his neighbour in circumstances exemplifying the conjunction of characteristics $Y_1 \wedge \ldots \wedge Y_m$. Let us further assume that for most actual or imagined exemplifications of $X_1 \wedge \ldots \wedge X_n$ and

$Y_1 \wedge \dots \wedge Y_m$ the two principles are congruent, i.e. that for them the two second level practical attitudes are not directed towards two opposed (not jointly realizable) first level practical attitudes, but that for some exceptional exemplifications of $X_1 \wedge \dots \wedge X_n$ and $Y_1 \wedge \dots \wedge Y_m$ they are incongruent. A person may favour a situation in which everybody favours keeping his promise and helping his neighbour and may find himself unable to keep an appointment unless he fails to save his neighbour from drowning.

This type of situation, which is familiar from real life, from literature and from often inadequate descriptions in textbooks on ethics, poses a problem for which at least the following solutions seem to suggest themselves, both in theory and practice. One is to locate the source of the apparent competition not in the actually accepted principles but in their imprecise formulation – say, a formulation which omits to mention circumstances in which a person is not bound by a promise. Another suggestion is to locate the source of the apparent competition in a failure to note the acceptance of a general rule of precedence determining for every case of competition which of the competing principles is to be applied. Such a rule might, for example, give precedence to that principle whose non-application causes a greater loss to society as measured in money. A third suggestion is to admit that there are genuinely competing principles whose joint acceptance burdens their acceptor in some situations with a decision which, although it is not arbitrary – as are decisions about genuine borderline cases – does nevertheless *not* consist in the application of a general principle. When the evaluative principles which are supposed so to compete are legal, lawyers, tend to speak of the judge's discretion; when the principles are moral, moral philosophers tend to invoke the chooser's moral sense or intuition. Lastly, it could be – and has been – suggested that the distinction between strict and competing principles is spurious and that all so-called 'evaluative principles' are nothing but backward looking summaries of past evaluations which in present or future evaluations can at best serve as rules of thumb.

Instead of deciding between these suggestions for dealing with *prima facie* competing evaluative principles, one may regard the proposals as a roundabout way of characterizing different actual or conceivable types of evaluative systems: systems consisting of strict principles only; systems consisting of competing principles only; mixed systems; and, lastly, collections of mere rules of thumb. A history of the development of divorce law in England from the

117

twelfth century to the present day might well show that whereas the early legislation was guided by strict principles only, the most recent legislation was guided by the conviction that ending a broken marriage is preferable to continuing it, but that the question whether a marriage has in fact broken down can only be decided *ad hoc*. The question as to which systems or subsystems of morality, prudential conduct or law are strict, not strict, mixed or *ad hoc*, has been of continuing interest to moral philosophers, theoretical jurists and others.

Principles of practical rationality or supreme principles of practical evaluation

All practically evaluative principles, with the possible exception of merely retrospective summaries of past practical evaluations, can in a weak sense of the term be regarded as rational. But there is also a strong sense of the term, which is based on the traditional metaphor of sovereign Reason and in which a practically evaluative principle must satisfy some further requirements if it is to deserve the title of a supreme principle of practical evaluation or of a principle of practical rationality. The most obvious of these requirements is (1) its supremacy over other practical principles. Among the other requirements are (2) the demand that it refer to all circumstances which are essential to it or, more precisely, to its undominated component; (3) the demand that it be simple and not a combination of two or more principles; (4) the demand that it be universally binding; and, usually though not always (5) the demand that it be strict, that is to say that it does not compete for application with other supreme principles of practical rationality. Having made a distinction between strict and competing evaluative principles, it seems best to distinguish in accordance with it between strict and competing principles of practical rationality. While this distinction is clear enough, the notions of supremacy, essentiality and simplicity need further comment.

The notion of supremacy can be defined in terms of the relation of domination, which is characteristic of any stratified system of practical attitudes, i.e. any system of attitudes with at least two, and at most a finite number of levels. Such a system must contain at least one supreme practical attitude, i.e. a practical attitude which, while it dominates one or more practical attitudes, is not dominated by any. In defining a supreme practical attitude as dominating but undominated, it is important to remember the difference between

118

negatively undominated – i.e. undominated, positively dominated or indifferently dominated – attitudes on the one hand and undominated attitudes on the other. Thus while any undominated attitude is by definition also negatively undominated, the converse may, or may not, be the case. Comparing the definition of a practical principle with that of a supreme practical principle, it is clear that, as intended, a practical principle is either supreme or else indifferently or positively dominated by a supreme principle.

In order to explain the other requirements it seems best to consider the schematic formulation of a supreme (practically) evaluative principle, say – as can be done without real loss of generality – a practical principle expressing an undominated practical pro-attitude of second level which negatively dominates a generic situation characterized by a certain conjunction of characteristics. Let us, in other words, consider the schematic statement $S + (U - X_1 \wedge \dots \wedge X_n)$ on the assumption that $\gamma [S * (S + (U - X_1 \wedge \dots \wedge X_n))]$. The conjunction of characteristics is roughly speaking essential to the attitude expressed by the principle if any change in the characteristics would involve a change in the attitude. More precisely, the conjunction is essential if, and only if, replacing any subconjunction by its negation would *not* involve a change of the first level attitude (e.g. from $-$ to $\pm$) but would involve a change in the second level attitude (e.g. from $+$ to $-$).

The requirement of simplicity can be expressed more precisely as demanding that a supreme principle, say $S + (U - X_1 \wedge \dots \wedge X_n)$, where $X_1 \wedge \dots \wedge X_n$ is essential, be not decomposable into two principles which differ from the original principle only in that each of the new principles contains a subconjunction of $X_1 \wedge \dots \wedge X_n$ in place of the whole conjunction, such that the two subconjunctions are mutually exclusive and jointly exhaustive of the whole conjunction. Thus the supreme principle $S + (U - X_1 \wedge \dots \wedge X_{10})$ is not simple if it can be decomposed into two supreme principles

$$S + (U - X_1 \wedge X_2 \wedge X_3) \quad \text{and} \quad S + (U - X_4 \wedge X_5 \wedge \dots \wedge X_{10}).$$

The requirement of personal universality is the demand that the class U of human beings – towards whose possession of a certain first level practical attitude S has a certain undominated second level attitude – contain all human beings. It does not imply that the generic situation towards which the first level attitude is directed has a specific content, e.g. that in this situation all human beings are treated as equal, as ends rather than as means etc. A Nietzschean's supreme practical principle might, for example, express a second level pro-attitude whose object is a universally held first level pro-attitude towards a generic situation in which some human beings are treated as slaves. And in defending such a principle he might well claim to expound a supreme principle of practical reason – even of morality, in a sense of the term which does not confuse 'true' morality with confused sentimentality.

Instead of demanding that a supreme principle of practical evaluation be strict – a point on which common and philosophical usage is less decisive – it seems, once again, best to admit both strict and competing supreme principles and not to prejudge the question whether 'in the last analysis' all or some supreme principles may turn out to be strict or, for that matter, to compete with other supreme principles.

It is important to be quite clear about two empirical assumptions which, if correct, guarantee that the notion of a supreme principle of practical evaluation is not empty. One is that a person's system of practical attitudes may be, and often is, stratified into a number of levels; the other that it may, and often does, contain personally general practical attitudes of at least second level which are directed towards circumstantially general attitudes of lower level. Since the evidence for these assumptions is mainly introspective or phenomenological, one might be inclined to ascribe a special kind of certainty or even self-evidence to them. They are, however, best regarded as belonging to philosophical anthropology – philosophical, because concerned with phenomena of a complex structure, whose investigation requires some logical and other philosophical equipment; anthropological because concerned with man as an individual and as a social being.

On the rationality or irrationality of a person's practical attitudes as judged by his own standards

In speaking of the rationality, irrationality, or non-rationality of a person's practical attitudes, one may be judging them either by one's own or by his standards. Yet once the latter kind of judgment is understood, the former presents no great difficulties. In judging a practical attitude to be rational, one judges it to be justifiable by a supreme principle of practical evaluation or a set of such principles, rather than by some subordinate rule, intuition or arbitrary decision. In the light of the preceding analyses the nature of both, the principles and the justification, can be made more precise. As regards the supreme principles, it is clear that if no room is to be left to intuitions or arbitrary decisions, they must be strict and mutually neither opposed to, nor incongruent with, each other.

As regards the manner in which a practical attitude is justified or 'covered' by a supreme principle of the kind described, some further comment is needed. Let us, in order to avoid unnecessary complications, consider the relation between on the one hand a certain practical attitude of first level, say $S - f$ (e.g. S has an anti-attitude towards the practicability described by a statement to the effect that he is smoking a cigarette which he believes to be harmful to his health) on the other hand a certain supreme practical principle of second level, say $S + (U - X_1 \wedge \ldots \wedge X_n)$ (e.g. S has an undominated pro-attitude of second level directed towards a situation in which every member of the class U of all rational human beings has an anti-anti-attitude towards any generic situation in which he is engaged in an activity which is harmful to his health). It will simplify matters further if we introduce the following transparent terminology which applies not only to our example but to all the cases which interest us here: we call the situation (described by) f 'the critical situation' of the practical attitude; the features described by $X_1 \wedge \ldots \wedge X_n$ the 'characteristic features' required by the principle; the practical attitude of S towards f 'the personal attitude' of S; and the practical attitude of (S and every other member of) U towards f 'the universalized attitude of S'.

Using these terms one can explain the sense in which a person's practical attitudes are covered by his supreme principles of practical evaluation; the sense in which some of the attitudes so covered are by his own standards rational while others are irrational; and the sense in which those of his practical attitudes which are not so covered are neither rational nor irrational or, briefly, non-rational. Limiting ourselves, as hitherto, to systems of attitudes with no more than three levels and considering only practical attitudes of first level of form $S * f$ and supreme practical principles of second level of form $S * (U * X_1 \wedge \ldots \wedge X_n)$, where $*$ stands indifferently for $+$, $-$ or $\pm$, we first of all define the statement that $S * f$ is covered by $S * (U * X_1 \wedge \ldots \wedge X_n)$ as meaning that the critical situation (described by f) has the characteristic features $X_1 \wedge \ldots \wedge X_n$ (required as essential by the supreme principle $S * (U * X_1 \wedge \ldots \wedge X_n)$). If the first level practical attitude is covered by the second level principle, then the former conforms to the latter or is *rational* by the standards of S if, and only if, (1) the (undominated) second level attitude is positive and the personal attitude has the same character as the universalized attitude (i.e. both are pro-, anti- or indifferent attitudes) or (2) the second level attitude is negative and the personal attitude differs in character from the universalized attitude or (3) the second level attitude is an indifferent attitude. Thus, to return to our example, S's practical anti-attitude towards smoking a cigarette is by his own standards rational.

Similarly, if the first level practical attitude is covered by the (undominated) second level principle then the former violates the latter or is *irrational* by the standards of S if, and only if, (1) the (undominated) second level attitude is positive and the personal attitude differs in character from the universalized attitude or (2) the second level attitude is negative and the personal attitude has the same character as the universalized attitude. Thus, keeping to our example S's practical pro-attitude towards smoking a cigarette would by his own standards be irrational.

On the non-rationality of a person's practical attitudes as judged by his own standards

If a person's practical attitude is not covered by any of his supreme principles of practical evaluation, then it is by his standards neither rational nor irrational but *non-rational* or, what is equivalent but sounds even worse, non-irrational. Because the general characterization of non-rational practical attitudes is obvious and because it is possible clearly to distinguish between different species of non-rationality, one might be tempted to arrange them on a scale between the extremes of rationality and irrationality. Instead of yielding to this temptation some characteristic examples of non-rational practical attitudes will be given.

An important example of a non-rational practical attitude is a practical attitude $S * f$ for whose coverage two supreme principles, say, $S * (U * X_1 \wedge \ldots \wedge X_n)$ and $S * (U * Y_1 \wedge \ldots \wedge Y_m)$ compete in such a manner that if it is rational by one of them it is irrational by the other (e.g. where f describes a situation in which the fulfilling of a promise *ipso facto* involves a failure to help a neighbour in distress). It is, of course, always possible so to reformulate the two competing principles that any competition appears to be excluded (e.g. to include

122

among the characteristic features of the supreme principle, which favours the favouring by everybody of promise keeping, a suitable exceptive clause in cases where promise keeping 'seriously' clashes with helping a neighbour in distress). Yet whether or not one decides on such a reformulation, that is to say on replacing the competing by apparently strict principles, one's second level attitude would after the reformulation, in the same instances as before, depend on an *ad hoc* intuition.

Another kind of a non-rational attitude $S * f$ is one which S is capable of universalizing personally but not circumstantially. That is to say that while he has the undominated second level attitude $S * (U * f)$, he is not able to consider the concrete situation as described, or rather indicated, by f as possessing any finite number of characteristic features. This inability of subsuming a particular under a conjunction of attributes without misrepresenting it is quite familiar in situations in which one tries to describe a painting, a piece of music or other work of art and yet feels certain that the particular whose unique nature one wishes to convey escapes subsumption under any finite conjunction of concepts.

A third kind of non-rational practical attitude is exemplified by a person's inability of personal universalization. Thus S might be able to regard his practical attitude $S * f$ as being covered by

$$S * (S * X_1 \wedge \ldots \wedge X_n),$$

but not by

$$S * (U * X_1 \wedge \ldots \wedge X_n).$$

A fourth kind of non-rational practical attitude is exemplified by a person who is unable to universalize either circumstantially or personally and is only capable of seeing $S * f$ as the object of $S * (S * f)$. A fifth kind is exemplified by a person who cannot ascend from $S * f$ to the second level but is capable of seeing $S * f$ as an instance of $S * X_1 \wedge \ldots \wedge X_n$. Lastly a sixth kind is exemplified by a person who is incapable of more than grasping what is expressed by $S * f$. The distinction between rational, irrational and non-rational practical attitudes, as well as the distinction between different species of non-rationality, can be expected to have some bearing on the analysis of morality.

Are a person's supreme principles of practical evaluation themselves rational? According to our definition they are not, because it demands of a rational attitude that it be covered by a supreme principle and because the practical attitude expressed by a supreme principle of practical evaluation is not so covered. Yet the purpose of the definition – namely to exhibit the relation between practical attitudes which are covered by supreme principles and the attitudes which are expressed by these principles – would also be achieved, if it were so modified that a practical attitude expressed by a supreme principle or indeed any practical attitude would by the modified definition cover itself.

On the rationality, irrationality or non-rationality of a person's practical attitudes as judged by another's standards

Different people may have different supreme principles of practical evaluation, so that one person's supreme principles, or attitudes which are rational by these principles, may by another person's supreme principles of practical evaluation be irrational or, at least, non-rational. Applying one's supreme principles of practical evaluation to another person's practical attitudes may be fairly complex, especially if the other person's system of practical attitudes is stratified into more levels than one's own. The relation between two such systems may be schematically characterized by assuming that a person Q (Quintus) whose supreme practical principles are $q_1, ..., q_n$ is applying them to the practical attitudes of S (Sextus) whose supreme practical principles are $s_1, ..., s_m$.

In order to judge S's supreme practical principles, i.e. $s_1, ..., s_m$, as well as S's other practical attitudes not by S's but by his own supreme principles, i.e. $q_1, ..., q_n$, Q adds them to S's system of practical attitudes, in such a manner that in the enlarged system of S the supreme principles $q_1, ..., q_n$ 'override' all practical attitudes of S *whatever their level.* Two main cases can be distinguished, namely (1) the case where Q compares his supreme principles (ascribed to Q by) $q_1, ..., q_n$ with S's supreme principles (ascribed to S by) $s_1, ..., s_m$ and (2) the case where Q compares his supreme principles with those of S's practical attitudes which are not his supreme principles (ascribed to him by) $s_1, ..., s_m$.

Within the first type of case we can distinguish three subcases. (1 *a*) A supreme principle q is of the same level as a principle s. In this case s is by Q's standards irrational, if and only if, q and s are either opposed to, or incongruent with, each other. Otherwise s is non-rational by Q's standards, that is to say its acceptance or rejection by Q depends on an *ad hoc* decision. (1*b*) A supreme principle q of Q is of higher level than a principle s of S. In this case we consider Q's system of practical attitudes as enlarged by the practical attitude (expressed by) s. The practical attitude s is by Q's standards rational, irrational or non-rational according to whether it is rational, irrational or non-rational in the enlarged system. (1*c*) A supreme practical principle q of Q is of lower level than a principle s of S. In this case we again consider Q's system of practical attitudes as enlarged by s. The practical attitude s is by Q's standards irrational if, and only if, in the enlarged system q is irrational (because covered by, and violating, s). Otherwise s is non-rational by Q's standards.

We now turn to the second type of case in which Q views those of S's practical attitudes, say (those ascribed to S by) $\sigma_1, ..., \sigma_n$ which are not expressed by S's supreme principles. Here again we can distinguish between three subcases. (2*a*) The practical attitude (expressed by, say), σ when added to Q's system of practical attitudes is in the so enlarged system rational or irrational. In this case σ is by the standards of Q rational or irrational. (2*b*) The practical attitude σ is rational in S's system of practical attitudes in virtue of a principle s which by Q's standards is irrational (see cases 1*a* and 1*c*). In this case σ too is by the standards of Q irrational. (2*c*) Using the preceding criteria (2*a* and 2*b*) σ is neither rational or irrational. In this case σ is by the standards of Q non-rational.

To sum up, if all Q's supreme principles of practical evaluation are of higher level than those of S, Q's evaluation of S's supreme principles and other practical attitudes is fairly straightforward. He simply proceeds by adding his own principles $q_1, ..., q_n$ to S's system and by applying them to S's practical attitudes. Complications arise when S's supreme principles, or some of his dominated practical attitudes, are of higher level than those of Q. For such cases the preceding account of what is involved when Q judges S's system of practical attitudes by applying his supreme principles of practical evaluation to it, may well turn out to be too crude. Yet, however refined, it would still have to rest on the reasonable assumption that Q understands S's practical attitudes and, more generally, that just as we occasionally understand each other's beliefs, so we occasionally also understand each other's practical attitudes. By assuming such understanding one raises the problem of its nature, but does nothing that contributes to its solution. Some steps towards this goal will be taken at a later stage of the inquiry (in chapter 18).

CHAPTER 10

ON THE RELATION BETWEEN EVALUATIVE AND REGULATIVE STANDARDS OF CONDUCT

Having discussed the logical structure of regulative maxims or regulations and of codes of conduct on the one hand (in chapter 2), and the structure of evaluative practical principles on the other (in chapter 9), we are ready to examine the relation between a person's evaluative and regulative standards in his acting and planning. The discussion will proceed as follows. After some partly retrospective remarks on the logical structure of practical evaluations and regulations, a distinction will be drawn between two kinds of sanction, associated with contravening a regulation, namely regulative and evaluative sanctions. It will then be argued that evaluative sanctions are not the only way in which evaluations may support regulations and some other kinds of evaluative support for regulative standards will be discussed. There follows an examination of the manner in which a person's supreme evaluative principles are related to his supreme codes of conduct – provided, of course, that his evaluations are based on supreme principles of evaluation and that he lives by at least one code of conduct. The chapter ends with some remarks on supreme codes of conduct which appear to be approved by a person's supreme evaluative principles, but are in fact so approved only on the assumption that certain tacit or implicit conditions are satisfied.

A comparison of the structure of practical evaluations and regulations

Both practical evaluations, i.e. practical preferences and the other practical attitudes defined in terms of them, and practical regulations are standards of conduct; and both may, and usually do, occur in stratified systems. Just as a practical attitude may be directed towards another practical attitude, so a regulation may be directed towards another regulation, for example by requiring its modification in order to restore the lost adequacy between a system of regulations

126

and the world for which it was intended. As regards practical attitudes it will again be sufficient to consider the trichotomy of practical pro- and anti-attitudes and the attitudes of practical indifference.

The fundamental difference between evaluations and regulations is that evaluations express a person's practical attitudes to what is practicable and that regulations express what, under given conditions, is required of him – whatever his practical attitudes may be. We write as before $S*f$ to express that S has a certain practical attitude, namely $+$, $-$ or $\pm$ towards the situation (described by) f; and $S*X_1 \wedge \ldots \wedge X_n$ to express that S has this attitude towards any situation characterized by $X_1 \wedge \ldots \wedge X_n$. We also write as before $m = f \xrightarrow{S} g!$ to express the regulative maxim or regulation by which it is required of S that he conduct himself in such a manner that if the situation described by f is the case, then the situation described by g (and referring to a period of time not preceding f) is also the case. We further write, say, $Y_1 \wedge \ldots \wedge Y_m \xrightarrow{S} Z_1 \wedge \ldots \wedge Z_r!$ in order to express a regulation whose descriptive antecedent is any situation characterized by $Y_1 \wedge \ldots \wedge Y_m$ and whose descriptive consequent any situation described by $Z_1 \wedge \ldots \wedge Z_r$. (Here, as elsewhere, an unpedantic use of the terminology explained in chapter 2 will help to avoid both cumbersomeness and misleading ambiguity.)

In spite of their fundamentally different structure regulations can be, and often are, objects of evaluations, and evaluations can be, and often are, components of regulations. It is a familiar fact that a person S may have a practical attitude towards a regulation whether or not it is addressed to him. A person may have a practical pro-attitude towards a law which forbids the use of dangerous drugs, or an anti-attitude towards a school regulation which requires his daughter to wear a school uniform on weekdays. It is an equally familiar fact that certain of our regulations refer to practical attitudes in their descriptive antecedents. Thus a regulation might well say that any person who has a practical pro-attitude towards smoking should occupy a smokers' compartment on certain trains. However, if a regulation is to be applicable and practicable in the world we live in (see pp. 29f.) then it cannot in its regulative consequent reasonably require the immediate presence of a practical pro-attitude. Consider for example the seeming counterinstance of a regulation which requires of S that he *have* a practical pro-attitude towards helping Q whenever Q needs his help. What makes this regulation unreasonable is that S either has this attitude or does not have it – whatever the regulations which he may have adopted. What makes this regulation *seem* reasonable is its being easily mistaken for – or its being taken for the slipshod formulation of – another regulation to the effect that S should *do* something rather than *have* or *be* something. It would, for example, be reasonable to require of S that he help Q whenever Q needs his help or that he conduct himself as if he had a practical pro-attitude towards helping Q whenever Q needs his help.

Regulations can be 'violated' or 'broken' in a sense of these terms which does not apply to evaluations. Thus a person who is subject – whether subjected by himself or others – to a regulation $f \xrightarrow{S} g!$, but nevertheless brings about $f \wedge \neg g$ is violating this regulation; whereas a person who has a practical attitude $S + X_1 \wedge \ldots \wedge X_n$, but is performing an action which lacks one or more of the features $X_1, \ldots, X_n$, is in performing it, either *ipso facto* changing his practical attitude or else making a mistake. Moreover, regulations, unlike evaluations, have sanctions. The difference is important since in order to clarify some of the complex interconnections between regulations and evaluations one must consider both the manner in which a sanction may be associated with the contravention of a regulation and the form it may take.

Regulative and evaluative sanctions of regulations

A certain regulation such as $m_0 = f_0 \to g_0!$ may belong to a certain code of conduct or system of regulations M_0, all of which are addressed to S_0. (Here, as elsewhere when an explicit distinction is needed between constants and variables, letters with subscripts stand for constants and letters without subscripts for the corresponding variables.) That a certain code of conduct is addressed to a certain person does not imply that he has made it his own code of conduct in the sense of living by it or seriously trying to do so. For what follows we shall, however, assume that M_0 has been adopted by its addressee or addressees and that the variable M ranges not over all codes of conducts, but only over such as have been adopted by their addressees. Thus in asserting that the regulation $m_0 = f_0 \xrightarrow{S_0} g_0!$ belongs to a certain code of conduct M_0 (adopted by S_0) – briefly $m_0 \in M_0$ – one is asserting an empirical proposition about S_0.

It is the truth of this empirical proposition which makes all the difference between S_0's mere non-satisfaction of a regulation m_0 (e.g. a pious Christian's non-observation of Jewish ritual) and his violation of it (e.g. a pious Christian's non-observation of Christian ritual). More precisely a person's action constitutes a case of his not satisfying a regulation (e.g. $m_0 = f_0 \rightarrow g_0!$) if, and only if, the action can be described by the negation of the regulation's descriptive counterpart (e.g. by $\gimel D(m_0) = f_0 \wedge \gimel g_0$). A person's action constitutes a case of his violating a regulation if, and only if, it constitutes a case of his not satisfying the regulation and if the regulation belongs to a code of conduct which he has adopted (e.g. if $\gimel D(m_0)$ and $m_0 \in M_0$).

By a sanction one understands an undesirable situation, or sequence of situations, which is associated with the violation – in the case of externally imposed rules, also the mere non-satisfaction – of a regulation. It is 'undesirable' in the sense that the person suffering it normally would prefer its absence to its presence, if he had a choice in the matter. According to whether the association between the violation of a regulation and its sanction is mediated by another regulation or an evaluation, one can distinguish between regulative and evaluative sanctions. Both are familiar phenomena. The regulative sanction of a regulation is a secondary regulation whose object is a primary regulation. More precisely, the descriptive antecedent of the secondary regulation is the negation of the descriptive counterpart of the primary regulation; the regulative consequent of the secondary obligation requires the realization of a painful or unpleasant situation or sequence of situations for the addressee of the primary regulation; the addressee of the secondary regulation may, but need not coincide, with the addressee of the primary regulation. Schematically these conditions can be represented by regulations of the following forms:

$$m = f \underset{S}{\overrightarrow{}} g! \quad \text{and} \quad m' = (\gimel (f \underset{S}{\overrightarrow{}} g) \underset{Q}{\overrightarrow{}} h!)$$

where m is a primary and m' a secondary regulation and where S and Q may coincide.

From regulative sanctions of regulations on the one hand, and from the evaluation of regulations on the other, one must distinguish what may be called their 'evaluative sanctions'. The evaluative sanction of a regulation is its addressee's practical anti-attitude towards its being violated by him. More precisely, the addressee of the regulation has adopted it as belonging to a code of conduct by which he lives or seriously tries to live; and he has a practical anti-attitude towards the violation of the regulation. Schematically, $m = f \underset{S}{\overrightarrow{}} g!$, $m \in M$ and $S - [\gimel (f \underset{S}{\overrightarrow{}} g) \wedge m \in M]$. In being associated with the violation of an adopted regulation the attitude expressed by $S - [\gimel (f \underset{S}{\overrightarrow{}} g!) \wedge m \in M]$

clearly fulfils the first condition which any sanction of a regulation must fulfil. It also fulfils the second condition, namely that it be undesirable. This is so not because $S - [\mathcal{7}\,(f\overrightarrow{\,_S}g) \wedge m \in M]$ expresses a practical anti-attitude, but because its object – the felt conflict between adopting and violating a regulation – is a painful state of mind the absence of which anybody would normally prefer to its presence, if he had a choice in the matter.

On the evaluation of code-dependent obligations

The preceding analysis and comparison of regulations and practical evaluations have among other things shown that a regulation can be the object of another regulation but that an evaluation cannot be the object of a regulation (though it may be a component of its descriptive antecedent). Recognition of this asymmetry is a prerequisite for the enquiry into the relation between practical attitudes which are directed towards the adoption of regulations or codes of conduct on the one hand and the obligations based on these regulations or codes of conduct on the other. It also emphasizes the difference between code- or regulation-dependent obligations and obligations which arise independently of regulations – of form $f \rightarrow g!$ – or systems of such, i.e. codes of conduct.

It seems best to start the analysis by noting two fundamental points namely (1) that a person's code-dependent obligations are logical consequences (of the descriptive counterparts) of the regulations and codes adopted by him and (2) that, therefore, any support given by a person's practical attitudes to these obligations, may be given not only directly, but also more or less indirectly via the support they give to the regulations and codes of conduct which he has adopted. The first of these points was made earlier, when the structure of codes of conduct, especially their applicability, practicability and adequacy in the situations for which they are designed and adopted was discussed in some detail. The upshot of that discussion can be formulated as the thesis that a statement $O_M f$ describes a person's code-dependent obligation to bring about the situation described by f if, and only if, (a) f is logically implied by the descriptive counterpart of a code of conduct M, briefly $D(M) \vdash f$; (b) M is adequate to the world of the code's addressees and (c) the code is adopted by whoever is designated in it as the person who is to bring about f (see chapter 2).

As regards the second point, namely the indirect evaluative support which a person's practical attitudes may give to his code-dependent obligations, it is clear that a person's practical attitude towards a regulation as part of an adopted code may differ from his practical attitude towards the regulation as such. Since a person's obligations are logical consequences of (the descriptive counterparts of) the codes of conduct which he has adopted, a similar distinction must be made between a person's practical attitude towards his obligations *qua* consequences of his codes of conduct and his practical attitudes towards the obligations independently of their following from his or indeed any codes of conduct. One may, for example, assume that a certain person has a practical pro-attitude towards his military code which contains a regulation requiring him to salute his superior officers when meeting them and also a regulation requiring him to take cover when under fire. Having a pro-attitude towards the code as a whole, he also has a pro-attitude towards all obligations *qua consequences of the code* and, hence, also towards the obligation to salute his superior officers while taking cover when meeting them under fire. Thus even a code-dependent obligation which by itself is considered obnoxious benefits from the evaluative support which is given to the code on which it depends.

A person's practical attitude towards a particular code of conduct and hence the obligations which follow from it, may or may not be in harmony with his practical attitudes towards these obligations considered by themselves. The great variety of possible degrees of harmony or disharmony becomes obvious, even if one restricts oneself to a person's first level practical attitudes and primary obligations, based on a code of conduct towards which he has a practical pro-attitude. At one extreme is the position of a person who has not only a practical pro-attitude towards the code, and hence towards every obligation based on it, but also towards each obligation by itself. (Thus if M_0 is the code and $O_M f_n$, i.e. $D(M_0) \vdash f_n$, it is not only the case that $S + M_0$, but also that for every n such that $D(M_0) \vdash f_n - S + [(\exists M) : (D(M) \vdash f_n)]$.) At the other extreme is the position of a person who has a practical pro-attitude towards the code, but a practical anti-attitude towards any of the obligations based on the code, when considering the obligations by themselves. (In other words $S + M_0$ but for every n such that $D(M_0) \vdash f_n - S - [(\exists M) : (D(M) \vdash f_n)]$.) Such a position is, for example, conceivable in a radical opponent of anarchism who prefers a legal code all of whose regulations are immoral to none at all. Between these two extremes intermediate positions are possible depending on the distribution of anti-attitudes and attitudes of indifference over $O_M f_1, ..., O_M f_n ...$.

Matters become more complicated if one considers also the possibility of a person's practical anti-attitudes and attitudes of indifference towards the acceptance of a code; and still more complicated if one considers a person's practical attitudes towards more than one code of conduct, especially as a person's attitude towards, say, the joint acceptance of two codes is not by itself sufficient evidence for his attitude towards each of them separately. In a similar manner a person's practical attitude towards each of two codes by itself is not sufficient evidence for his practical attitude towards their joint acceptance. But matters become again comparatively simple if one considers only supreme evaluations on the one hand and supreme regulations and obligations on the other. The examination of their relationship, which will be our next topic, is presupposed by any attempt at characterizing various types of morality.

On the relation of supreme evaluative principles to supreme codes of conduct, regulations and code-dependent obligations

Although a person's having practical attitudes implies his having at least one undominated practical attitude, it does not also imply that his attitude is a supreme principle, i.e. personally universal, circumstantially general and essential, as well as simple and strict. And to assume that a person's conduct is guided by one or more such principles is to make an empirical assumption. In the following analysis of the relation between supreme evaluations and supreme regulations this assumption will be made. For the sake of expository simplicity it will – without loss of generality – be further assumed that all supreme principles of evaluation are of second level and that they moreover are of form: $S + [U + X_1 \wedge ... \wedge X_n]$.

Instead of saying explicitly and correctly that this formula indicates the evaluation of a practicability by a supreme principle of evaluation of second level whose personal, second level attitude and whose universalized, first level attitude are both positive, one may say – more briefly, but still correctly – that it indicates supreme approval of the positive evaluation of the practicability, or that the practicability is the object of a supremely approved positive evaluation. When considering only evaluative principles of form

$$S + [U + X_1 \wedge ... \wedge X_n]$$

132

no harm will be done by saying somewhat imprecisely that the practicability is a supreme value. (This manner of speaking would not do when comparing supreme principles of form $S + [U + X_1 \wedge \ldots \wedge X_n]$ with supreme principles of form $S - [U + X_1 \wedge \ldots \wedge X_n]$ or of form $S - [U - X_1 \wedge \ldots \wedge X_n]$. When engaged on such a comparison one would have to distinguish explicitly between supremely approved positive evaluations, supremely disapproved positive evaluations and supremely disapproved negative evaluations.)

In considering the structure of codes of conduct it became clear that a person may live by more than one code of conduct, for example by a number of professional codes. A person's code is supreme if, and only if, the obligations following from it override the obligations following from any other code in every conceivable case of conflict. To assume that a person's conduct is guided by one or more supreme codes – two codes being supreme only if they cannot conceivably come into conflict – is to make an empirical assumption. For it is quite possible that a person should live by conflicting codes in such a manner that he resolves any conflict between them by *ad hoc* decisions; or that a person should have no codes of conduct but simply a system of rules of thumb, or not even such a system. If one wishes to examine the relation between a person's supreme principles of evaluation and his supreme regulations one must assume that he lives by a supreme code of conduct consisting of at least one regulation.

What has been said in general about the need to distinguish between on the one hand evaluating a code of conduct and *thereby* the regulations it contains and the obligations it implies, and on the other evaluating these regulations and obligations independently of this particular code, applies of course to the special, and especially interesting case, of evaluating supreme codes by supreme principles of evaluation. We must in particular distinguish between the supreme value (the supremely approved positive evaluation) of a practicability which consists in bringing about the continued acceptance of supreme regulations and obligations *qua* elements and consequences of a *particular* supreme code and the supreme value of a practicability which consists in bringing about their continued acceptance *qua* elements of *some* (possibly not yet accepted or even specified) code.

It seems useful to represent this distinction schematically. For this purpose let $\mathfrak{M}$ be a variable ranging over a person's supreme codes of conduct and those codes which he could adopt as supreme;

let $\mathfrak{M}_0$ be a particular supreme code adopted by the person; let m range over the class of regulations and f over the class of practicabilities. Assume further that m_0 is a particular regulation which belongs to $\mathfrak{M}_0$, i.e. that $m_0 \in \mathfrak{M}_0$ and that f_0 is a particular state of affairs, which the person is obliged to bring about by conforming to $\mathfrak{M}_0$, i.e. $O_{\mathfrak{M}_0} f_0$ or, equivalently, $D(\mathfrak{M}_0) \vdash f_0$. The distinction is then represented by the following schematic expressions

(1) $S + [U + \mathfrak{M}_0]$

(2a) $S + [U + (\exists \mathfrak{M}) : (m_0 \in \mathfrak{M})]$

(2b) $S + [U + (\exists \mathfrak{M}) : D(\mathfrak{M}) \vdash f_0]$

all of which are assumed to refer to undominated practical attitudes. Clearly, (1) logically implies (2a) and (2b) while (2a) and (2b) neither separately nor jointly imply (1).

As to (1) it is conceivable, and seems a fact, that some person or group of persons regards a particular code of conduct as supreme – e.g. a military code of honour, as in the case of the Japanese Samurai, or a religious code as in the case of Agamemnon in Euripides' *Iphigeneia in Aulis*. As to (2a) it is again conceivable, and a fact, that some people may regard a certain regulation or maxim – e.g. when meeting a distressed person not to increase his distress for reasons of idle curiosity – as belonging to *some* supreme code, the continued adoption of which is or would be a supreme value for them. Lastly, as regards (2b) similar remarks apply as to (2a).

It is worth noting that (2a) and (2b) are instances of more general principles, namely

(3a) $S + [U + (\forall m)(\exists \mathfrak{M}) : m \in \mathfrak{M}]$ and

(3b) $S + [U + (\forall f)(\exists \mathfrak{M}) : (D(\mathfrak{M}) \vdash f]$

and that (3a) can be considered as an approximative formulation of the principle of Kantian morality. For a maxim of a person's action or, as Kant also puts it, of a person's will is moral in the Kantian sense if, and only if, the person can regard it as (or will it to be) a principle of a universal supreme legislation. How far this approximation does justice to Kant's categorical imperative is an exegetic matter whose detailed discussion is here out of question. Our formulation does not, and is not meant to suggest that applying (3a) would lead necessarily to one and only one code of supreme value, especially as this uniqueness claim is, as will be argued, mistaken. It is, moreover, arguable how far the meaning of 'S has an undominated practical pro- (or anti-) attitude towards everybody's having a practical pro- (or anti-) attitude towards a maxim m' coincides with what Kant means by 'm is a maxim of S's will', especially as the meaning of the Kantian concept of will is by no means uncontroversial.

It is conceivable that a person might adopt the following principles which are stronger than $(2a)$ and $(2b)$, namely

$(4a)$ $S + [U + (\forall m)\,(\forall \mathfrak{M}) : m \in \mathfrak{M}]$ and

$(4b)$ $S + [U + (\forall f)\,(\forall \mathfrak{M}) : D(\mathfrak{M}) \vdash f]$,

which formulae express that any regulation m which is contained in every supreme code is a supreme value and that the same is true of an obligation which follows from every supreme code. If one regarded $(4a)$ as the definition of 'super-Kantian' morality of a maxim, then a maxim would be moral in this sense only if S can regard it as (or will it to be) a principle of *every* universal supreme legislation. Although Kant's categorical imperative corresponds to the weaker $(3a)$, his arguments are meant to support also the stronger formulation $(4a)$.

On supreme codes of conduct of apparently supreme value

A person's code of conduct is one of his supreme codes if, and only if, its regulations are not overriden by those of any other code which he has adopted. And a person's supreme code of conduct is one of his supreme values if, and only if, the continued adoption by him of the code is the object of one of his supremely approved positive evaluations. Hence a person's supreme code of conduct may, or may not be, one of his supreme values. Although this is by now obvious, it is of interest to consider some cases in which a person's supreme code of conduct, though not one of his supreme values, may appear to be among them because of some tacit or implicit condition which can be normally ignored.

Let us, as before, use $\mathfrak{M}_0$ for a particular code adopted by a person S or rather for the practicability of the continued adoption of $\mathfrak{M}_0$ by S; and $S + [U + \mathfrak{M}_0]$ to indicate that S has a practical pro-attitude towards everybody's having a practical pro-attitude towards the continued adoption of $\mathfrak{M}_0$. Now this practicability is one of S's supreme values only if the second level attitude is a practical principle, i.e. undominated, personally universal, circumstantially general and essential, simple and strict. Among these demands, of which the formula shows only the demand of personal universality to be fulfilled, the demand of essentiality is for the moment of particular interest.

This is the requirement that the practicability (which is the object of the universalized first level attitude) be characterized by all its essential features and by no feature which is inessential. Moreover, of the two ways in which the characterization may fail to be essential, namely incompleteness and superfluity, only the former needs to be considered.

When one speaks of a code of conduct as adopted by oneself or by others, one sometimes takes it as understood that its continued adoption depends on the continuation of 'ordinary circumstances' which may be more or less clearly defined. Thus a code of conduct which forbids one to take the law in one's own hands because it is lodged in the capable hands of certain authorities, is adopted for ordinary circumstances which exclude civil war. A code of conduct which demands that one must obey the government of one's country is adopted for ordinary circumstances which exclude a situation in which it is one of the government's aims to 'liquidate' all citizens belonging to one's own race or indeed to some other race.

In these and similar cases one must distinguish between, on the one hand, the merely apparent supreme value of the continued adoption of a certain supreme code, i.e. a merely apparent supreme evaluative principle $S + [U + \mathfrak{M}_0]$ of S, and, on the other hand, the actual supreme value of the continued adoption of the code by S in *certain ordinary circumstances*, i.e. an actual supreme principle of his $S + [U + \mathfrak{M}_0 \wedge c_0]$. That c_0 is an essential feature of the practicability $\mathfrak{M}_0 \wedge c_0$ and that $\mathfrak{M}_0$ by itself is, therefore, an incomplete indication of it, can be schematically expressed by the conjunction

$$S + [U + \mathfrak{M}_0 \wedge c_0] \quad \text{and} \quad S - [U + \mathfrak{M}_0 \wedge 7\, c_0].$$

The conjunction expresses, one might say, not supreme, but qualified, supreme approval of the continued adoption of $\mathfrak{M}_0$. The distinction between ordinary and extraordinary circumstances need not be exclusive or sharp, as might be exemplified by $S + [U + \mathfrak{M}_0 \wedge c_0]$ and $S - [U + \mathfrak{M} \wedge d_0]$, where c_0 describes a society free from internal *and* external conflict and d_0 describes a society in utter chaos. And there are other possibilities, consideration of which is best postponed until we are ready to discuss the relationship between legality and morality.

CHAPTER 11

MORALITY

Much of the preceding discussion has been devoted to exhibiting the complex structure of systems of practical attitudes, in particular by showing how practical attitudes may differ in kind, level and generality, in the objects towards which they are directed and in the relations which they bear to codes of conduct. A morality is a part or aspect of a practical system, as one might call any system comprising all the practical attitudes of a person or of a group of persons who share the same practical attitudes. For this reason some of the differences between practical systems are reflected in differences between various types of morality. To draw some of these distinctions is one task of this chapter. Another is to show that, and why, even the simplest morality presupposes social life. The chapter begins with a minimal definition of moral standards. It proceeds to show that, and why, even such standards are social. It ends with a characterization of some 'pure' and some 'mixed' types of morality.

A minimal definition of 'moral standard' and 'morality'

A practical system is, or contains, a morality if it comprises one or more moral standards. As has been pointed out in similar cases, the definition of these terms must to some extent be stipulative, since neither their ordinary nor their technical uses are uniform. What can, however, be properly demanded of it, is that it should be convenient, that it should emphasize rather than obscure relevant distinctions and that it should have some foundation in ordinary and specialist usage. The following definition is intended to define a moral standard as any practical standard which at least one major Western philosopher – and possibly some minor ones – regard as moral; and a morality as any practical system which contains at least one moral standard. The Western philosophical tradition, which forms the background of these definitions, ranges from what are sometimes called 'situationalists', who deny that any truly moral attitude can be circumstantially general, to rigorous prescriptivists for whom any moral standard is a categorical imperative.

With these *provisos* a moral standard can be defined as an undominated, personally universal, practical *pro-* or *anti-*attitude. It will be convenient to take as examples of moral standards only practical attitudes of second level which are simple and essential. Because of this convenient restriction and because moral attitudes are by definition undominated, the possession of a moral standard by a person S can be schematically represented by expressions of form $S + [U * f]$ or $S - [U * f]$. The terminological reason why $S \pm [U * f]$ is not regarded as (expressing) a moral standard, but rather 'a standard of moral indifference', is that a practical system would not be considered as containing a morality, unless it contained at least one positive or negative moral standard.

In accordance with the minimal definition of a moral standard, we can now define a practical system as being, or containing, a morality or as having a moral aspect if, and only if, it contains at least one moral standard, i.e. at least one undominated, personally universal, practical *pro-* or *anti-*attitude of at least second level. This definition, especially in this lengthy restatement, is clearly seen not to exclude the possibility that a moral standard, say (that ascribed to S by) $S + [U * f]$, which belongs to a practical system should be an instance of a moral standard which has the additional feature of circumstantial generality – for example of

$$S + [U * X_1 \wedge ... \wedge X_m] \quad \text{or of} \quad S + [U * \mathfrak{M}_0].$$

In other words a moral standard which satisfies the minimal definition may be an instance of a moral standard which apart from satisfying this definition fulfils some other relevant requirements.

Yet it is conceivable that a practical system is, or contains, a 'concrete' morality in the sense that it comprises only moral standards which lack any sort of circumstantial generality. Whether such practical systems in fact exist, is an empirical question. My own inclination would be to regard their existence as fairly plausible: introspective evidence shows that in some cases of moral decision circumstantial generalization is enormously difficult, if not impossible. It thus seems reasonable to assume that some people though capable of personal generalization are not capable of circumstantial generalization at all. But since moral evaluations cannot be done by proxy, the morality of people who cannot formulate standards of form

$$S + [U * X_1 \wedge \ldots \wedge X_n] \quad \text{or} \quad S - [U * X_1 \wedge \ldots \wedge X_n]$$

can at most be concrete or situational.

It is similarly conceivable, and empirically plausible, that a person's practical system should comprise only undominated practical attitudes of at most second level which moreover lack not only circumstantial, but also personal generality. Such a system might for example comprise practical attitudes of form $S + [S + f]$ and of form $S - [U' + f]$, where U' differs from U by not having S among its members. Thus a person may have a pro-attitude towards his, but nobody's else's, proattitude towards joining the army in a concrete, circumstantially ungeneralizable situation; or he may have a pro-attitude towards everybody else's, but not his own, pro-attitude towards joining the army in this situation. In neither of these two cases would he – or would he be said to – employ a moral standard because the application of a moral standard by a person implies that it be in principle applicable to everybody. To deny the name of a moral standard to practical attitudes which lack personal generality and to deny that a practical system containing only such undominated practical attitudes contains a morality is not – to repeat it once more – to deny that such systems exist. We might emphasize this by saying that they contain a sub-morality, which is a perfectly proper subject of enquiry.

On the social content of morality

If a person's practical system contains not even a submorality, his actions – if he is capable of acting – still have a social content. They are, as became clear in examining their internal and external perspectives, chosen interventions or non-interventions not only in the course of nature, but also in the course of social life (see chapter 6). The internal perspective of our actions is determined by the way in which we physically, cognitively and evaluatively demarcate our chosen bodily conduct, the external perspectives are determined by the way in which those who observe us and interact with us demarcate those aspects of our bodily conduct which appear chosen to them. We normally try to achieve concurrence between the internal and external perspectives of our actions, although we sometimes secretively or deceitfully try to prevent such concurrence. Attempts at achieving or preventing concurrence in the internal and external perspectives of actions are particularly important when the demarcated chosen bodily conduct is speech and writing, which most obviously are, and depend on, social institutions.

A person's minimal moral standards are social not only by being standards of action, but also by virtue of the personal universality which is built into their very structures. If $S + [U * f]$ expresses a moral standard of S, then the class U of everybody, including himself, towards whose first level practical attitude he has a practical attitude of second level, is not a mere aggregate of persons. In making it the object of his second level attitude he assumes U to consist of persons who, like himself, are capable of acting and interacting, of using language, of classifying situations, of understanding the classifications of others, and last, but by no means least, are capable of adopting, and of living by, moral standards. Depending on the extension of U, having a morality is being aware of oneself as belonging to a social group, a society or mankind.

While even a minimal moral standard, such as $S + [U * f]$, has a social character in virtue of its personal universality, there are particular kinds of moral standards whose social character is further strengthened by the object of the universalized attitude. This is so especially when this object is the qualified or unqualified continued adoption of a code of conduct regulating the actions and interaction of a social group or society – in particular of a supreme code of conduct. Moral standards of this type form an important topic of sociological inquiry, even if the sociologists' proper interest in their genesis tends to make them pay insufficient attention to their structure.

A notable exception is Emile Durkheim whose analysis of what he calls moral facts fits moral standards, in which the universalized attitude is directed towards the adoption of some supreme code of conduct, i.e. moral standards such as $S + [U * \mathfrak{M}]$, fairly well. He distinguishes between two aspects of morality. One of them finds expression in moral rules which give rise to moral obligations conceived very much in Kantian fashion. The other aspect is a *sui generis* desirability. While the former aspect according to Durkheim (1951) corresponds to what is commonly called 'morally right', the latter corresponds to what is commonly called 'morally good'. Yet although he thus correctly distinguishes between moral evaluations and moral regulations, his analysis of the moral facts is too crude to exhibit the general relationship between a morality and the practical system to which it belongs, and hence the various forms this relationship may take. A finer analysis is primarily a philosophical task. But it may well be that in performing it one enables the genetic explanation to become more specific and more amenable to empirical tests.

On systems of morality comprising only minimal moral standards

Starting from the proposed definition of a minimal moral standard and looking back at the analyses of supreme evaluative principles, supreme codes of conduct and their mutual interconnections, as well as at the distinction between strict and competing evaluative principles and regulations, one is quite naturally led to a classification of pure and mixed moralities which corresponds fairly well to what Durkheim called 'moral facts' and what philosophers of varous schools have propounded as 'moral truths'. Apart from making contact with the philosophical literature, the classification is meant to emphasize the thesis that a person's moral standards – just as his prudential or professional standards – constitute merely a part or aspect of his total practical system and cannot be understood in isolation from it.

If by a pure type of morality one understands a morality comprising moral standards of only one of the distinguished kinds, then a minimal or concrete morality is a pure type. It is minimal not in the sense of imposing minimal burdens, but in the sense of being least general since the moral standards which it comprises lack all circumstantial generality. The personal universality of a minimal standard may give a spurious impression of circumstantial generality. Thus if $S + [U + f]$ is a minimal moral standard of S, it may with perfect correctness be expressed by saying that S has an undominated pro-attitude towards everybody's having a pro-attitude towards *the concrete situation* described by f and, hence, towards any situation which is 'precisely like' this situation. However, no fully concrete situation is precisely like any other fully concrete situation, so that a practical attitude which is directed towards a fully concrete situation is *eo ipso* not circumstantially general.

There are weaker senses in which two situations may be 'precisely alike', for example if one assumes that two such situations may differ, *only* spatio-temporally. This assumption is by no means clear and is, for example, incompatible with any view of space and time which regards them with Leibniz not as independent of, but as relations between, the entities which apparently occupy them. The assertion of a circumstantial generality which is the result of abstracting from

141

a situation's spatio-temporal characteristics may thus be quite empty and merely an elaborate and misleading way of referring to a practicability in its full circumstantial concreteness.

Indeed any apparently general demarcation of a class of situations as being alike in all respects except for a finite number of characteristics may not be general at all since, if the number of characteristics possessed by each of two situations is infinite or indefinite, it may be impossible to decide whether they share all these characteristics apart from the explicitly mentioned exceptions. The circumstantial generality of a moral standard is clearly indicated only by the enumeration of a finite number of attributes of the practicability towards which the universalized attitude is directed, i.e. schematically by the finite conjunction $X_1 \wedge \ldots \wedge X_n$ in $S * [U * X_1 \wedge \ldots \wedge X_n]$. It may, of course, be doubtful whether a moral standard lacks circumstantial generality or whether what is lacking is its clear characterization.

If, in accordance with common usage and the practice adopted earlier, one regards a moral standard as rational only if it is both personally and circumstantially general, then minimal moral standards and a minimal of concrete morality are not rational, but non-rational. Moral philosophers who hold that a person's moral evaluations are not circumstantially general, but depend on *ad hoc* intuitions about concrete situations often appeal to a moral intuition or a moral sense rather than to Reason. This is so because intuition and sense are regarded as apprehending the concrete and particular, while Reason is regarded as apprehending the abstract and the general. Yet intuition and sense though traditionally opposed to Reason are nevertheless not considered as irrational.

On purely axiological systems of morality

To be rational, a moral standard has to be a moral principle, that is to say not merely an undominated, personally universal, practical pro- or anti-attitude of at least second level, but in addition also circumstantially general, simple, and essential. Laying particular emphasis on its personal and circumstantial generality, and taking its other features for granted, (the ascription to a person S of) a rational evaluative principle can be schematically represented by, say,

$$S + [U * X_1 \wedge \ldots \wedge X_n].$$

Among the principles of this genus we may, in accordance with our

142

earlier inquiry into regulations, codes of conduct and code-dependent obligations distinguish those moral principles whose universalized practical attitude is directed towards the continued adoption of a particular supreme code of conduct, of a regulation belonging to a specified or unspecified supreme code of conduct or of an obligation following from a specified or unspecified supreme code of conduct. Such moral principles will be called 'deontic' moral principles as opposed to non-deontic or 'axiological' moral principles. Deontic moral principles have been schematically represented by

$$S + [U + m_0], \quad S + [U + (\exists \mathfrak{M})(m_0 \in \mathfrak{M})], \quad S + [U + (\exists \mathfrak{M}) : D(M) \vdash f_0]$$

etc.

A purely axiological system of morality comprises some axiological principles but no other moral standards. It does in particular comprise neither deontic moral principles nor minimal moral standards and leaves no room for *ad hoc* intuitions about the morality or immorality of any action not covered by its axiological principles.

One important point of interest in considering the possibility of a purely axiological system of morality is that it forces us to notice the difference between two senses of moral obligation, namely moral obligations which follow from an adopted supreme code of conduct and moral obligations which are independent of such a code. Since, according to those who hold that every morality is in the last analysis purely axiological, we nevertheless have genuine moral obligations, it is incumbent on them to explain a sense of moral obligation in which it is not code-dependent. But even if these philosophers have ignored the question, it must not be ignored by anybody who wishes to speak of moral obligations arising in purely axiological systems.

The difference between the two kinds of moral obligation namely code-dependent and code-independent moral obligations, becomes clear when we examine the sense of supererogatory actions in such systems. A supererogatory action, for example a certain type of self-sacrifice, might well be a supreme value of a person living by a purely axiological morality. Schematically, it might be the case that $S + [U + self\text{-}sacrifice]$. What makes the supremely valued action supererogatory for S is that while the action itself is one of his supreme values, requiring it of everybody including himself is not. Schematically, $\gamma \, [S + [U + requiring \ self\text{-}sacrifice]]$. Indeed, it may well be that while S judges self-sacrifice to be moral, he judges that to require it of anybody as immoral.

143

By contrast S judges a moral action as at the same time directly obligatory if he judges not only the action but also the requiring of it as moral. Schematically, not only (1) $S + [U + X]$ but also (2) $S + [U + requiring\ X]$ – e.g. S has a moral pro-attitude not only towards truthfulness in certain circumstances, but also towards demanding it in these circumstances. While the distinction between code-independent and code-dependent moral obligation is not always sharp, and while there may be borderline cases, which it would be improper to define out of existence, the distinction is by no means artificial, as can be seen from a comparison between the clear cases on the two sides of the border. Without making the distinction one could not, for example, explain the familiar situation in which a person considers (bringing about) f his moral obligation because it depends on a code towards whose continued acceptance he has a moral pro-attitude, while at the same time he considers it his (code-independent) moral obligation to bring about a change of this code so that f would no longer be a (code-dependent) moral obligation.

On purely deontic systems of morality

A purely deontic system of morality comprises only deontic moral principles. For those who live by a morality of this type, if there are any such, an action or other practicability has moral value only in so far as it fulfils a moral obligation which follows from a code of conduct the continued adoption of which is a supreme value. In accordance with our discussion of the relations between supreme evaluative and supreme regulative principles (in chapter 10) we may distinguish between three varieties of pure deontic morality, namely a substantive variety, a formal variety and a variety which is both formal and substantive.

A person lives by a substantive variety of a purely deontic morality if all his moral obligations follow from a particular supreme code, say, $\mathfrak{M}_0$, i.e. if, say, $S + [U + \mathfrak{M}_0]$. A simple example would be the Decalogue for any person who lived by it, acknowledged no other supreme code and no other supreme value than its continued adoption. In adducing this particular example one has, of course, to interpret those commandments which seem to regulate practical attitudes as regulating conduct, e.g. the commandment not to covet one's neighbour's wife as the commandment not to follow one's desire, and to do one's best to make it vanish if one has it, as well as to do one's best to prevent its emergence if one does not have it.

A person lives by a formal variety of a purely deontic morality, if he has a more or less determinate idea of what a moral code should be like and if his only supreme value is that his actions should conform to regulations fit for incorporation into such a code, i.e., say,

$$S + [U + (\forall f)(\forall \mathfrak{M}) : D(\mathfrak{M}) \vdash f].$$

The most important example of such a morality is, as has been noted earlier, to be found in Kant's ethical writings. His doctrine that a person's ability to will a regulation or code of conduct to become a universal law is a necessary and sufficient condition of its morality, may adequately represent the morality of *some* people. Admitting this possibility is perfectly compatible with rejecting the more characteristic Kantian theses that everybody's morality is of this type and that the universalizability test does, or would lead to, exactly the same results for everybody. In other words, although Kant and others may have lived, or may be living, by a Kantian morality, its description must not be confused with a description of morality in general.

The formal test by which the morality or otherwise of a regulation is to be decided may be more specific. The following, rather implausible, version of a so-called 'rule-utilitarianism' may serve as an example of a more specific test. According to it a regulation or code of conduct is moral if, and only if, its continued adoption would produce the greatest possible amount of utility for everybody. A person living by such a morality would have to possess a clear conception of utility and of a method for measuring it personally and interpersonally, as well as of a method of aggregating individual utilities into social utilities. To make the test purely formal he would have to make the further, very implausible, assumption that it is applicable to every regulation by itself, i.e. independently of any already adopted and implemented regulations. The type of morality just described differs from the Kantian merely by implying that a person's ability to will a regulation or code of conduct to become a universal law is limited by his inability to will this for any regulation or code of conduct whose continued adoption would not produce the greatest amount of utility for everybody.

Schematically such a deontic morality could be represented as containing only one moral principle say,

$$S + [U + (\forall f)(\forall \mathfrak{M}) : (\mathfrak{M} \in F) \wedge D(\mathfrak{M}) \vdash f],$$

145

where F is a conjunction of characteristics required of any supreme code $\mathfrak{M}$ – the moral principle being accepted on the assumption that its application does not lead to contradictions between the obligations which arise for S by applying it in his choices. This assumption is contingent and concerns both the characteristics F and the world in which S has occasion to apply the principle. As with any distinction between form and substance, the distinction between characterizing the form and characterizing the substance of a supreme code of conduct is not absolute.

It may sometimes be difficult, if not impossible, to distinguish between the requirement that any supreme code of conduct must satisfy certain formal conditions if it is to be adopted; and the requirement that a given supreme code of conduct be adopted only so long as circumstances are normal. Yet if the normality or otherwise of the circumstances does not depend on the code but on non-deontic standards, the morality of a person who lives by his code is not exhausted by it; and is thus not a purely deontic morality.

Drawing the line between the substantive and the formal variety of purely deontic moral systems is to some extent a matter of convention. But once the line is drawn, it is not difficult to conceive of a morality which contains both substantive and formal deontic principles. An example would be a morality which comprises the Decalogue and a suitable version of the categorical imperative.

On 'mixed' systems of morality

Of the 'pure' systems of morality the purely deontic type is the least stable in the sense that its moral standards must satisfy not only the conditions satisfied by axiological principles, in particular personal universality and circumstantial generality, but must in addition be directed to one kind of practicability only, namely the continued adoption of a supreme code of conduct. A purely deontic system thus loses its purity if two of its supreme regulations compete for application to the same situation, since in this case the supreme code of conduct must be supplemented by other moral standards. These may be axiological principles, i.e. supreme evaluative principles directed towards practicabilities other than the continued adoption of the supreme code, minimal moral standards, i.e. undominated practical attitudes lacking circumstantial generality, or even *ad hoc* intuitions.

The next pure type of moral system in decreasing order of stability is

146

the purely axiological type. Such a system loses its purity if two of its supreme axiological principles compete for application to the same situation. In that case the supplementation may consist in a minimal principle or an *ad hoc* decision or – somewhat implausibly – in a supreme regulation arbitrating between the competing axiological principles. A crude example of such a moral system would consist of a set of supreme evaluative principles and a regulation to resolve any conflict between two or more competing principles by drawing lots or throwing dice. Similar remarks apply to a purely minimal morality and its loss of purity through the competition of two or more minimal standards.

It is quite possible that a person's morality comprises strict standards of more than one kind. Of mixed systems those comprising strict deontic and strict axiological standards have attracted much philosophical attention. In such a morality the deontic principles, such as $S + [U + \mathfrak{M}_0]$, determine a person's code-dependent obligations or duties, as well as what is permitted or forbidden to him; whereas the axiological principles, such as $S + [U + X_1 \wedge \ldots \wedge X_n]$ – with $X, \ldots, X_n$ characterizing practicabilities other than the continued adoption of a supreme code – determine what is morally good, bad or indifferent for him to do. If his morality is consistent or, more precisely, if no two of his moral principles are opposed to or incongruent with each other, then no obligatory action can be morally bad and no forbidden action morally good.

Though conceivable, it seems humanly impossible that every morally good action should be obligatory, for example that the heroic conduct of the Christian martyrs should be judged everybody's duty. On the other hand, it is both conceivable and humanly possible that some morally bad actions, for example a certain type of fairly harmless malicious gossip, should not be forbidden by moral regulations. Yet, whatever the proper relationship between the forbidden and the morally bad, a morality which acknowledges both, moral duties and moral goodness beyond the call of duty seems to be particularly suited to human nature.

There is no need to elaborate all the possible combinations between the various pure types of morality. One further possibility is a moral system comprising in addition to deontic and axiological principles also minimal moral standards; another a morality which comprises all these and explicitly leaves room for *ad hoc* intuitions to fill in any gaps. Again one might, by suitably extending the distinction

147

between axiological and deontic principles to minimal moral standards, distinguish even within a minimal morality between the morally good and the morally obligatory. And there are other more or less interesting distinctions which could be added to those already drawn, by using and refining them indefinitely.

CHAPTER 12

JUSTICE

The idea of justice held by a person or prevalent in a society has an ideal and a deontic component. The ideal component is the conception of a society which enables the members of all social classes or of some clearly specified ones to have certain kinds of practical interests and in which the conflicting practical interests of different people are adjusted to each other in accordance with certain standards. The deontic component consists of moral obligations the satisfaction of which by their addressees is believed to decrease the differences, if any, between the existing and the ideal society. It is the main purpose of this chapter to elaborate this rather empty sketch of the notion of justice into an account of the place of justice in morality.

The chapter starts with an examination of the possible formal relations between the ideal and the deontic component in a conception of justice. There follows an argument to the effect that any notion of justice – as well as its traditional species of distributive, commutative and punitive justice – involves a prior demarcation of equivalence classes and, hence, a prior classification of persons and interests and that this classification is, moreover, not only factual but evaluative. This thesis is then exemplified by comparing various principles of justice. The chapter ends with an examination of the place of justice in purely deontic, axiological and mixed moralities.

On some possible formal relations between the ideal and the deontic component in a conception of justice

Before considering the interrelation between the two components in any conception of justice, it seems advisable to guard the characterization of the ideal society against some misunderstandings. It is first of all important that a person's being enabled by his social circumstances to have a certain practical interest be distinguished on the one hand from his having the practical interest and on the other hand from his

149

having an impracticable pro-attitude towards its object. For example, a middle class child in Victorian England was enabled by its social surroundings to have a practical interest in a university education even if it preferred some other option to it; while a child of the same intelligence belonging to a lower social stratum might have had a pro-attitude towards a university education but was unable to pursue it.

As regards the second characterization of the ideal society, namely its standards of adjusting the conflicting interests of different people, one must not confuse interpersonally conflicting with intrapersonally opposed practical interests. Thus while a person's practical pro-attitudes to, and hence his practical interests in, taking and not taking a holiday tomorrow are opposed, the practical interest of one person in taking and another person's interest in not taking a holiday may, but need not conflict. They conflict, for example, if the two people are married and enjoy only holidays taken together.

A precise definition of the conflict between the practical interests of two people is suggested by the definition, proposed earlier on, of a person's social interest as a self-regarding practical attitude the realization of which depends on the conduct of one or more other people (see p. 106). A social interest of a person S conflicts unilaterally with a social interest of a person Q if, and only if, the realization of S's interest depends on Q's conduct in such a manner that in so far as Q's conduct realizes Q's interest it is (empirically) incompatible with the realization of S's interest. A social interest of S and a social interest of Q conflict bilaterally if, and only if, the interest of either conflicts unilaterally with the interest of the other. The definition can be, and has been, extended to conflicts between more than two pepole and to conflicts which involve various combinations of people with common as well as with conflicting interests. Yet the more the definitions are designed to describe such situations in all their complexity the greater the difficulty of applying them to reality.

As has been mentioned earlier (p. 107) the social theorist who wishes to predict the development of an actual social system often follows the example of the natural scientist in trying to devise an idealized version of the actual system which, though simpler in structure, can yet for the purpose of social prediction be identified with it. The practical social thinker who wishes to change an actual society which falls short of his ideal of justice into a society which falls less short of it must have that ideal in mind. This ideal society must – like the natural or social scientist's ideal systems – be both intellectually simple and applicable to the real world.

The intellectual simplicity of the ideal just society consists in a sufficiently transparent system of social interests which it enables its members to have, as well as in a sufficiently transparent set of standards according to which any possible conflicts are, or can be, adjusted. The applicability of the ideal society to the actual world does not, however, consist in identifying the actual with the ideal system – as is done in the theoretical natural or social sciences – but in devising, adopting, proposing and (in a morally approved way) imposing a system of obligations, in particular a legal code, on the members of the society.

A very simple system of obligations for so changing an actual society that it becomes less removed from the ideal just society would consist of the one code-independent obligation to do everything in one's power to bring the just society nearer realization. Yet in many actual situations such an obligation would turn out to be immoral, to defeat its purpose or both. Thus it may be in a person's power to kill a pernicious tyrant and thereby to bring the just society a great step nearer – but only in circumstances in which killing the tyrant means certain death for his killer. In such circumstances many people who judge the tyrannicide moral may yet judge requiring it to be immoral. For such people the tyrannicide and, hence the single obligation to do everything in one's power to bring the just society nearer, is not a (code-independent) moral obligation since such an obligation implies not only the morality of the obligatory act, but also the morality of requiring it.

Even when the one obligation to bring the just society nearer appears to be moral – for example because the existing society would not turn its fulfilment into martyrdom – it could be self-defeating, because different people might, in trying to fulfil it, prevent each other from doing so. More generally whenever the realization of a practicability can be achieved by different, mutually exclusive, kinds of collaboration, the adoption of a common code of conduct becomes desirable. An obvious example is the regulation of traffic in a crowded city. Clearly, the more complex the mutually exclusive strategies for achieving a certain social situation, and the greater their number, the greater also is the need for the adoption of a common code of conduct, which is deontologically consistent, adequate to the actual word and, of course, suitable for bringing about the desired change.

In order to judge the suitability of the deontic component of one's idea of justice to its ideal component, one has to rely on one's common sense and theoretical knowledge of the structure of the society in which one lives, of the laws of social change, of man's capacity to intervene in its course, as well as of the features which any society having the characteristics of a just society would necessarily also possess. In all these respects our knowledge is far from adequate and history shows that even those among us who, like the Marxists, claim to know the course of history in broad outline, cannot agree on the code of conduct which, in a given historical situation, is suitable to bringing nearer, or at least not removing farther, the realization of their ideal of justice. A conservative who holds that his society is just or as nearly just as is humanly possible will tend to identify the laws of his country with the deontic component of his idea of justice. In some societies, in which the law of the land contains practicable provisions for its own change, the gradualist reformer might agree with the conservative on the deontic component of justice, however much they disagree on its ideal component. The revolutionary who regards the law of the land as a safeguard of injustice will disagree with both of them. But his idea of justice, if it is to have any change of being realized, will also have to contain a code of conduct adopted by him and his collaborators, whether this code be formulated in a theoretical treatise, a political manifesto, the constitution of his party or by some other means.

Ideas of justice as depending on evaluative classifications and equivalence classes

In referring to unspecified kinds of interests which unspecified kinds of people are enabled to possess by their social circumstances, and to unspecified standards by which conflicting practical interests of different people are adjusted to each other, the proposed general definition leaves room for a great variety of substantively different conceptions of justice. It is nevertheless more specific than the classical and admirably concise definition of Ulpianus that *justitia est constans et perpetua voluntas jus suum cuique tribuendi* (that justice is the ever present will to give everybody what is due to him). The proposed definition, unlike the classical, emphasizes the distinction between the ideal and the deontic component in any conception of justice and thereby implies the important possibility that a change in the existing society – for example an industrial or medical revolution – may call

for a change in the deontic component of one's conception of justice
if one's ideal component is to remain unchanged. Again, the proposed
definition indicates more clearly than the classical the manner in
which the substantive differences between various conceptions of
justice depend on prior moral evaluations, expressed in evaluative
classifications.

In order to explain one's conception of an ideal society, in which
everybody has what is due to him and in which nobody has or takes
what is not due to him, one has (1) to distinguish between anti-social
practical interests, i.e. practical interests which in the ideal society
nobody would be able to have (e.g. killing people for pleasure) and
interests which are not anti-social; (2) to classify the members of
the society into social classes according to the social interests which in
the ideal society they are enabled to have (e.g. the class of all people,
of children, of people with exceptionally high intelligence); (3) to
provide criteria for deciding when the social interests of two people
belonging to the same social class (every member of the society, two
orphaned infants, two judges) are or are not equivalent. The explanation of each of these points may be more or less detailed. Yet even
a very general explanation of them may reveal very great differences
in the conceptions of justice held by different people. Thus Aristotle
in the fifth book of *The Nicomachean Ethics*, which is still one of the
best formal analyses of justice, nevertheless ascribes just social
interests only to those 'who share equally in ruling and being ruled'
which excludes slaves, children and wives.

Clearly, a person's conception of the ideal just society – and hence of
the classifications and criteria needed for characterizing it – is a moral
conception, since bringing it about, or at least bringing it nearer, is the
object of a system of moral obligations. Yet even considered by themselves the classifications and criteria rest on moral evaluations. Anti-
social practical interests are obviously practical attitudes towards
which a moral anti-attitude is directed. The assignment of a set of social
interests to a social class in preference to any other such assignment –
for example the assignment expressed by 'children, kitchen and
church' to women – again implies a moral judgment. As to the criteria
of equivalence, by which the justice or injustice of a social interest is
determined, they too depend on moral attitudes, as becomes clear
when one considers, for example, the morality of different tax systems
or social security.

Compared with the possible differences in the ideal components of various concepts of justice, the possible differences in the deontic components are, from the point of view of this essay, of minor importance – even though the same ideal component may be associated with different deontic components and the question of the most suitable one may be crucial for anybody who has to choose between them. In characterizing the purely formal structure of the deontic component of any conception of justice, one may follow the traditional, Aristotelian distinction between distributive and corrective justice. Distributive justice is exercised 'in the distribution of honour, wealth and the other divisible assets of the community' in such a manner that their actual distribution approximates as nearly as possible to their distribution in the ideal, just society. Corrective justice 'supplies a corrective principle' either in transactions into which all the parties concerned enter voluntarily such as 'selling, buying, lending at interest...' or in transactions into which not all the parties concerned enter voluntarily because they are furtive like 'theft, adultery, poisoning, procuring...' or violent like 'assault, imprisonment, murder, robbery with violence...'.

It would be tempting to continue the comparison between our analysis of any conception of justice as based on the dependence of a deontic on an ideal component, and Aristotle's analysis of it. But it is in any case worth pointing out, or recalling, that Aristotle is aware of the possibility of different conceptions of justice, supported by different moral evaluations as expressed by different social classifications and criteria of equivalence. To quote only one relevant passage, he says that while 'all are agreed that justice in distributions must be based on desert of some sort' they 'do not all mean the same sort of desert' since 'democrats', such as Aristotle himself, 'make the criterion free birth; those of oligarchical sympathies wealth, or in other cases birth; and upholders of aristocracy make it virtue'. (The relevance of the quotation is in no way affected by the sense in which Aristotle uses 'democracy' and 'aristocracy' and which is quite different from their present sense.)

What applies to the formula 'To each according to his deserts' applies also to similar pithy formulae such as 'To each according to his works', 'To each according to his rank', 'To each according to his legal entitlement', 'To each the same'. Each of them admits of different and mutually incompatible interpretations, as is well shown by Perelman (1945) and each of the various interpretations depends in the manner explained on prior moral evaluations.

*On Kant's categorical imperative and Nelson's principle of balance
as allegedly independent, substantive criteria of justice*

Ulpianus' definition of justice and the other definitions considered are, as would be generally agreed, quite insufficient to serve as criteria for deciding whether any concrete action is or is not just. Indeed the preceding analysis of any notion of justice as consisting of an ideal component, based on prior moral evaluations, and a deontic component determining one of a number of conceivable strategies for bringing the realization of the ideal nearer, makes it appear highly unlikely that a criterion could be produced which would determine for everybody the justice or otherwise of any action in the same way and without presupposing other moral criteria or principles. Yet, since such apparently independent criteria have been proposed, it seems necessary to consider some plausible candidates.

The best known among them is Kant's categorical imperative when restricted to actions which affect the adjustment to each other of conflicting interests of different people. This is so because Kant regards the categorical imperative as a necessary and sufficient criterion of the morality of all actions – whether or not they affect the adjustment of conflicting interests – and because for him the morality of an action coincides with its justice to the extent to which it affects the adjustment of conflicting interests. To put it in a slightly different way, for Kant justice is a species of morality, namely the morality of a species of actions. Since, as has been argued earlier (p. 145), not every morality, not even every deontic morality, is Kantian, the categorical imperative is not a criterion for everybody. It may, moreover, for those who accept it lead to different results. Whether this is so because they implicitly employ additional moral criteria, is an empirical question to which I should be inclined to give an affirmative answer.

Another apparently independent criterion of the justice or injustice of concrete actions has been proposed by Leonard Nelson as a result of a thoughtful critique and reconstruction of the practical philosophy of Kant. Nelson (1917: pp. 216ff.) replaces Kant's principle for testing the justice of an action through the universalizability of its maxim by a principle of balance and a principle of retribution the applicability of which presupposes that the principle of balance has been violated. The principle of balance is a particularly clear representative of an important class of allegedly independent principles of justice whose application by a person demands that he imagine his system of practical attitudes to be different from what it in fact is. This demand differs both from the Kantian demand to assume the rôle of universal legislator and the ordinary demand for sympathy or empathy – i.e. attitudes which one possesses or does not possess and towards the presence or absence of which one also possesses or does not possess attitudes of higher level.

The principle of balance is formulated as follows (Nelson 1917: p. 133): 'Never act in such a manner, that you could not consent to your conduct if the interests of those affected by your conduct were your own.' Nelson's explanatory comments show that the addressee of the imperative is required to imagine *not* that he no longer possesses his own interests but that without changing his own interests he adds the conflicting interests of the other persons to his own and then decides as if all these interests 'were united in one and the same person'. Thus, at least part of what the principle of balance requires is that one should treat conflicting practical interests as practically opposed.

Now, quite apart from the impossibility or, at least, sometimes insuperable difficulty of so uniting the conflicting interests of two persons, for example those of a catholic opponent and an atheist defender of abortion, the insufficiency of the principle of balance follows from its incompatibility with any realistic description of a person's system of practical attitudes. To see this it is convenient to distinguish between two cases in which a person S adds a conflicting practical interest of a person Q to his system of practical attitudes, namely (1) the case where the added conflicting attitude of Q is dominated by one of S's moral attitudes (e.g. where Q's first level pro-attitude towards abortion in certain circumstances is dominated by S's higher level moral anti-attitude towards any pro-attitude directed towards the deliberate shortening of the life of any animal organism); and (2) the case where the conflict is one between a moral attitude of S and a moral attitude of Q (e.g. between S's patriotic moral pro-attitude towards any pro-attitude directed towards defensive war and S's pacifist moral anti-attitude towards any pro-attitude directed towards war of any kind).

In the first case the balance is struck not by applying the principle of balance but by S's adherence to a different moral principle. In the second case the outcome is either undecided or else – if we unrealistically assume that S can not only add Q's conflicting interest to his own system of interests, but also compare their strength – dependent on which of the two interests is the stronger. But then the possibility must be admitted that in some cases S's moral attitude will outweigh Q's, that in other cases Q's moral attitude will outweigh S's, and that in a third kind of case the two moral principles will balance each other in strength. Thus Nelson's principle of balance, like Kant's categorical imperative, may for its acceptors lead to different results (e.g. to the pacifist moral principle overriding the patriotic, to the patriotic overriding the pacifist or to a stalemate between the two). If we admit the possibility that of two conflicting attitudes of any level neither outweighs the other and if, with Nelson, we accept the thesis that every conflict of practical attitudes is rationally decidable, then it follows that the principle of balance is not a sufficient criterion for deciding the justice or otherwise of all concrete actions. (See pp. 122f.)

On Locke's conception of a social contract and Rawls's conception of fairness as allegedly independent, substantive criteria of justice

All so-called contract theories of government are based on the assumption or fiction of a prepolitical or natural state of society in which its members can, and do, consent to the formation of a political society, whose institutions guarantee a certain adjustment of the conflicting interests of its members. Whether the contract which results from the consent of the members of the pre-political society can serve as an independent criterion of the justice of social institutions and, indirectly, of actions depends on the nature of the contract, which in turn depends on the mental abilities and practical attitudes of the members of the prepolitical society. If they greatly differ in political foresight, lust for power and in the degree to which they possess it in the prepolitical society, it is likely that, for example, most contemporary English liberals, socialists and conservatives would not accept their social contract as a criterion of justice.

Locke's *Second Treatise of Government* can be interpreted as an attempt at outlining a social contract which could serve as a test for the justice of political institutions and actions. This is so because of the special assumptions he makes about the contracting parties on the one hand and the purpose of their contract on the other. Of the contracting members of the prepolitical society he assumes that they are 'all free, equal and independent' and so situated that 'no-one can be put out of his estate and subjected to the political power of another without his own consent'. About the purpose of their agreeing with each other, he assumes that it is 'to join and unite into a community for their comfortable, safe and peaceable living, one amongst another, in a secure enjoyment of their properties, and a greater security against any that are not of it' (§ 95).

That this account of the contract and the circumstances of the contracting parties does not provide us with a substantive criterion of social justice follows from the indeterminate sense of the notions of freedom, equality and independence which can be specified in a variety of conflicting ways. They could, for example, in accordance with Aristotle's political *credo* be so specified that a slave-owning society would be just. Locke is aware of this and supplements his account by a doctrine of inalienable, natural rights and by indicating reasons for a revolutionary dissolution of a political society. If, as seems plausible, Locke's doctrine of natural rights is a statement of moral principles – rather than of certain general human characteristics which, like the instinct for survival, are not specifically moral – then *the* social contract is not an independent criterion of justice, but a contract whose justice or injustice is judged by other moral criteria. On this interpretation, which implies that Locke's ethics is inconsistent with his epistemological rejection of innate ideas, Locke's conception of a social contract would be very similar to that of Rousseau and Kant (1797: §§ 43ff.), both of whom regard the justice of a social contract, which changes a prepolitical into a political society, as dependent on moral principles which are independent of the circumstances or content of any contract.

Recently a contract theory of social justice has been proposed and worked out in impressive detail by John Rawls in a number of papers and a book (Rawls 1972). This theory too gives rise to the question whether the assumptions made about the situation in which, and the persons by which, the contract is made depend on unstated moral principles which are either as a matter of fact or as a matter of some special non-logical necessity adopted by every human or every rational human being. Although Rawls (1972: p. 579) leaves this question deliberately aside, even a very brief examination of a very brief outline of his theory implies an affirmative answer.

About the prepolitical society Rawls makes the heuristic assumption that no member knows 'his place in society, his class position or social status...his fortune in the distribution of natural assets and abilities, his intelligence, strength and the like'. He assumes even 'that the parties do not know their conceptions of the good or their special psychological propensities' (1972: p. 12). As regards a social contract made by people in such circumstances he holds that *if* they are rational or fair, they will adopt as its overriding principle of justice 'that all social values – liberty and opportunity, income and wealth and the bases of self-respect – are to be distributed equally unless an unequal distribution of any, or all, of these values is to everyone's advantage' (1972: p. 62).

The imaginative effort imposed by Rawls on the contracting parties is at least as difficult as that imposed by Nelson on those applying the principle of balance. It is, moreover, in some respects less clear. It is in particular doubtful whether a person who is supposed not to know his conception of the good or his special psychological propensities, has any conception of the good or any psychological propensities; and if not, whether he can in any normal sense be fair. Yet even apart from the doubt whether Rawls's heuristic assumptions about the pre-political society logically imply this, or any, principle of justice, the principle is not the only one which can be chosen 'rationally' or 'fairly' by a person who has, as it were, rid himself of himself as far as is humanly possible, without losing interest in arriving at a principle of social justice.

Thus a theory of justice, which is a simplification of, and hence rather different from, the Rawlsian theory, might conceive a fair social contract as a set of rules governing an all embracing social game, in which everybody's chances are equal – for example in accordance with de Finetti's principle (see p. 44). This definition of a fair social game or a fair political society will be acceptable to some people, such as the *aut Caesar aut nihil* types. But it will be too weak for those for whom fair play is not a sufficient guarantee of justice. Such people (of whom I am one) would, for example, consider Russian roulette an immoral game although they admit that the players chances in it are equal. A stronger conception of the justice of a social game, and another competitor for Rawls's theory, could be defined by adding to the condition that everybody's chances be equal the further condition that the principles of the game or the social contract be not immoral.

Yet this further condition, which plainly implies the dependence of a person's conception of justice on his whole morality, could be specified in very different ways. Thus one might adopt Rawls's egalitarian standpoint for certain practical interests, for example by guaranteeing to every member of the society equality in housing, income and education while otherwise allowing social life to be competitive and fair in the narrow sense of the probabilistic definition. Again, a limited Rawlsian egalitarianism might be supplemented by a social organization in which some persons hold high office assigned to them by a lottery in which the chances of all citizens are equal, a procedure adopted for some offices in the classical period of Athens.

There are also conceptions of justice – dependent on other moralities – which lack both the egalitarian element and the element of fairness in the sense of equal chances for everybody. One of them is expressed by Plato's principle 'that one man should practice one thing only, namely the thing to which his nature is best adapted'. (*Republic* I, 366). It could nevertheless be argued that Plato's derivation of his principle of justice is compatible with Rawls's heuristic assumption about the prepolitical society; and that the reason why their conceptions of justice are so different lies in their different moral principles.

On the place of justice in deontic and other types of morality

Although every conception of justice contains an ideal and a deontic component, the place of justice in a person's morality is likely to be particularly clear if his morality is purely deontic. This is so because in this case the deontic component of his conception of morality is a part of his supreme code of conduct. If such a person lives by a substantive variety of a deontic morality – say the Decalogue or another deontic morality which can be schematically expressed by $S + [U + \mathfrak{M}_0]$ – then the deontic component of his conception of justice will be either the whole or part of his supreme code of conduct. It may not, of course, always be easy or even possible to decide which of the code-dependent obligations are obligations of justice and which are wider moral obligations. Thus if a person whose supreme code of conduct is the Decalogue, has a conception of justice whose ideal component refers only to human relations, then the fifth commandment, namely 'not to take the name of the Lord, your God, in vain', expresses for him a moral obligation, but not also an obligation of justice.

If a person lives by a Kantian or other formal variety of a deontic morality, schematically $S + [U + (\forall f)\,(\forall \mathfrak{M}): (\mathfrak{M} \in F) \wedge D(\mathfrak{M}) \vdash f]$, then all his moral obligations will satisfy the criterion of being derivable from a code of conduct of a certain kind, while his obligations of justice will be included in, but will not include, the class of all his moral obligations. Thus a person stranded on a distant star without any chance of rejoining a political society will, if his morality is Kantian, still have moral obligations even though at least some of them will not be obligations of justice. Yet, whatever the correct exegesis of Kant's ethical theory, one must admit the possibility of a person's deontic morality which coincides with the deontic component of his conception of justice.

If a person lives by a minimal or purely axiological morality, schematically if all his moral principles are either of form $S * [U * f]$ or of form $S * [U * X_1 \wedge ... \wedge X_n]$, then the deontic component of his conception of justice, if any, will consist of code-independent moral obligations, whose satisfaction he believes will bring nearer, or at least not to remove any further, the ideal just society. And his code-independent obligations of justice will be included in his other moral obligations, all of which are code-independent.

However, a person who does not adopt deontic moral principles in the strict sense may nevertheless have a moral pro-attitude towards the *qualified* adoption of a code of conduct in *ordinary* circumstances (see p. 136) even though in the case of a minimal or purely axiological morality no sharp dividing line can be drawn between ordinary and extraordinary circumstances. (If such a division could be drawn, the qualification could be incorporated into the code of conduct, thus giving rise to deontic principles on one side of the dividing line.) The moral pro-attitude towards such qualified adoption of a code of conduct is a moral pro-attitude towards determining one's own or others' obligations of justice by the application of the code in circumstances when not doing so would *almost certainly* lead to delays, confusions, disputes, or other avoidable occurrences which are believed to retard rather than to promote the realization of the ideal just society.

Because within an axiological morality a code of moral conduct can only be applied in circumstances the precise demarcation of which is not possible, one cannot exclude the possiblity that an action which conforms to the code is by the axiological morality immoral and, hence, unjust. The only effective precaution against this possibility is to be aware of it and to make sure that an exception be admitted whenever strict satisfaction of the code would be immoral. To allow for such exceptions, when the strict application of the code of conduct would result in immorality and hence, in injustice, and to put them into effect is the function of equity. The need for introducing it as a corrective to a strict code of conduct adopted within a pure axiological morality was emphasized by Aristotle (*Nicomachean Ethics*, V) whose own

161

morality was a combination of an axiological morality with the merely qualified adoption of a code of conduct expressing the deontic component of his ideal of justice.

Because the line between cases falling under the code and cases which are to be treated in equity as exceptions is not sharp and cannot in the nature of things be defined by the code, the decision must lie with the person – be he a professional judge or a layman trying to do or to decide what is just – who is applying the code. It is up to him, 'where the law-giver's pronouncement because of its absoluteness is defective and erroneous, to rectify the defect by deciding as the law-giver would himself decide if he were present on the occasion, and would have enacted if he had been acquainted with the case in question' (*Nichomachean Ethics*, V). What has been said about the place of code-dependent obligations expressing in a merely qualified manner the deontic component of a conception of justice in an axiological morality, holds to some extent also for certain mixed types of morality. More precisely, in so far as the deontic component of a conception of morality is expressed by regulations whose adoption is merely qualified, there is room and need for equity.

There are, then, many conceptions of justice which, like the moralities to which they belong, differ from each other both in form and substance. This view differs both from the position of Plato and other absolutists who hold that there can be only one adequate, genuine, or correct concept of justice, and from the position of Hobbes and other positivist philosophers of law who argue that the concept of justice is either empty or else identical with the concept of legality. While both the absolutists' and the positivists' doctrine are incompatible with the preceding analysis, the positivists' doctrine has in addition the absurd consequence that in their view the expression 'unjust law' is a contradiction in terms.

CHAPTER 13

PRUDENCE AND WELFARE

Within the great variety of practical attitudes which – in harmony or conflict with each other – govern human conduct, we may distinguish, at one extreme, rational attitudes which are personally and circumstantially universal and undominated, and at the other extreme, purely selfish attitudes which a person has towards a concrete situation without regard to any interests other than his own. Between these extremes lie attitudes which, so to speak, combine some features of the purely selfish with some features of the rational attitudes. These mixed attitudes are often called by the name of prudence – a propensity which Bishop Butler (1736: I. IV. 4) characterizes as that 'reasonable self-love the end of which is our worldly interest'. The main aim of this chapter is to elaborate Butler's characterization of prudence and in doing so to determine the place of prudential evaluations, principles and values in systems of practical attitudes.

The discussion will proceed as follows. After defining the notions of a prudent practical attitude and contrasting practical with theoretical prudence, the formal structure of a person's system of prudential attitudes – a subsystem of the system of all his practical attitudes – will be examined and the possibility of substantively different notions of prudence explained. Next the relation between prudence and various kinds of welfare – private, extended private, and social – will be considered. The chapter ends with a brief examination of the manner in which practical preferences and social welfare are treated in the social sciences.

On prudent attitudes and prudential principles

Self-regard is normally considered to be compatible with prudence and with morality, but different from either. Yet although most people would admit the possibility of self-regarding actions being either prudent or imprudent and either moral or immoral, there are some who under the pressure of certain moral theories would reject this classification. Among the dissidents are some who take self-regard to imply, or even to be equivalent with, prudence; some who take self-regard to imply, or even to be equivalent with, morality; and a very small, eccentric minority who take self-regard to be equivalent with both prudence and morality. If, under the influence of such theories, the concept which will here be called 'prudence' is considered unfit to bear this name, it nevertheless has – well named or ill named – important applications which make it indispensable in describing the complex structure of practical attitudes.

Before defining the notion of a prudent practical attitude it is necessary to recall the more general notion of a self-regarding practical attitude. A person S has a self-regarding practical attitude towards a practicability (described by), say, f if, and only if, the practicability involves himself and the attitude is directed towards f as essentially involving himself either as an individual or as a member of a class of persons. Thus S has a self-regarding pro-attitude towards paying less taxes on his royalties, whether or not his attitude is directed towards this tax reduction for himself as a person or as an author. A second level practical attitude $S*[S*f]$ is self-regarding if it is directed towards a self-regarding first level practical attitude of S qua S or S qua member of a wider class, e.g. S qua author, qua citizen or qua human being. Higher level self-regarding attitudes are defined analogously.

We can now define the notion of a principle of prudence and, thereby, of a prudent practical attitude as one which is, or is covered by, a principle of prudence. A practical attitude of a person S is a principle of prudence if, and only if, (1) it is self-regarding; (2) it is personally and circumstantially general; (3) its personal generality is restricted to a class of persons qua member of which S has the self-regarding attitude; and (4) it is either positively or indifferently dominated by a moral attitude. Of these conditions, the first which needs no further comment, is intended to capture the element of the self-love which Butler discerns in prudence, the others its reasonableness or rationality.

The second and third simply express the generality which is characteristic of all practical principles, and without which they could not be applied to particular cases. The third condition requires that what is prudent for a person qua member of a class of persons must in his view be prudent for every member of this 'prudential class'. The last condition expresses a reasonable limitation of prudence by excluding immoral attitudes from prudent ones. One does not regard an efficient businessman who pursues his business in an immoral fashion as a prudent businessman, an efficiently stealing thief as a prudent thief or an efficient embezzler as a prudent embezzler.

Together these conditions distinguish practical prudence, or prudence *simpliciter*, from efficiency which concerns the choice of suitable means to given ends – be they moral or immoral, prudent or imprudent. Efficiency, or mere technical prudence, depends for its exercise on prior practical attitudes, whereas prudence in Butler's (and our) sense is, like morality or pure – i.e. personally ungeneralized – self-regard, a feature of some practical attitudes. Again prudential principles express practical attitudes towards practical attitudes, whereas methodological maxims express the technical know-how by which practical attitudes may be realized.

Leaving unexpressed the requirement that a prudential principle be positively or indifferently dominated by a moral attitude, and distinguishing explicitly between constants and variables (by using letters with subscripts for constants and letters without subscripts for variables) we can represent the form of a prudential principle by $S * [G(S) * X]$ and a specific or constant prudential principle by, say, $S_0 + [G_0(S) - X_0]$. Here '$G(S)$' stands for a prudential class *qua* member of which a person S has a self-regarding second level attitude $S *$ towards a self-regarding first level attitude $G(S) *$ towards a practicability X. If in our specific prudential principle S_0 is a certain historian, say Sextus, $G_0(S)$ the prudential class of historians *qua* member of which Sextus has the second level self-regarding attitude, and X_0 a practicability characterized as a careless checking of references, then $S_0 + [G_0(S) - X_0]$ represents the statement: Sextus has *qua* member of the prudential class of historians a self-regarding pro-attitude towards a situation in which every member of the (prudential) class of historians, including himself, has a self-regarding anti-attitude towards the careless checking of references.

Prudential principles differ from each other in the nature of the first and higher level attitudes (positive, negative or indifferent), in the type of practicability which is the object of the self-regarding attitude of first level, and in the prudential class which is the subject of the first level attitude. As regards this prudential class, it may be any class *qua* member of which a person has a self-regarding attitude. It may be in particular a class comprising all human beings or only one. If, however, the subject of the self-regarding second level attitude is S *qua* S – if $S * [S * X]$ – then the attitude is purely self-regarding or selfish and, hence, not prudent.

165

On the structure of a person's system of prudential principles

The structure of a person's system of prudential principles is best discussed by assuming that his system of practical attitudes comprises both prudential principles and moral principles and by comparing the two. Prudential principles differ, by definition, from moral principles in their personal generality, which is restricted to prudential classes (and may, but need not, be universal), and in their being dominated by higher, namely moral, attitudes. A person's prudential principle expresses part of what he considers as reasonably self-regarding conduct for any member of a prudential class *qua* member of his class, himself included, and hence what he considers as one of the conditions of well-being for any member of the prudential class *qua* member of it. To make explicit a person's conception of prudence and, thereby, of well-being would imply exhibiting all the prudential classes of which he considers himself to be a member and for each prudential class the prudential principles which he associates with it. A person's principles of prudence may, of course, conflict with each other and some of them may be incapable of exact or unambiguous formulation.

Consider, as before, the prudential principle of our historian $S_0 + [G_0(S) - X_0]$ which expresses his pro-attitude towards any self-regarding historian's anti-attitude towards the careless checking of references. Another prudential principle of this historian is, we assume, the principle $S_0 - [G_0(S) + X_1]$ which expresses his anti-attitude towards any self-regarding historian's pro-attitude towards relying on hearsay evidence. The set of all prudential principles held by S_0 as a historian consists of all the correct substitution instances of $S_0 * [G_0(S) * X]$ in which the first and second level variable $*$ is replaced by $+$, $-$ or $\pm$ and the variable X is replaced by a constant describing a kind of practicability confronting S_0 as a historian. Of the specific prudential principles arrived at in this manner, and adopted by S_0, some will be included in others and thus be redundant.

S_0 will very likely adhere to other prudential principles, in which the place of $G_0(S)$ is taken by other prudential classes. And just as a person's prudence *qua* historian is a condition of his well-being as a historian, so his prudence *qua* businessman or stamp-collector is a condition of his well-being in these capacities. If the prudential class $G_0(S)$ coincides with the class of all self-regarding human beings, then any prudential principle associated with it expresses what in the view of S_0 is a condition of everybody's happiness – in a sense of the term in which happiness can be neither unreasonable nor immoral.

Yet, while a prudent action – i.e. an action covered by a prudential principle, which in turn is positively or indifferently dominated by a moral attitude – cannot be immoral, it is possible for a moral action not to be prudent. If Socrates after his unjust trial had followed Crito's advice to flee from Athens he would have acted prudently and not immorally. In not following Crito's advice he acted morally, though not prudently. There are, of course, many examples of moral and imprudent actions which are far from approaching the heroism of Socrates. Moral actions, which are not prudent, are a species of supererogatory actions; i.e. of actions which are the object of a moral pro-attitude, but the requiring of which is not also the object of a pro-attitude (see p. 143).

Apart from being, in the manner described, associated with his prudential classes, a person's prudential principles have the same structure as any other personally and circumstantially general dominated practical attitudes of, at least, second level. It is thus quite easy to apply what has been said about such attitudes in general to the analysis of a person's system of prudential principles. The key concepts used are the stratification, inconsistency and domination of practical attitudes. As attitudes of, at least, second level, prudential principles may, or may not, manifest all three kinds of inconsistency (explained in chapter 7). Thus two prudential principles belonging to a person's practical system may, or may not, be opposed to each other or incongruent with each other. Again, a practical attitude covered by a prudential principle may, or may not, be discordant with, i.e. negatively dominated by, it. Lastly, although a prudential principle is by definition required to be positively or indifferently dominated by some moral principle, this requirement may be violated by mistake. That is to say a person may not be aware that a principle which he regards as prudential is in fact negatively dominated by one of his moral attitudes – just as a person may not be aware that some of his theoretical beliefs which he regards as consistent are in fact inconsistent.

Some further distinctions drawn earlier are also useful in demarcating a person's conception of prudence. One is the distinction between evaluative principles which are, and evaluative distinctions which are not, simple and essential. Its point is that all evaluative principles can be represented as either simple and essential or as having such principles as their components (see chapter 9). Another distinction of importance is that between strict and competing evaluative principles (explained in chapter 9). Less important in demarcating a person's conception of prudence is the distinction between evaluative and regulative standards of conduct (explained in chapter 10), since codes of prudential conduct and code-independent prudential obligations play a much smaller rôle than do codes of moral conduct or code-independent moral obligations. Because of this a typology of prudential practical systems distinguishing (after the fashion of chapter 11) purely axiological, pure deontic and mixed systems of prudential standards would appear rather pointless.

On the content of different conceptions of prudence and personal welfare

Just as the formal structure of a person's conception of prudence is determined by the place of his prudential principles in the hierarchy of his practical attitudes, namely below the moral attitudes by which they are dominated and above the self-regarding attitudes which are dominated by them, so the content of his conception of prudence depends on the influence exerted from below by the content of his self-regarding attitudes and from above by the content of his moral attitudes. It is not among the tasks of this inquiry to describe the genesis of specific concepts of prudence and of the rôle played in it by the interaction of a person's self-regard and his morality. But it seems well within the limits of a logico-philosophical analysis of the structure of practical systems to consider the position of a person, say S, who is fully aware of his first level self-regarding attitudes and of his moral attitudes and who in the light of them is trying to determine the prudential principles which would be appropriate for him.

Since whoever adheres to a prudential principle adheres to it *qua* member of a prudential class, S must first of all acknowledge a classification of people into prudential classes. As a rule he will, apart from possible minor details, find such a classification ready made in the language describing the various more or less permanent functions which the members of his society may assume. To these functions correspond classes comprising everybody belonging to a certain profession, everybody having a certain family status, everybody having a certain position of political responsibility etc. and, lastly, the class of all members of the society. These prudential classes will as a rule be coextensive with other social classes, whose members are the subjects or objects of certain practical attitudes and social interests – for example of 'justicial' classes of persons to whom equal treatment is due according to the ideal and the deontic component of the conception of justice which is prevalent in S's society.

If S, for example when choosing or changing his career, is confronted with the possibility of effectively choosing to become, or not to become, a member of one or more prudential classes, his choice may or may not be subject to prudential principles. It is subject to such principles if he makes the choice *qua* member of a prudential class, membership of which he either cannot or does not wish to relinquish. For example a person who *qua* member of the class of (what he regards as) normal human beings, or *qua* member of an oppressed or underprivileged minority, chooses to enter a profession (and with it to accept its associated prudential principles), chooses so not only from self-regard and subject to his moral attitudes, but also subject to some already accepted prudential principles. Such a choice of prudential principles under previously accepted prudential principles implies a stratification of prudential principles, and with it the possibility of discordance between them. It may also be the case that the effective choice of membership in one or more prudential classes is not subject to any prior principles of prudence. This is so when a person does not consider himself a member of any specific prudential class, or when he decides no longer to choose *qua* member of the prudential classes as a member of which he has so far made his choices. An example would be the choice of a person who severs all his connections with his previous social existence and joins the foreign legion, a community of drop-outs, a religious order etc.

A prudent pro-attitude towards a practicability implies a pro-attitude towards its competent realization. Thus, if S *qua* historian has a pro-attitude towards checking his references, he *ipso facto* has a pro-attitude towards doing so competently rather than incompetently, i.e. doing so in the light of the best available factual and technical knowledge. Yet, although prudence implies a pro-attitude towards competence it does not, as has been pointed out earlier, imply competence. A person may have prudent attitudes and yet be incompetent in their realization. There is, of course, no objection to defining prudence in a wider sense by requiring that, like prudence in the narrow sense, it be incompatible with immorality, and by requiring in addition that it be incompatible with incompetence. Prudence in this wider

sense of a generalized self-regard which is made both morally reasonable by the exclusion of immorality and technically reasonable by the
exclusion of incompetence, is often called 'practical wisdom'.

Private and extended private welfare

The object of a person's moral attitudes is to bring about what from the
point of view of his practical system is a situation of moral value or
a moral value. A moral value is either a private moral good, if the
situation involves only the person having the attitude, or a public
moral good, if it involves others besides him. Similarly the object of
a person's prudent attitude is to bring about what from the point of
view of his practical system is a situation of prudential value or a prudential value. A prudential value is (constitutive of or conducive to)
private welfare or public welfare according to whether only the person
having the attitude or others besides him are involved in the situation.

It helps to avoid unnecessary confusion if one distinguishes two
notions of public welfare, namely a notion of extended private welfare
and a notion of interpersonal or social welfare. A person's notion of
extended private welfare is characterized both by the prudential
principles which he accepts *qua* member of certain prudential classes
(e.g. *qua* normal human being, scholar and teacher, if he is either), and
by the prudential principles which in his view he would accept if he
were a member of certain prudential classes which he acknowledges
as such, but of which he is not a member (e.g. professional sportsman
or opera singer, if he is neither). A person's notion of interpersonal or
social welfare is not merely the acknowledgment of prudential classes
of which he does not regard himself as a member but also (1) the
acknowledgment of the fact that others differ from him in accepting
for themselves and others prudential classifications and corresponding
prudential principles which are different from his own as well as
(2) the adoption of principles of justice for resolving the conflicts
arising from this difference in prudential classifications and principles.

In order to understand the manner in which a person's conception of
his private welfare, as determined by his prudential principles, sets
limits to his selfishness, it is useful to consider how he 'maximizes' his
first level preferences or how he chooses his first level best. His first
level practical attitudes are, we recall, those of his practical attitudes
which are directed towards practicabilities not involving any of his
practical attitudes. Thus a person who has a preference for smoking

over non-smoking after dinner has a first level preference – quite apart from, and independently of, any second level strong or weak preference which he may have towards the presence of the first level preference over its absence or towards the absence of the first level preference over its presence. Again he has his first level preference for smoking over non-smoking after dinner, whether or not he does anything to realize the second level preference, i.e. to change or to preserve his first level preference.

To maximize one's first level preferences or to choose one's first level best (whenever one is confronted with a set of mutually exclusive and jointly exhaustive practicabilities which are the objects of these preferences) is (a) to establish at least a weak ordering among these preferences and (b) to realize a practicability which is maximal in that ordering. (See chapter 4 on the $\mathfrak{R}$–$\mathfrak{T}$–$\mathfrak{C}$, or weak, ordering of preferences and on maximal elements of such an ordering.) It should be noted that a person may be aware of his first level preferences, but make a mistake in trying to maximize them – e.g. by violating the requirement of transivitity. He may try to choose his first level best but fail to do so.

A person who in correctly maximizing his first level preferences is choosing his first level best, may nevertheless in doing so fail to choose his prudent best and thus choose contrary to his private welfare. This happens whenever in maximizing his first level preferences he violates one or more of his prudential principles or, more precisely, whenever the practical attitude which is the result of the maximization of his first level preferences is negatively dominated by one or more of his prudential principles. Prudence – which like morality consists in practical attitudes of at least second level directed towards practical attitudes of first level – must be distinguished from maximization of first level preference. Just as such a maximization may be moral or immoral, so it may be prudent or imprudent.

In characterizing a person's choice in accordance with his conception of private welfare, it has been tacitly assumed that his prudential principles are not opposed to, or incongruent with, each other. This consistency assumption for practical systems corresponds to the analogous consistency assumption for systems of beliefs. Making it does not imply any confidence that it will always be satisfied, but is necessary to any inquiry into the structure of practical systems and their subsystems. Another point which deserves to be explicitly mentioned is the possibility of competing prudential principles. Here, as in the case of competing moral principles, the competition of two principles for application to the same practical attitude must be, and can only be, resolved by *ad hoc* intuition.

What has been said about the maximization of private welfare in accordance with one's prudential principles, applies with obvious modifications to public welfare in the sense of extended private welfare. The modifications are all based on a person's considering not only the prudential principles associated with the prudential classes of which he is a member, but also prudential principles associated with prudential classes of which he is not a member. To put it differently, when concerned with his private welfare he deliberates *qua* member of the prudential classes to which he belongs and hence on his own behalf, whereas when concerned with extended private welfare he does not only deliberate on his own behalf but also, sympathetically, on behalf of others *qua* members of prudential classes, if any, to which he does not belong. The latter type of deliberation is characteristic of the adviser rather than the agent.

It raises the question of the extent to which a person may usefully advise another about prudent behaviour in a sphere of life – or prudential class – of which he has no experience. How, for example, should a scholar who is only moderately musical advise an opera singer about his or her prudent choices? One extreme answer would be that there really is only one prudential class, namely the comprehensive class of all human beings, and that the alleged other prudential classes are defined by prudential principles which are deducible from the prudential principles associated with the comprehensive class, in conjunction with a detailed description of the activities of an opera singer. Another answer is that while both the scholar and the opera singer share membership in the comprehensive class, and while the prudential classes of scholars and opera singers are associated with principles not deducible in the way mentioned, it is nevertheless possible for the scholar to imagine more or less adequately what it is to belong to the prudential class of opera singers and thus to give useful advice. Whether or not, as some philosophers assume, there is ultimately only one prudential class, namely the comprehensive prudential class of all human beings, is an empirical question which – it seems – has different answers for different people.

Social welfare

A person who considers himself a member of more than one prudential class and thus acknowledges more than one set of prudential principles may, in determining his private welfare, not only have to decide on his first level preferences but may also have to make an *ad hoc* decision between competing prudential principles. This difficulty arises because, as has been pointed out, prudential principles, like other evaluative principles, may be strict or competing; and because just as there are moralities which contain only strict, only competing or both strict and competing principles, so the totality of a person's prudential principles may also comprise one or both of these two types. (For an analysis of the competition of principles see p. 116.) A person who considers the public welfare of many persons in the light of his own prudential classification – of public in the sense of extended private welfare – may have a more difficult task. For it is one thing to decide for oneself which of two prudential principles, of which in a given instance only one is satisfiable, is to be satisfied. It is another thing to make such an *ad hoc* decision for two fellow human beings, and still another to make it for oneself and a second person. There is, for example, a difference between deciding a conflict between the demands of prudent scholarship and prudent teaching for oneself, on behalf of two colleagues each of whom fulfils one of these functions or on behalf of oneself in one of these functions and a colleague in the other. Lastly a person who considers the social welfare of many people in the light of *their* different prudential classifications – assuming such a difference – has the still more complex task of somehow doing justice to all of them. He has to find an adequate combination of, or compromise between, the ways in which each person orders his own preferences within the limits of his own prudential principles. More precisely, a person S has a conception of social welfare for a group of persons, $S_1, ..., S_n$, in which he may, or may not, be included if, and only if, (1) he has a method for combining the individual orderings of each person into a social ordering, i.e. a method for combining all the orderings R_i of each person S_i into a social ordering R and (2) if he has a conception of social justice which must not be violated by R.

This quasi-mathematical formulation of the problem of combining individual orderings into a social ordering, which is borrowed from Arrow (1951), must not mislead us into believing that the problem has a simple solution or that it has only one solution. People's

actual conceptions of social welfare are not expressed by a mathematical function of individual orderings but by their more or less
qualified approval of various actual or ideal political systems which
– more or less in harmony with their conception of justice – adjust the
individual orderings to each other.

An example is the ideal dictatorship of Plato's guardians to whose
prudential and moral attitudes it is considered moral to subject
everybody, or the dictatorship of a Hitler who is supposed to know
what is useful to his people and 'hence' moral. Another example is
a *laissez faire* economy combined with a political democracy. Yet
another is a 'welfare state' after the British model in which parlia-
mentary democracy is combined with a limited free market system,
limited nationalized industry and a system of social welfare. And
there are many other possible systems. While it is one of the main
aspects of any political society to function as a method for combining
individual orderings of practical preferences into a social ordering,
it is one of the main aspects of political philosophy to criticize this
method and to propose improvements or more radical changes. In all
these systems, including absolute dictatorship, the social adjustment
of individual preferences is beyond the power of any individual. But
the appraisal of its morality can only rest with individuals.

Practical preferences and social welfare in the social sciences

In so far as the natural sciences are concerned only with certain aspects
of the natural universe, they can often with great advantage neglect
others. Although, for example, classical mechanics describes an ideal
world, it can with much success be applied to the movements of
material bodies in the world of ordinary experience. The application
consists in treating the descriptions of the ideal world *as if* they were
descriptions of the world of ordinary experience. While this procedure
is within its proper limits justified both by its rationale and by its
success, it can lead to great confusion in regions of experience in which
the features which are neglected by the theory are no longer negligible.
This happens, for example, when classical mechanics is used to show
that man is not responsible for his actions because the movements of
his body are like those of every other material body fully determined
by the past states of the universe.

The situation in the social sciences is similar even though their
theories have been less successful. An idealizing feature, common to

many economic and other social theories, which is of interest in the present context is their explicit or implicit neglect of the stratified structure of practical systems. Treating people's systems of practical attitudes *as if* they were not stratified, that is to say *as if* all practical attitudes were of first level is harmless and may even be useful in certain regions of choice. Thus a large part of man's economic conduct, for example much of his buying and selling, expresses first level practical preferences or attitudes which are either undominated or indifferently dominated by higher level attitudes, especially prudential or moral ones. In these regions of conduct the first level best (the most preferred practicability, is the only best and stratification can be safely neglected. Its neglect may even pave the way for further useful idealizations – for example such as make it possible to measure preferences (see chapter 4).

Yet, since people's moral and prudential appraisals depend not only on their practical systems being stratified but on the specific manner of this stratification, this fact cannot safely be ignored in those spheres of conduct where first level practical attitudes can conflict with prudential and moral attitudes. Thus it is simply a gross error to regard the principle of the maximization of first level preferences as the supreme principle of rational conduct. It is, therefore, encouraging to notice that, unlike their classical predecessors, at least some contemporary economists tend to restrict the applicability of the principle to more narrowly economic contexts.

Neglecting the stratification of individual practical systems may clearly affect and vitiate accounts of combining individual preferences into social welfare. An example is Arrow's famous impossibility theorem. Arrow (1951) considers the mathematical problem of combining the weak preference orderings $R_1, ..., R_n$ of a number of persons $S_1, ..., S_n$ into a social ordering R subject to certain conditions which he regards as intuitively obvious, and proves that the combination is logically impossible. The proof is correct, but one of the conditions is either immoral or unclear. This condition is the so-called principle of Pareto to the effect that if the alternative x is preferred to alternative y by every single individual according to his ordering, then the social ordering also ranks x above y.

If the compared preferences of the individuals are first level preferences then the principle is immoral from the point of view of anybody who is aware of possible conflicts between his first level and his higher level prudential or moral attitudes. Assuming, for example, that all the members of a society have a first level preference for smoking over non-smoking which conflicts with their prudential and moral principles then they must regard the application of Pareto's principle as, in this instance, immoral. If on the other hand the compared preferences of the individuals include both first level and higher level preferences, then the principle leaves it quite unclear whether or not a first level preference shared by all individuals and conflicting with a moral preference also shared by all individuals should become the social preference. It is thus not surprising that people's actual conceptions of social welfare (as discussed in the preceding section) do not imply Pareto's principle – even though they may contain some more or less severely restricted versions of it.

CHAPTER 14

MORALITY, PRUDENCE AND LEGALITY

From principles of prudence and morality, which are personal standards of conduct in the sense that they are part of a person's system of practical attitudes, we must distinguish external standards of conduct, which require a person's obedience independently of his prudential or moral attitudes. Most important among external standards – at least in countries with developed legal systems – are legal standards. It is the main purpose of this chapter to examine the manner in which the demands of legality on the one hand and of morality and prudence on the other may reinforce or weaken each other. In doing so one is exposed to two opposite dangers. One is to neglect the social aspects of prudence and morality and, consequently, to underestimate their rôle in the creation and application of the law. The other is to ignore the simple fact that the law, by claiming obedience, invites assent or dissent in the light of morality and prudence and thereby enforces the formation or, at least, the clear formulation of the prudential and moral principles of those who are subject to the law.

After a brief attempt at characterizing legal systems we shall examine the notions of legal and moral institutions and show how the former can be relevant to morality and the latter to the law. Next the function of prudence and morality in the development of customary or 'unwritten' law and of 'written' law will be considered. This discussion will enable us, among other things, to distinguish between regulative principles, evaluative principles and some other components of a legal system. The chapter ends with an examination of the morality of obeying and of breaking the law of the land.

On the nature of legal systems

While in some so-called primitive societies there is no difference between legal and other public standards of conduct, the distinction

177

between them presents no practical difficulty in societies like our own. The history of Roman Law exemplifies both types of society, namely early Rome where *ius* and *fas* almost, or wholly, coincide, and imperial Rome, where the distinction between them is quite clear. That one is able to distinguish between legal and other standards of conduct does not imply that there is an agreed answer to the highly controversial theoretical question as to what makes a standard of conduct legal or legally valid. The brief answer which will be proposed here, though conciliatory in tone and intention, is unlikely to end the controversy.

The question whether or not a standard of conduct is legally valid can only be answered by reference to a particular system of law, just as the question whether or not an empirical proposition is scientifically valid can only be answered by reference to a particular system of scientific beliefs and methods of inquiry. The comparison between such scientific and legal systems throws some light on the structure and function of both, and is worth pursuing. However, in order to analyse the notion of legal validity, the comparison need not be taken too far. The main point for the present purpose is that both legal and scientific systems comprise – apart from logical and ontological assumptions – two kinds of components, namely (1) principles of authorization, which authorize the introduction of components into, or the elimination of components from, the system (where the components may, or may not, themselves be principles of authorization); and (2) substantive components (which are not principles of authorization).

The principles of authorization may be more or less precise and more or less explicit. In the case of scientific systems they include so-called rules of scientific method, such as principles connecting experimental evidence with theoretical assertions, as well as metaphysical assumptions, such as the principles of causality or complementarity, coupled with the demand that no scientific proposition be incompatible with them. In the case of legal systems, the principles of authorization include, on the one hand, principles about the manner in which legal validity can be conferred upon standards of conduct by authoritative declaration (as when a bill becomes law in parliament), by authoritative application (e.g. by judges to particular cases) or by authoritative publication (e.g. in a special series of published laws); on the other hand they include fundamental principles of legality, such as the principles *nullum crimen sine lege* or *nulla poena sine lege*, coupled with the demand that no legal standard of conduct be incompatible with them.

The substantive components of a scientific system include general empirical propositions, such as the general propositions of applied mechanics or the theory of evolution, and singular propositions about natural constants. The distinction between metaphysical assumptions and substantive components is not sharp. The substantive components of a legal system include general legal standards, such as the provisions of the law of contract or the criminal law, and singular propositions such as concrete judicial decisions about the rights and duties of a certain person. Again, the distinction between the fundamental principles of legality and general legal standards may not be sharp.

The principles of authorization determine the extent to which a legal or scientific system may change. It is generally agreed that certain changes must be excluded as depriving a system of its legal or scientific character. Thus no jurist would regard as legal a system in which the only principle of authorization would be the whim of one person; and no scientist would regard as scientific a system in which authorization by an oracle would be a condition of the scientific validity of every component of the system. However, jurists disagree as to whether, for example, the so-called laws of Nazi Germany constituted a legal system and scientists disagree as to whether psychoanalysis is part of any scientific system; and these examples are not the only indication of disagreement about the essential characteristics of legal or scientific systems.

The notions of legal and scientific validity, as characterized by reference to particular legal or scientific systems, are relative notions. More precisely, a component of such a system is *internally valid* if, and only if, its being part of the system is authorized by the system's authorizing principles. This explanation raises the question whether the ultimate authorizing principles from which all components of the system derive their validity but which are themselves not authorized by principles of the system, should be called 'internally valid'. To call them 'internally valid' or 'internally invalid' is to extend the meaning of these terms. The position of the ultimate authorizing principles of a legal or scientific system is the same as that of the axioms of a system of logic or any other axiomatic theory. Following the analogous custom of calling not only the derived theorems, but also the underivable axioms of such a theory 'valid', the ultimate authorizing principles of legal or scientific systems will also be called 'internally valid'.

Even if there were no plurality of conflicting legal or scientific systems, one would have to distinguish the merely internal validity

179

of a system from its acceptance or external validity. The plurality of conflicting systems and the possibility of abandoning one such system for another without internal authorization, make the distinction between internal and external validity quite obvious. (It is worth noting that a similar distinction is necessary in ontology and even in logic, where the recognition of the internal logical validity of a proposition with respect to one logic (e.g. L) is compatible with the acceptance of another logic (e.g. I) with respect to which the proposition is not internally valid.)

The acceptance or external validity of a legal or scientific system by a person or group of persons is an empirical fact. It is, moreover, a social fact since the effective acceptance of either type of system presupposes a high degree of cooperation between many people, organized in various kinds of legal or scientific institutions. The need for such organization does not, however, exclude the possibility that two or more legal or scientific systems are accepted within a society. Thus during some periods in the middle ages canon and secular law were both accepted in Europe without either being regarded as superior to the other. The possible coexistence of different scientific systems besides each other seems to be even more obvious. The possibility of different legal systems in one society is denied by Austin and his followers who regard law as the totality of commands issuing from a sovereign whose sovereignty is by definition indivisible. The possibility of different scientific systems is disliked by some totalitarian governments, so much so that heretical scientists who reject certain authorizing principles are persecuted.

This is not the place to discuss the complex problem of why people accept the legal or the scientific system which they do accept or, more precisely, why they prefer accepting to rejecting it. It seems quite wrong to assert that the sole or main reason for accepting a legal system is the serious threat of its being enforced by punishing those who break it. It seems similarly wrong to exclude fear of punishment or unpleasantness from the reasons for accepting rather than rejecting a scientific system by one's conduct. Yet it must be admitted that in spite of some similarities in the reasons for accepting a legal or a scientific system, there are also some more or less obvious dissimilarities.

The last point to be made in characterizing legal systems is that even those which contain one or more clearly formulated codes of conduct (in the strict sense of chapter 4) contain in addition a variety of other components, in particular principles of evaluation, interpretation and application which are not derivable from any of the codes of conduct. Here again legal and scientific systems show an interesting analogy, namely the analogy between codes of conduct in legal and theories in scientific systems. For any scientific system containing theories (in particular mathematized theories) also contains principles of evaluation, interpretation, and application which are not deducible from the theories. In examining the relation between legality on the one hand and prudence and morality on the other, it is important to consider not only legal codes of conduct but also the principles for their interpretation and evaluation.

What makes one acknowledge a standard of conduct as a legal standard is not its having a certain place in one's personal practical system, but its being an internally valid component of an externally valid legal system. In any society in which a particular legal system is externally valid the question of how far one's personal practical system and the legal system coincide may not merely be a question of theoretical interest but become a moral question of life and death.

On the relevance of legal and public moral institutions to each other

A person's prudential and moral standards are aspects of his system of practical attitudes and are as such private to him. The legal standards of conduct which he acknowledges as externally valid are part of his social environment and as such are public facts. This opposition between private morality and prudence on the one hand and public legality on the other must not blind one to the existence of other public standards of conduct, in particular public morality which consists in a fairly substantial interpersonal agreement between the private moralities of the members of one's society; as well as the public conception of prudence which consists in a similar agreement between their private prudential standards. (The use of the deliberately vague term 'substantial agreement' is meant to indicate that neither the sets of standards about which there is agreement, nor the sets of people who agree about any of these sets of standards are precisely fixed.) Since public institutions are stable or recurrent social relationships, governed by public standards, one may – according to the nature of these standards – distinguish between legal, moral and prudential public institutions.

The standards of public morality and public prudence – like the standards of private morality and prudence – embrace evaluative practical principles and regulative principles and may give rise to code-dependent and code-independent obligations. In most developed legal systems regulative principles and code-dependent obligations outweigh the practical evaluative principles and code-independent obligations. Private morality and prudence may, or may not, be satisfied by the same actions which satisfy public morality or the law. Practical decisions are easiest when one's first level preferences, one's private morality, public morality and the law pull in the same direction. They are most difficult when one's private morality pulls in one direction while one's first level preferences, public morality and the law pull together in the opposite direction. Between these extremes there is an unlimited number of possibilities of these forces differing in direction and weight.

Where public morality and the law diverge, one may be in advance of the other. It seems, for example, that in England public morality was in advance of the law permitting homosexual acts between consenting adults, while the law abolishing the death penalty seems to be in advance of public morality. It may be the case that public morality contains principles which divide its concerns from those of the law and that the law contains similar principles. Thus in England public morality seems at present to encourage a contraction of legal concern with sexual mores and an expansion of legal concern with financial mores. On the other hand the law, by permitting hitherto proscribed forms of gambling, encourages public morality – especially through its more vocal representatives – to take a closer interest in them.

The relevance of public morality and the law to each other is not exhausted by a possible parallelism or divergence of standards. Another important interconnection between the two systems is the possibility of their acknowledging each other's institutions without fully accepting the standards by which they are governed. An example of a legal acknowledgment of an institution of public morality is the Roman legal doctrine of *obligatio naturalis* according to which certain specified actions, which gave rise to moral obligations, did not give rise to enforceable legal obligations but were recognized to the extent that if the morally obliged person who had fulfilled his obligation wanted to undo its fulfilment, he could not legally do so. Thus, according to Roman civil law, if a person had paid a debt based on an informal contract (*nudum pactum*) which was not legally enforceable, recovery of the payment was nevertheless also not legally enforceable (see Sohm 1884: § 84).

Just as the law may acknowledge the social fact of the predominance of certain moral standards or a public morality, so it may also acknowledge the social fact of the predominance of certain prudential standards in the society governed by the law. Examples, drawn again from Roman law, are so-called *bona fide* contracts which, unlike contracts *stricti juris*, impose duties which are not explicitly mentioned in the contract, especially the duty of care or *diligentia* (Sohm 1884: § 76). Although this duty admits of gradation, what is normally required is *omnis diligentia*, i.e. that the contracting parties behave 'as any careful man would behave in the circumstances'. It is clear that the law not only acknowledges, and presupposes, moral and prudential institutions, but also their being, as so much else in man's social and physical environment, subject to change.

If it is obvious that moral and prudential institutions are part of the environment in which the law is being applied, then it is no less obvious that legal institutions in turn are part of the world in which one's morality and prudence are exercised. Examples are the legal institutions of public law, such as citizenship; of family law, such as marriage; of private law, such as property. Their relevance to morality and prudence may be twofold. On the one hand they may be facts which, though acknowledged by morality or prudence, have no *general* bearing on their content. Thus a person may morally bind himself to perform a certain action one day after his marriage, in the same way in which he may morally bind himself to perform a certain action one day after reaching his thirtieth birthday – where the legal fact as well as the biological fact have no other function than to fix the time, if any, at which his obligation becomes effective. On the other hand a legal institution may have a special bearing on morality or prudence. Being married, for example, may be an essential condition of a purely moral obligation to realize certain practical interests of one's wife, which one would not be morally bound to realize if one were not married at all or married to another woman.

On the modification of the law by morality and prudence

Apart from their obvious interaction by reinforcing or weakening each other through parallel or divergent standards of conduct and by acknowledging each other's institutions, a society's legal system and its public morality interact also in less obvious ways, especially by modifying each other. The law modifies private and thus indirectly public morality by a complex process transforming external or heteronomous standards of conduct into internal or autonomous ones. The description and explanation of this process of internalization is a psychological or sociological task and it seems that our understanding of it is not greatly enhanced by a logico-philosophical analysis of the structure of legal and moral systems. Morality on the other hand supplements and modifies the law, at least partly, because of the characteristic structure of legal systems. It is this structure which allows the infiltration of moral standards into the law either through explicitly authorized channels or through more or less hidden interstices from which no legal system is entirely free.

One of the many examples of an explicitly authorized channel for the reception of moral standards into the law is the Roman *ius gentium*, which unlike the civil law, regulated the conduct of aliens in their relations to each other and to Roman citizens. Since the *ius gentium* was conceived by Gaius and other jurists to contain standards of conduct common to all men, i.e. – in accordance with their philosophy – moral standards, it was obvious that those who applied this part of the law were expected to supplement it by their moral standards, whenever supplementation was necessary. More generally, a legal system may, and often does, show awareness of its incompleteness and demand explicitly that in cases which are not covered by a clear legal standard those whose function it is to apply 'the law' should do so by following their common and moral sense.

The manner in which the moral and prudential convictions of judges and other practitioners of the law infiltrate it through its interstices, depends largely on the determinacy of its formulation. Clearly, if a region of conduct is governed by a wholly unwritten, customary law, which like the Roman *ius non scriptum* is characterized *only* as inveterate custom (*consuetudo longa*) and a general conviction of its necessity (*opinio necessitatis*), the content of this law will be largely moulded by the morality of those who apply it. Usually the customary law is shot through with regulative and evaluative standards which are generally acknowledged as legal and are more or less reliably and more or less authoritatively recorded as limiting the deliberation of the judges and administrators. If, as in Anglo-American common law, all judicial decisions are authoritatively recorded together with their justification by general principles, it may become controversial, whether such a law is still customary. While this is a matter for stipulation, it seems that common law on the whole allows more scope to a judge's moral convictions than a legal code.

184

It must be emphasized that not every legal code or set of regulations such as, say, the *Code Napoléon* or the *Preussisches Landrecht* is a code of conduct in the strict sense (of chapter 4), i.e. deontically consistent and adequate to the world. Even if a code of conduct when created is adequate to the world, it is likely to lose this adequacy in some respects, in which case its applicability may depend on a judge's reinterpretation in the light of his moral and prudential convictions. Again, if a legal system comprises more than one code of conduct, if two such codes compete for application, if no legal regulation determines the priority of one code over the other, if a judge determines this priority in the light of his morality or prudence, if this decision is justified by a general standard of conduct, and if this decision together with its justification is reliably and authoritatively recorded, then the judge's moral standard may give rise to a legal one.

Another feature of legal systems which explains their openness to infiltration by the morality and prudence of judges and administrators of the law, is the distinction between code-dependent and code-independent legal obligations. The distinction is quite similar to the distinction between code-dependent and code-independent moral obligations (see chapter 12). We remember that a so-called deontic morality comprises only code-dependent moral obligations, a so-called axiological morality only code-independent moral obligations. If a person's morality is deontic, that is to say if he has adopted a supreme code $\mathfrak{M}$ as comprising all his moral standards, then his having a code-*dependent* obligation to bring about f can be schematically represented by the conjunction of $S + [U + \mathfrak{M}]$ and $D(\mathfrak{M}) \vdash f$ (where the second level practical attitude is undominated). If a person's morality is axiological, then his code-*independent* obligation to bring about f consists in his not only having a moral pro-attitude towards f, but also towards requiring f, schematically $S + [U + f]$ and $S + [U + \text{Req} f]$ (where both second order attitudes are undominated). Lastly, the possibility of a partly deontic and a partly axiological morality had to be admitted, as well as the qualified adoption of a moral code, i.e. its adoption in 'normal circumstances'.

What has been said about deontic, axiological and mixed moral systems applies *mutatis mutandis* also to legal systems. The place of S is taken by the principles of authorization of the legal system, sometimes personified as the legislator, say L; the place of U is taken by the judges and other officials applying the law, say J; and the schematic representation of code-dependent and code-independent legal obligations take the following form: (1) (bringing about the situation described by) f is a code-dependent legal obligation if, and only if, $L + [J + \mathfrak{M}]$ and $D(\mathfrak{M}) \vdash f$ (if, and only if, the legislator authorizes a practical pro-attitude of the judges J towards the continued adoption of $\mathfrak{M}$ and if $D(\mathfrak{M})$, i.e. the descriptive counterpart of $\mathfrak{M}$, logically implies f). (2) f is a code-independent legal obligation if, and only if, $L + [J + f]$ and $L + [J + \text{Req} f]$ (if, and only if, the legislator authorizes a practical pro-attitude by J not only towards f but also towards requiring f). Most legal systems are mixed in the sense of containing both code-dependent and code-independent obligations and it seems perfectly possible for the law to authorize the merely qualified adoption of a certain code in normal circumstances.

The distinction between code-dependent and code-independent legal obligations might, even without being further elaborated, help theoretical lawyers and philosophers of law to settle their dispute as to whether all legal obligations are based on 'rules' or whether some of them are based on 'principles' which are not rules (see e.g. Dworkin 1970). One cannot be sure about this since the notions of rule and principle employed in the controversy are not clear. If by 'rules' one means regulations of form $a \xrightarrow{i} b!$ organized in deontically consistent and adequate codes, and by 'principles' evaluative principles of form $S * [X * f]$ and, perhaps, other propositions which are not regulations, then one must in any case reject as too narrow any view of the law as comprising only regulations and code-dependent obligations.

In practice the distinction between a set of code-independent and a set of code-dependent obligations is not always sharp. A legally controlled sphere of conduct may first of all be controlled only by very general evaluative principles which may suggest the codification of clear-cut regulations, whose actual acceptance may, for lack of any reliable and authoritative publication, remain in doubt. Yet here as elsewhere the existence of borderline cases does not imply the absence of clear positive or negative ones. What makes these differences important to the problem of the relation between the law on the one hand and morality and prudence on the other, is that the further removed a set of legal standards is from being a code of conduct in the strict sense, the greater the need for judges and other administrators to depend on their own sense of what is just and prudent.

A detailed description of a legal system's written and unwritten parts (of its evaluative principles, which give rise to code-independent

186

obligations, and of its codified regulative principles, which give rise to code-dependent obligations, as well as of various practical difficulties of distinguishing between different types of standard) *ipso facto* reveals the interstices through which public morality and prudence via the private morality and prudence of the law's practitioners, may supplement and modify the law. It is not, however, an indication of all of them. The reason why there are further possibilities for such infiltration is that, apart from imprecisely formulated standards of conduct, the law also contains other porous components.

Among them are various presumptions and fictions employed in determining the legally relevant facts. Instead of elaborating this obvious point at length, it seems preferable to exemplify it briefly. In the presumption of Roman law to the effect that, unless clear evidence to the contrary is produced, the wedding ceremony indicates the father of a child (*pater est quem nuptiae demonstrant*) a great deal depends on what is regarded as a wedding. The laxer the interpretation of what constitutes a wedding, the more men will be affected by the presumption – a fact which together with others might well change the conduct of paternity disputes and the character of paternal responsibility according to the law. Similarly, the legal fiction to the effect that certain types of association and institution are in certain respects, e.g. as regards commercial contracts, to be treated as persons depends on the interpretation of what constitutes the relevant type of association or institution. And this interpretation may modify the content of the law governing the commercial conduct of those subject to it.

On the morality of obeying the law

Legal standards of conduct are a species of external standards. The subject which authorizes an external standard is, unlike the subject which authorizes a moral standard, not necessarily among its addressees. While it may happen that the external authority is, or is personified by, one of the addressees, the connection is not necessary. Thus while it may be that a judge, a gangleader or a fashion expert authorizes a standard to which he is subject, their function as addressees is clearly separable from their authorizing function. The positive characterization and identification of the external authority varies with the type of external standard and within each type. It may be as clearly determined as the person of the Pope or as obscurely determined as the best writers now alive. Again, the manner in which

187

an external standard is authorized is, unlike the manner by which moral standards are authorized, not the awareness of an undominated practical pro-attitude towards the standard (which in the case of a moral standard is itself a practical attitude). In other respects the authorization may take many different forms such as the proper promulgation of a papal bull or the use of split infinitives by a fair number of the best writers now alive.

The satisfaction or non-satisfaction of an external standard may itself be the object of selfish, prudent or moral attitudes. It is clear that the satisfaction of an external standard may at the same time be the satisfaction of a moral standard and that otherwise its morality depends both on the content and context in which the external standard is being satisfied. A general analysis of the relation between regulations and evaluations (in chapter 11) implies, for example, that it may be moral to satisfy a regulation which is part of a certain code of conduct, even though it would be immoral to satisfy it if it were part of a different code of conduct. In the case of legal standards the morality or immorality of fulfilling one's legal obligations depends in particular on the morality or immorality of the social order, which is protected by the external validity of the legal system.

In almost every society two extreme positions are bound to be mistaken, namely an extreme moralism which regards any externally valid legal system as morally irrelevant, and an extreme legalism which regards only an externally valid legal system as fit to regulate the conduct of the members of the society. The extreme moralist is prepared to acknowledge all kinds of facts except those which are implied by the external validity of the legal system. Yet even the most irreconcilable enemy of the Nazi social order might acknowledge the legal institution of marriage and legal inheritance in order to fulfil what in the light of his moral and prudential principles is a duty to his children. On the other hand, it is hardly conceivable that an extreme legalist would not draw the line at some legally obligatory horror and thereby discover that he has overriding moral obligations.

Between the two untenable extremes lies the position according to which it may be moral and even morally obligatory in some cases to obey and in others to disobey the law. The demarcation of the two kinds of case depends on the one hand on the nature of the legal system and the social order to which a person is subject, and on the other on the person's moral and prudential convictions. Without such demarcation and indeed without a casuistic attention to detail one must be content with the following remarks which, because of their generality, are theoretically almost empty and practically almost useless.

On the reasonable empirical assumption that breaking a law, especially when this is done to express moral disapproval of the social order which it protects, is likely to weaken the external authority of the legal system to which it belongs, we can distinguish between a number of possibilities in which the breaking law may be considered moral. One of them, which has been exemplified during the Vietnam war, is to consider the breaking of a certain law – e.g. a law of con- scription – moral even if it is normally considered immoral to work towards the abolition of the legal system to which it belongs. Another possibility, which has been exemplified during the last days of British rule in India, is to consider as moral the breaking of some laws, which by themselves are considered moral or morally indifferent, because the legal system to which they belong is considered immoral. It is, of course, generally agreed that anarchy is a great evil. But just as death may be preferable to certain kinds of life, so total anarchy may be preferable to certain kinds of order. However, to the question as to the criteria for deciding that this point has been reached no helpful answer can be given here.

CHAPTER 15

ON PRAGMATIC AND PRACTICAL
IDEALIZATIONS

The weakness which prevents a person from living by his morality may be intellectual or moral. Intellectual weakness prevents him from clearly recognizing his moral principles or the circumstances in which they apply. Moral weakness prevents him from acting in accordance with clearly recognized moral principles in circumstances to which they are clearly applicable. There are no unfailing recipes for over-coming either weakness. But that there are some methods for doing so is an assumption made by most of those who are concerned with the education of children or adults. Among those methods at least two fall within the scope of this essay. One, which is meant to overcome the intellectual weakness and may be called 'pragmatic idealization', consists in the imaginative replacement of complex features of one's actual world or morality by ideal features which are more easily intelligible and can for the purpose in hand be identified with the actual ones. The other, which is meant to overcome the moral weak-ness and may be called 'practical idealization', consists in the imagina-tive replacement of one's actual by an ideal way of life which can to some extent be approximated by one's conduct and which in so far as it is so approximated, makes for greater harmony between one's morality and one's conduct.

The present chapter examines both pragmatic and practical idealiza-tion. After contrasting pragmatic idealization in scientific and moral contexts two kinds of pragmatic idealization in moral contexts will be considered, namely idealizations of the social world in which moral principles are applied and idealizations of these principles themselves. Next the nature of practical idealizations and ideals will be explained and briefly exemplified. The chapter ends by distinguishing the unrealizable, or at most approximately realizable, ideals, which are the result of pragmatic and practical idealization, from ideals which are in principle fully realizable.

On pragmatic idealizations in scientific and moral contexts

When, at the beginning of this essay, a natural sequence of its topics had to be determined, the fairly obvious point was made that the morality or immorality of an action presupposes its practical possibility, which presupposes its empirical possibility, which in turn presupposes its logical possibility. In this connection it was also pointed out that, as one proceeds from logical via empirical to moral questions, it is important to distinguish all along the line between commonsense and specialist thinking, in particular specialist thinking employing idealizations. The most effective mode of specialist thinking about empirical matters is scientific thinking whose most highly organized pragmatic idealizations are scientific theories. Although the analysis of scientific theories belongs to the philosophy of science, some understanding of their structure and function is presupposed by the present inquiry (see p. 5).

Their structure was briefly characterized as resulting from general modifications imposed on commonsense experience by their logico-mathematical framework and from special modifications due to deductive abstraction and conceptual innovation. Their main function was characterized as consisting of the identification of theoretical and commonsense statements in appropriate contexts and for appropriate purposes, of which predicting the course of nature as the most obvious one. The reason for taking note of the structure and function of scientific theories in an inquiry into systems of practical attitudes and morality is twofold. For one thing, science with its theories and some of its less highly organized pragmatic idealizations is a powerful instrument in determining what is practicable and, hence, subject to moral evaluations and regulations. For another, the pragmatic idealizations of science are sufficiently similar to those of specifically moral thinking to make a comparison rewarding.

The main point of similarity is that in some scientific as well as in some moral contexts the actual world, or a part of it, is replaced by an idealized simplification in such a manner that treating the actual world *as if* it were the idealized world is justifiable in the context and for the purpose in which they are so identified. The main difference between pragmatic idealizations of the actual world in scientific contexts on the one hand, and moral contexts on the other, concerns the manner of their justification and the aspects of experience selected for idealization. That idealization in scientific contexts is morally justified is usually taken for granted. Trying to predict what is going to happen or would happen under certain circumstances is, like trying to find out the truth in general, in itself not immoral and normally not attended by immoral actions. Until the recent past exceptions were almost wholly restricted to certain physiological or medical experiments on humans or animals, whereas nowadays even physical experiments, such as those which increase dangerous radiation, may be immoral. Yet be this as it may, the moral justification of applying scientific theories for prediction is subsidiary to its theoretical justification. That is to say, if the application of a theory, i.e. the identification of its idealized with the actual world, is not theoretically justified, then the question of its moral justification does not arise.

Where moral evaluation presupposes prediction of the course of nature, scientific idealization may *ipso facto* lighten the evaluative task. But moral evaluation also faces complexities of its own which call for different types of idealizing simplification. Thus doing our moral duty by our neighbours, or going beyond it by supererogatory actions may presuppose that among other things, we know their practical attitudes – in particular whether or not they conflict with our own and whether or not they are from the point of view of our own morality immoral. Such knowledge is often unattainable, because the practical systems of different people, though similar in structure, often differ greatly in content. In order to overcome this obstacle, it is sometimes necessary and theoretically and morally justifiable to ascribe to the members of a society or mankind an idealized practical system, and to determine the morality of one's actions towards them *as if* the ascription were true. As in the physical sciences, such idealizations may prove more or less adequate to our purpose.

Pragmatic idealizations of the social world in moral contexts

A systematic inquiry into pragmatic idealizations of the social world in contexts of moral decision for the purposes of moral evaluation might model itself on a similar inquiry into scientific idealizations of the physical world (see Körner 1966). Thus, one of its tasks would be the exhibition of commonsense practical, especially moral, thinking. This task has to some extent been undertaken in the second part of the present essay. A second task would be to exhibit the manner in which commonsense systems of practical attitudes are subject to general modifications by a stricter logico-mathematical framework than that which is their natural habitat, and to special modifications which – independently of the general ones – lead to a variety of different idealizations. In performing this task one would be able to draw extensively on our earlier examination (in part I) of the logical structure of factual, constructive, preferential and deontic thinking. The third task would be to exhibit the relation between commonsense and idealized practical systems and to justify their identification in certain specific contexts of moral decision for the purpose of certain specific moral evaluations. Although a systematic execution of the three tasks cannot be undertaken here, it may be useful to make some very brief remarks on it.

To begin with one would have to describe some commonsense practical systems, for example some of the systems dominant in Western culture. One might then select one of them as one's main example, say 'bourgeois morality', as described, among others, by M. Ossowska (1971). This example would have the additional advantage of having various versions, namely axiological, deontological and mixed ones – a fact for which there is good evidence in the writings of Western moral thinkers. In characterizing the logical structure of commonsense practical systems one would then have to describe in some detail the 'inexactness' of its concepts, especially of the concepts of practical preference, practical indifference, (code-dependent and code-independent) obligation and concepts defined in terms of these. Connected with their inexactness, i.e. their admitting of positive, negative and neutral instances, is in particular the non-transitivity of practical indifference. Thus, just as in the case of, say, perceptual indistinguishability in weight, as tested by a pair of scales, it is often possible to find three objects a, b, c such that while a is indistinguishable from b and b is indistinguishable from c, a and c are distinguishable, so – as has been pointed out earlier (chapter 4) – in the case of practical indifference it is possible that in the case of three options a, b, c a person may be indifferent between a and b and between b and c but not between a and c.

The general modifications of a practical system by one of the current logical systems L or I or a combination of both (see chapter 1 for a description of these logics) leads to a replacement of inexact concepts by exact ones and of non-transitive commonsense by transitive idealized indifference. In so far as one regards any of the current theories of preferential and deontic reasoning as a general logic, the general modifications also involve a replacement of the more or less indeterminate commonsense principles governing preferential and deontic reasoning by the exact principles of these theories. (See chapters 2 and 4.) It goes without saying that *if* the commonsense practical system is inconsistent or troubled by antinomies, its idealization is – or is at least intended to be – free from these shortcomings.

As to the special modifications of commonsense practical systems by deductive abstraction, which removes some of the deductive connections of a concept, and conceptual innovation, which introduces new concepts into practical systems, two examples will have to suffice. The first exemplifies deductive abstraction. We have seen that practical attitudes are stratified into levels, that is to say that some practical attitudes are dominated and that 'being a dominated attitude of a person S' entails 'being positively, negatively or indifferently dominated by an attitude (of next higher level) of S'. To abstract from the stratification of practical attitudes and to consider them all as being of first level, is to engender great philosophical confusion – as has been shown in discussing Arrow's acceptance of Pareto's principle as intuitively obvious (p. 175). Yet the same deductive abstraction, i.e. considering only first level preferences, might under certain circumstances be a useful idealization in attempts at devising a morally justified entertainment tax.

The second example is of theoretical innovation. It is an empirical mistake to assume that everybody is accepting a set of principles for measuring his first level preferences on an interval scale (as explained in chapter 4). Yet, imputing the acceptance of these principles to everybody may in some contexts be a justifiable conceptual innovation – for example in attempts at justly reorganizing a pension scheme.

Having described commonsense practical systems as well as their idealizations by general and special modifications, one would have to determine the circumstances in which the application of a specific pragmatic idealization to the real world of practical systems, that is to say the identification of idealized and actual systems, is morally justifiable. The justification would consist in showing that while in the given circumstances a better mind than ours would, in trying to apply moral principles to the actual social world, have no need to pretend that this world is simpler than it is, we have the moral duty to do so because we are less likely to make moral mistakes if we make the relevant idealization than if we do not. Thus some people might argue that one is morally obliged to use welfare economics or decision theory in certain complex political matters, since not using them is more likely to result in the misapplication of one's moral convictions than using them. The cogency of the argument depends, of course, not only on the circumstances in which these theories are proposed for application, but also on their reliability. And there is much less agreement about their scope and reliability than there is about the scope and reliability of the theories of physics and the natural sciences in general.

On the pragmatic idealization of moral principles

Just as morality may allow or demand the identification of the actual with a simplified world in order to avoid moral mistakes based on intellectual weakness, so it may, for the same reason, allow or demand the identification of one's moral principles with simpler ones. The distinction between simplifying the world to which moral principles are being applied and simplifying the principles themselves is by no means clear cut. Thus in trying to devise a just distribution of wealth it makes no difference whether we identify the social world of complex human beings with a world consisting of economic men, or whether we identify moral attitudes dominating practical attitudes directed to options of all sorts with moral attitudes dominating practical attitudes directed to essentially economic options only. If our moral principle is schematically represented by $S * [U * X]$, where S is a human being, U the class of human beings and X the characteristic of a practicability which is not purely economic, then $S_e * [U_e * X]$ would represent a simplification of the world into one of economic men U_e only; and $S * [U * X_e]$ would represent a simplification of a moral principle into one in which a possibly non-economic or not purely economic practicability is simplified into a purely economic one characterized by X_e.

But there are pragmatic idealizations which are more naturally conceived as idealizations of moral principles than of the world. We are, for example, frequently faced with the moral problem of deciding between standards of action which are simple but inaccurate and standards of action which though complex are accurate. This problem arises not only when the standards in question are moral standards, but also, for example, in designing a technical handbook for motorists or ambulance men, since it may be morally preferable to act in accordance with simple inaccurate rules if by so doing less harm is caused to those in whose interest the handbook was designed than by acting in accordance with accurate but complex rules.

195

There is a great variety of circumstances in which replacing a moral standard by a simplified standard is morally justified. Obvious examples are situations in which the misapplication of the complex moral standard may lead to irreparable harm while the application or misapplication of the simplified standard may only lead to reparable harm. Another example would be the situation of a person whose moral convictions are so complex that his constant need for moral deliberation about his options would seriously impair his capacity for acting morally. A special case of this difficulty would be the situation of a person whose morality required him to spend his life helping others in the proper way, but which defined 'the proper way' in too complex a manner to allow him to help anybody in the ordinary sense of the word.

A different kind of example in which the replacement of a complex moral standard by a simplified standard of conduct is morally justifiable is the situation in which social co-operation is one's moral duty, but can be achieved only when the complex standard is simplified. This is so when a plurality of divergent personal standards prevents any effective co-operation between a group of people whereas their simplification to a common inter-personal standard guarantees *some* success in their attempt at co-operating on the lines determined by their personal standards. Another special case of this kind is a person's replacement of a complex moral standard which requires him to give his own answers to various subordinate factual or moral questions by a simplified standard in which somebody else's, e.g. an appointed arbitrator's, answers to these questions are accepted by him.

That the replacement of a complex moral standard, say s, by a simpler standard of conduct, say s', is morally justifiable, does not imply that s' itself is – or becomes as a result of the replacement – a moral standard. To see this one has to consider the way in which the pragmatic idealization of s into s' can be, and usually is, justified. The justification concerns on the one hand the adoption of s' as a standard in circumstances which are generally characterized by the intellectual weakness of the person adopting s' in place of s, and on the other hand the actions which this person performs in accordance with s' rather than with s. The moral justification of adopting s' in circumstances of intellectual weakness is, as the examples indicate, based on the conviction that by trying to conform to s' instead of s, fewer violations of s are likely than by trying to conform to s and that it is morally preferable to bring about a world in which the likelihood of

196

such violations is smaller to bringing about a world in which it is greater. It must be emphasized that this kind of justification, which reminds one of the way in which subjective probability theorists maximize utility (see chapter 3), is not always available.

As regards the actions performed in accordance with s' rather than with s, we must distinguish between those which violate s and those which do not violate s. The latter do not stand in need of justification. If a person in conforming to s' violates s then – assuming that the pragmatic idealization of s into s' is justified – his violation of s is considered 'excusable'. This means that one has a moral pro-attitude towards not blaming the person for the violation of s, perhaps even towards consoling him, trying to persuade him not to blame himself, etc.

If a legal system is intended to embody a certain morality, if this morality or the world or both are too complex for a single decree to pronounce the morality to be the law of the land, then the legislator will have to resort to pragmatic idealizations of the world or of the principles of this morality. An example of a legal system of his kind is canon law which is meant to legalize Christian morality, i.e. turn the moral teachings of the Jewish prophets and of Jesus, as far as is humanly possible, into a legal system with its own legal code of conduct, its own principles of authorization and its other components. It may seem paradoxical for a Christian to regard canon law as in any way 'simpler' than the moral demand that he should in all circumstances do his duty as a Christian. Yet one can think of many circumstances in which, say, a devout catholic in Elizabethan England or Stalinist Russia would find it intellectually much simpler to determine his conduct by relying on the regulations of the *codex iuris canonici* than on his own understanding of his Christian duties – especially if he has good reason to assume that fear might weaken his intellectual powers. Such a person might, for example, be greatly helped by the canon law doctrine acknowledging fear as a legitimate cause of a moral impossibility to obey the law.

In the attempt to implement Christian morality, canon law employs not only the pragmatic idealization of more complex moral into less complex legal standards, but also of a more complex into a less complex world. A means of achieving the latter is the use of legal fictions, such as the so-called *sanatio in radice* of an invalid marriage, i.e. a retrospective replacement, under certain conditions, of an invalid consent to a marriage by a valid consent to it.

Practical idealizations and morally ideal ways of life

In order to understand the nature of practical idealization and the manner in which it may strengthen the harmony between a person's moral convictions and his conduct, it seems best to start with some fairly obvious observations on the relation between a person's morality and his manner of life. Consider, for example, a person who tries to live by the morality of the Decalogue and who is faced with a decision to change his way of life – by changing his occupation, by changing his residence or in some other way. In making the decision he may be, and often is, interested in finding out whether the new way of life will make it easier or more difficult for him to live by his moral code or whether it will make no difference to his conduct. He will, for example, assume that if he chooses the occupation of a farmer he will have fewer opportunities and temptations to violate his moral principles than if he chooses the occupation of a waiter in a nightclub. He will similarly assume that certain ways of life will not only lead to fewer violations of his moral principles but also to more deeds of moral supererogation and thus be morally preferable. His judgments about the effect of his way of life on the morality or otherwise of his conduct are empirical conjectures, which may be false. But it will do no harm if we assume that his introspective psychology and knowledge of the world are on the whole sound.

What has been said so far is compatible with most views of the nature of morality. If one accepts the analysis of practical systems as stratified and the consequent possibility of discordance between moral and lower level practical attitudes, another possible effect of a person's way of life on its moral adequacy must be considered. To see this point clearly we might enlarge our example by supposing that the person mentioned in it has a first level pro-attitude towards committing adultery and that in accordance with the Decalogue this first level pro-attitude is negatively dominated by a moral attitude, i.e. that he has an undominated anti-attitude towards his first level pro-attitude towards adultery. It is again clear that some changes of his way of life might lead to a more or less speedy realization of his moral attitude, i.e. to the replacement of his first level pro-attitude towards adultery by an anti-attitude; that other changes of his way of life, such as leaving his occupation as a farmer in the land of Uz to become a waiter in one of the nightclubs of Sodom, might lead to a replacement of his anti-attitude towards his practical pro-attitude towards adultery by

198

a pro-attitude or an attitude of indifference; and that still other changes might leave the original discordance between his first level pro-attitude and his moral anti-attitude unchanged.

In choosing one way of life over another a person may thus improve the moral content of his life, that is to say make it from the point of view of his morality more perfect by making it poorer in violations of (code-independent or code-dependent) moral obligations, by making it richer in moral actions beyond the call of duty and by making it less troubled by discordances between his moral attitudes and the lower attitudes dominated by them. Some such discordance is part of the human predicament and has inspired a great deal of theological and philosophical speculation. It lies for example at the root of St Matthew's contrasting the willingness of the spirit and the weakness of the flesh, or of Kant's opposing a holy will in which duty and inclination necessarily coincide to the will of human beings which does not necessarily coincide with their inclinations and indeed necessarily conflicts with some of them.

The possibility of comparing different ways of life from the point of view of a given morality and of deciding, at least for some of them, which is morally more perfect than the others – a decision on which it may even be practicable to act – suggests the ideal of an absolutely perfect way of life which, though unrealizable, is yet capable of being approximated to by human conduct. A way of life is from the point of view of a given morality (absolutely) perfect if, and only if, it is free from any violation of (code-independent or code-dependent) moral obligations; it is not poorer in supererogatory moral actions (i.e. actions beyond the call of moral duty) than any other way of life; and is free from any discordance between moral and lower attitudes.

It is worth emphasizing that although a morally ideal way of life is defined with respect to a morality it does not coincide with it, but has some other non-moral characteristics. In other words, while leading the morally perfect life involves conforming to one's moral principles, conforming to one's moral principles does not in turn involve leading the morally perfect life – if only because of some discordance between one's moral and one's other practical attitudes. Spinoza saw this point very clearly and expresses it at the end of the last 'proof' of the *Ethics* when he asserts that nobody lives a life of blessedness, i.e. the ideal life according to his philosophy, because he has restrained his emotions, but that on the contrary the power to restrain one's desires arises from the blessed life itself. (. . . *nemo beatitudine gaudet quia affectus coërcuit, sed contra potestas libidines coërcendi ex ipsa beatitudine oritur.* QED.)

The following minor points about the notion of a morally ideal life may serve to guard its definition against misunderstanding. If, as is done here, one regards the human predicament as not allowing for complete concordance between moral and other practical attitudes, then a morally ideal life, though it may be approximated to more or less closely, is unrealizable by actual men in the actual world. If a person's morality is purely deontic, then the second clause of the definition of a morally ideal life is superfluous since a purely deontic morality has no room for supererogatory actions. Lastly, the assumption that actual ways of life may approximate to an ideal way of life more or less closely, does not imply that it is always possible to establish a strict or weak ordering of ways of life according to their relative distance from the ideal.

Some examples of morally ideal ways of life

The most familiar examples of moralities and ways of life which perfectly conform to them are found in the world religions. But there are others, such as that found in the philosophy of Spinoza. His main moral principle, which he briefly explains in the *Treatise on the Correction of the Understanding*, and fully in the *Ethics*, is to strive for himself 'together with other individuals, if this can be' after 'knowledge of the union which the mind has with the whole of nature'(*cognitionem unionis quam mens cum tota natura habet*). His subsidiary moral principles include the obligations 'to speak in a manner which is intelligible to ordinary people and to do for them all those things, that do not prevent us from attaining our supreme end...to enjoy only such pleasures as are necessary for the preservation of our health...to seek only enough money or other things as are needed for the preservation of health and life...and for imitating those customs of one's society which are not incompatible with the supreme goal'. The ideal way of life itself is a life in which consciousness of the mind's union with the whole of nature is always present. Spinoza considers such a state of mind realizable – although 'like all excellent things, which are as difficult to achieve as they are rare'. But it is doubtful whether he thought that it can last without interruption or whether he would claim to have had more than temporary experiences of the blessed state of mind.

Examples of religious moralities and ideal ways of life which perfectly conform to them are Christianity and Buddhism. According to both these religions the ideal life is unrealizable in this world – although men can strive after this ideal and in doing so conform to morality. According to both religions the ideal can only be reached through salvation towards which the Christian strives by following the divine example of Christ, the Buddhist by following the divine example of Buddha. The two religions differ fundamentally in their conceptions both of the world and of salvation. The Christian world is a world created by God and one which, having created it, God found 'very good'. Yet man is, as the result of his fall, imperfect because sinful and mortal. His salvation consists in the resurrection of the body after death and in eternal sinless and blessed life. The Buddhist world is a world of illusion (*maya*) and connected with it of an endless series of reincarnations, in which every reincarnated being is punished or rewarded for the deeds of its immediately preceding incarnation (*karma*). And man's salvation consists in being freed from illusion and incarnation by the submergence of his (illusory) individuality in absolute reality.

The point of this brief comparison of Christianity and Buddhism – or rather of two superficial sketches of these two profound and influential religions – is to show that their ideal ways of life correspond to different moralities. The main difference arises from the important rôle which the love of one's neighbours plays in Christianity and which the detachment from the illusory world of illusory individuals plays in Buddhism. The difference is clearly stated by a Christian scholar (Streeter 1932: p. 70): '...for the Buddhist's aim is the eradication of all desire – desire of things good as well as evil. Hence the Buddhist may not let pity pass the border-line that separates it from love; to love is to readmit desire; it is to jeopardize the tranquility which is the goal, for the attainment of which the ethical discipline exists.' It is the Buddhist's and the Christian's main moral principle to follow their divine examples in order to achieve salvation. But their content and the content of their subsidiary moral standards differ because the kinds of salvation at which they aim are very different.

Spinoza's philosophy, Christianity and Buddhism are thus examples of practical idealizations containing (*a*) the description of an ideal way of life which is unrealizable by ordinary people in the ordinary world; (*b*) a morality to which this ideal way of life would conform perfectly, in particular without discordances, but which can be adopted and imperfectly observed by ordinary people in the ordinary world; and (c) the promise that if man strives after the ideal, and thereby implicitly conforms to the morality associated with it, he may through salvation or in some other supernatural way achieve the ideal. In so far as a person regards this promise as a true and welcome message, it may help him to overcome his moral weakness and to conform to those moral standards conformity to which is implicit in his striving towards the ideal.

Unrealizable and realizable ideals

According to the preceding analysis of pragmatic and practical idealization each of them leads from a concept which is exemplified or realizable in the actual world (e.g. a feature of our physical or social environment, a standard of practicable conduct, an actual person's way of life) to a concept which is incapable of being actually exemplified or realized (a concept of pure geometry, an unrealizable legal fiction, a superhuman standard of conduct or way of life). Concepts of the latter kind remind one of Platonic Forms, concepts of the former kind of Plato's empirical concepts whose instances he regarded as 'participating' in, or as 'approximating' to or 'imitating' the Forms. One is even further reminded of Plato's philosophy when one remembers that in his later life he admitted only two kinds of Forms, namely mathematical Forms which are 'approximated' to by features of the physical world and moral Forms which are 'imitated' by human beings in their endeavour to act morally (see Field 1949).

There is, however, a fundamental difference between the results of pragmatic and practical idealization, as here exhibited and analysed, and Plato's Forms. For according to Plato there is only one set of Forms which corresponds to the concepts which are exemplified or realizable in the actual world, whereas pragmatic and practical idealizations may lead to different, and mutually inconsistent ideal concepts, and, hence, to different mathematical, physical and social theories, different legal systems, different philosophical and religious conceptions of morally ideal ways of life.

Neither the Platonic notion of ideal Forms, nor the present notions of pragmatic and practical idealization exclude another sense of the term 'ideal', namely the sense in which an ideal feature or state of affairs is simply a feature or state which is the object of a practical or moral pro-attitude and which, though not yet realized, is yet in

202

principle realizable. It must moreover be admitted that the distinction between realizable and unrealizable ideals is not always clear nor always important. Thus when, in analysing the general concept of justice in (chapter 12) a distinction was made between its deontic and its ideal component, the question of the realizability or otherwise of the ideal component was left open – thereby allowing for the possibility that the ideal components of some concepts of justice are realizable and that the ideal components of other concepts of justice are unrealizable.

PART III

ON THE EPISTEMOLOGY AND METAPHYSICS OF PRACTICAL THINKING

CHAPTER 16

ON THE RELATION BETWEEN COGNITIVE AND PRACTICAL RATIONALITY

Just as the logical questions, which were discussed in the first part of this essay, could not be ignored without inviting misunderstandings about the presuppositions of practical thinking, so the epistemological and metaphysical questions, which will be discussed in this, its third part, cannot be ignored without inviting misunderstandings about the wider implications of practical thinking. And to invite either kind of misunderstanding is to endanger the intelligibility of the main purpose and results of the enquiry. The epistemological problems to be examined are the relation between cognitive and practical rationality (in this chapter), the nature of moral evidence, moral argument and moral conversion (in chapter 17) and the limits of moral relativism (in chapter 18). The metaphysical problems to be briefly explored are the problems of the adequacy of any cognitive or practical position to reality and the problem of freedom (in chapter 19).

This chapter begins by developing further the purely formal distinctions drawn earlier between the consistency and the coherence of a person's beliefs (in chapter 2), and between the consistency and the coherence of his practical attitudes (in chapter 7). This is done by identifying the standards of cognitive coherence with the principles which define a person's categorial framework, and the standards of practical coherence with the principles defining his morality (in so far as his morality is defined by moral principles rather than concrete moral attitudes).

There follows an examination of the interdependence of cognitive and practical coherence, in particular of the manner in which the application of practical principles presupposes the application of cognitive principles and of the manner in which the acceptance and acceptability of cognitive principles is subject to accepted practical principles. The chapter ends with the examination of two opposite speculations: one of which reduces all thinking to an awareness of practical attitudes and their implementation, while the other reduces all practical attitudes to an awareness of preexistent or predetermined facts.

On the logical consistency and the coherence of beliefs

Just as the logical consistency of a set of beliefs lies in their not violating the principles of an accepted logic, so the coherence of a set of beliefs consists in their not violating certain accepted non-logical principles. The necessity, if any, of these non-logical principles was called 'ontological necessity' in order to distinguish it from the formal necessity of logical principles and their consequences. The intellectual history of mankind, especially the history of philosophy and science, contains many examples of different, more or less widely accepted principles of ontological necessity and, correspondingly, of different notions of coherence.

A systematic attempt at characterizing the principles of ontological necessity, which determine a person's conception of coherence, leads to the notion of a categorial framework. This notion rests on a number of empirical facts and can be conceived of as the relativization of some well-established philosophical distinctions.† The main facts are that human beings distinguish in their experience between particulars and attributes; that they classify the particulars and in doing so distinguish between categories or maximal kinds which (apart from possible common borderline cases) are mutually exclusive and jointly exhaustive of all particulars; that they associate with each maximal kind certain constitutive principles, i.e. propositions to the effect that being a member of this kind logically implies having certain (constitutive) attributes as well as certain individuating principles, i.e. propositions to the effect that being a distinct member of this kind logically implies possessing one or more (individuating) attributes; that they distinguish between independent particulars or substances, which exist independently of other particulars, and dependent particulars which exist only as features of independent ones; lastly that they employ a certain logic, used among other things in formulating the distinctions and principles mentioned. It should be noted that in accordance with these definitions, constitutive and individuating principles may be transcategorial, in the sense of being associated with two or more maximal kinds. Based on these empirical facts, a person's categorial framework is defined by his categorization of

† No more than a rough explanation is needed here. For greater detail see Körner (1971c).

particulars into maximal kinds with their associated constitutive and individuating principles, by his distinction between dependent and independent particulars and by his logic. The principles demarcating a categorial framework and their logical consequences might be called its 'framework principles'.

That people do in fact think within categorial frameworks, that is to say that they require their beliefs to be consistent with the corresponding framework principles, makes them into conditions of coherence and accounts for their 'ontological' necessity. That, on the other hand, the principles defining a categorial framework are necessary only for those who think within it and that more than one framework has been employed by different people and societies, is a cogent reason for rejecting – at least provisionally – the doctrine that a particular categorial framework is absolute and that the corresponding framework principles are absolute conditions of coherence.

A person's adherence to a categorial framework may be more or less explicit, more or less definite, and more or less confident. His confidence in it may vary from unquestioning acceptance to vacillation between its continued acceptance and its rejection in favour of an alternative framework which for some reason may prove more attractive to him. One might expect that the notion of a categorial framework would be a useful piece of theoretical equipment for the historian of ideas, since he is particularly concerned with intellectual changes which are both fundamental and sufficiently widespread to be of historical rather than merely biographical interest. It might, for example, enable him to make the idea of an intellectual or a scientific revolution clearer by defining it as a change of, rather than within, a categorial framework. Thus the almost universal rejection of Aristotelianism in favour of ways of thinking inspired by Galileo and his scientific successors is a change of categorial framework. So is the replacement of Newtonian and Kantian ways of thinking by ways of thinking which are inspired by orthodox quantum mechanics – even though this change of framework is as yet very far from universal and from having seeped into commonsense thinking.

The competition between the two frameworks is nevertheless part of the contemporary intellectual background and their comparison thus provides a living illustration of the concept of a categorial framework; of the ontological necessity of its framework principles as conditions of coherent thought for anybody who thinks within this framework and last but not least, of its possible replacement by another.

209

Maximal kinds of entities in the older framework are natural pheno-mena, i.e. events or situations with which there are associated as their constitutive principles a principle of causality, a principle of the conservation of matter and others which are less important in the present context; and with which there are associated as their indi-viduating principles the principle of their continuous occupation of a certain region of three-dimensional Euclidean space throughout an interval of Newtonian time. The competing framework differs radically from the old one in that the principle of causality is replaced by a probabilistic principle; the principle of the conservation of matter by a principle of the conservation of matter or energy; and the principle of continuous occupation of a region of three-dimensional Euclidean space throughout an interval of Newtonian time by a principle of a possibly discontinuous occupation by a natural phenomenon of a region in a four-dimensional Riemannian space–time continuum. While some philosophers are still trying to demonstrate the impossi-bility of this change of framework, there is good evidence that it has been made – or occurred in the minds of – some thinkers.

For the acceptor of a categorial framework defined by the conjunc-tion of its framework principles, say, F any logical consequence of this conjunction is not only true but ontologically necessary. Writing $\Box_F f$ for 'f is ontologically necessary with respect to F', we may symbolize the definition by

(1) $\Box_F f \underset{D}{=} (F \vdash f) \wedge f.$

The ontological possibility or coherence of f with respect to F is equivalent to the denial of the ontological necessity of $\daleth f$. In symbols

(2) $\Diamond_F f \underset{D}{=} \daleth\Box_F \daleth f = \daleth[(F \vdash \daleth f) \wedge \daleth f],$ i.e.

(3) $\Diamond_F f \underset{D}{=} \daleth(F \vdash \daleth f) \vee f.$

The only difference between these formulae and those of chapter 2 (p. 26) is the replacement of N, which does not imply any special concept of an ontological principle, by F, which identifies ontological with framework principles.

On the practical consistency and coherence of practical attitudes

The structure of a person's cognitive system, as one might call his system of beliefs, and the structure of his practical system, i.e. his system of practical attitudes, show certain analogies, which are worth recalling before enquiring into the interconnection and interdependence of the two systems. Thus the comparatively simple notion of cognitive or logical inconsistency has an analogous, though rather complex counterpart in the three kinds of practical inconsistency, which have been distinguished earlier (in chapter 7) as practical opposition, practical discordance and practical incongruence and give rise to the following definitions. Two practical attitudes are practically consistent if, and only if, they are neither opposed, nor incongruent, nor discordant; a set of practical attitudes is practically consistent if, and only if, it contains no two practically inconsistent attitudes; and a statement expressing a practical attitude is practically consistent if, and only if, it cannot be decomposed into statements expressing practical attitudes which together form a practically inconsistent set.

Just as the framework principles defining a certain categorial framework are for any person thinking within it conditions of cognitive coherence, i.e. the coherence of his beliefs, so his supreme practical principles are conditions of the practical coherence of his practical attitudes. In order to emphasize the analogy between cognitive and practical coherence we might speak of a person's supreme practical principles as defining the framework of his practical attitudes or his practical framework. And what has been said about a person's adherence, to a categorial framework or its framework principles – that it may be more or less explicit, more or less definite and more or less confident – applies *mutatis mutandis* to his adherence to a practical framework or the supreme practical principles defining it.

A supreme practical principle has been characterized earlier (in chapter 9) as being (or expressing) an undominated practical attitude which is personally universal, circumstantially general, essential, simple and strict. The requirement of strictness may be too restrictive. It conforms to a desire to make the principles of coherence as rigid as those of mere consistency and may be dropped without causing any inconvenience other than a fairly superficial rearrangement of definitions. As regards the form of supreme practical principles they may be non-deontic, i.e. directed towards lower-level attitudes without at the same time being directed towards requiring their being brought about or eliminated; they may be (or express) code-independent obligations, i.e. be directed towards lower attitudes *and also* towards requiring their being brought about or eliminated; and they may be (or express) code-dependent obligations, based on a supreme pro-attitude towards the continued acceptance of a certain code of conduct. As regards the content of the supreme practical principles, they admit the same variation as morality – provided that we consider only moralities consisting of such principles and not also minimal moralities which consist of supreme practical attitudes which are circumstantially concrete, i.e. not circumstantially general.

Cognitive coherence has, in accordance with commonsense and philosophical usage, been defined as implying cognitive consistency and as being implied by truth. It is similarly appropriate to define practical coherence as implying practical consistency and as being implied by morality. For a person who accepts, say, the Kantian categorial framework, the truth of his beliefs implies their coherence (with respect to the Kantian framework principles) and their coherence implies their consistency. Similarly for a person who accepts, say, the Benthamite practical framework, the morality of his attitudes implies their practical coherence (with respect to Bentham's principle of utility and his other supreme practical principles) and their practical coherence also implies their practical consistency. Since the notion of practical consistency of two attitudes, i.e. their non-opposition, concordance and congruence, differs quite radically from the notion of cognitive or logical consistency, the notions of practical necessity, of practical implication, and of practical coherence which are defined in terms of this notion, also differ radically from the corresponding cognitive notions.

These differences can be made even more obvious by the following schematic formulae which differ from the corresponding formulae of chapter 7 (p. 99) mainly by containing the variable Π in place of the variable P. The latter ranges over unanalysed supreme practical principles, while the former ranges over supreme practical principles in the sense of the preceding analyses. Let a, b, etc. indicate that S has a certain attitude (e.g. a pro-attitude towards formalization), γa that he has an attitude which is practically inconsistent with that expressed by a (e.g. that he has an anti-attitude or attitude of indifference towards formalization) and let us write '$\Diamond a$' for 'the attitude expressed by a cannot be decomposed into a set of attitudes of which at least two are practically inconsistent'. We can then define practical necessity by

(4) $\quad \square\, a \underset{D}{=} \gamma \Diamond\, \gamma a$

and practical implication by

(5) $\quad a \mathrel{\prec\!\!\cdot} b \underset{D}{=} \gamma \Diamond\, (a \wedge \gamma b).$

Before going further it must again be emphasized that practical implication, i.e. $a \dashv\!\!\cdot b$, though formally analogous to logical implication, i.e. $f \vdash g$, is substantively quite different from it. Apart from the obvious difference arising from that between cognitive and practical consistency, the following psychological or anthropological difference is also important. Whereas a person who fully and consciously believes f and $f \vdash g$ cannot as a matter of fact at the same time also fully and consciously believe that γg, a person may – and because of the human predicament manifested by discordances between attitudes often does – have an attitude a of which he is fully aware, have full awareness of $a \dashv\!\!\cdot b$ and yet also have γb. And this practical inconsistency may even be to his credit – for example if he accepts a supreme principle a, which is repellent to us, acknowledges that it practically implies b, which is equally repellent to us, but yet has the practical attitude γb.

Just as ontological necessity with respect to certain framework principles implies, but is not implied by truth, so practical necessity with respect to certain supreme practical principles implies, but is not implied by, morality – e.g. in the case of practical attitudes which are covered by competing rather than strict moral principles or in the case of a morality which is at least partly concrete, i.e. not circumstantially general. Writing $\mathrm{Mor}(a)$ for 'the attitude of S expressed by a is moral in S's system of practical attitudes', we may define practical necessity with respect to a set of supreme principles, say Π, by

(6) $\boxdot_\Pi a \underset{D}{=} (\Pi \dashv\!\!\cdot a) \wedge \mathrm{Mor}(a)$

and practical possibility or coherence with respect to Π by

(7) $\Diamond_\Pi a \underset{D}{=} \gamma(\Pi \dashv\!\!\cdot \gamma a) \vee \mathrm{Mor}(a)$.

(The corresponding more general formulae on p. 100 contain $\mathrm{Acc}(a)$, which symbolizes a more general notion of practical acceptability, in place of the more specific $\mathrm{Mor}(a)$.)

On practical coherence as partly presupposing cognitive coherence

A person's choosing to realize one of the practicabilities which he regards as open to him depends on his beliefs about a preexisting world of facts and about the course of events in which he may, or may not, be able to intervene. The assumption of such dependence enters the very notion of an intervention in the course of nature. In analysing it, particular stress had to be laid on the general notion of predetermination and its various species, especially empirical necessitation and probabilification of various kinds, as well as on the distinction between the cognitive and the evaluative attributes of an intervention in the course of nature (chapter 5). Since at that stage of the enquiry the concepts of practical and cognitive coherence were not yet available, the dependence of practical on cognitive coherence could only be hinted at. Even now there is no need for a detailed discussion and a few remarks on the dependence of practical coherence on the cognitive coherence of commonsense and scientific thinking about matters of fact will be sufficient. It seems, moreover, permissible and advisable to concentrate on a familiar categorial framework implicit in contemporary commonsense.

The courses of action through which one intervenes by one's chosen bodily conduct in the course of events take place in a world which according to this commonsense consists of material objects and persons, located in a Euclidean three-dimensional space and a one-dimensional time, and governed by causal laws. The categorial framework implicitly accepted by contemporary commonsense is thus not very different from the Kantian categorial framework – especially if one drops the Kantian distinction between phenomena and noumena and *somehow* finds room for freedom of choice in the phenomenal world. Attempts at adjusting commonsense and a modified Kantian framework to each other have become fairly common in the English-speaking world – ever since Oxford linguistic philosophers have started to pay attention to Kant and have put forward their combination of Kantianism and commonsense as containing the allegedly permanent conditions of cognitive coherence. (See, for example, Strawson 1966.)

A person who thinks within this framework finds himself in a certain situation involving himself, other persons and material objects, and considers the probability with which his situation will be replaced by another situation or sequence of situations, be it as a result of his intervention or independently of it. The actual situation in which he finds himself and the situations which he considers as its empirically or practically possible successors may differ in a variety of ways. Thus the material objects and persons involved in the various possible situations may differ from those in the actual situation in their spatial relations, in their personal relations – e.g. hatred between two persons having given way to love – and in their quality or quantity. On the other hand, the assumption of certain other changes, namely those which are inconsistent with the principles defining the commonsense framework, would be 'incoherent' or ontologically impossible. It

214

would, for example, be incoherent to assume that a practical thinker's original situation can be followed by another situation which has a feature uncaused by its predecessors or that as a result of these changes – whether or not they be the partial effect of his intervention – the total amount of matter in the universe has either decreased or increased. This is so because the principle of causality and the principle of the conservation of matter are constitutive principles associated with the maximal kind (or kinds) of material objects. (The two commonsense principles correspond, of course, respectively to the second and first analogy of the *Critique of Pure Reason*.)

On cognitive coherence as partly presupposing practical coherence

Just as coherent practical attitudes presuppose coherent beliefs, so at least some coherent beliefs presuppose coherent practical attitudes. The following classification of 'practical beliefs', which presuppose, or involve, practical attitudes and thus are subject to supreme practical principles, is not meant to be either exclusive or exhaustive because, while each of the distinguished classes is not empty, their precise demarcation may be controversial. There is, first of all, little doubt that at least some of our beliefs are instrumental in the sense that to have such a belief involves preferring to act as if it were true over acting as if it were false (*not*, preferring its being true to its being false). Thus my belief that a certain object is a pen, a hammer or some other instrument, needed in achieving an end which I wish to promote or thwart, is an instrumental belief.

A second class of practical beliefs are justificatory practical beliefs, i.e. beliefs that other beliefs are justified because they have been acquired, and could be acquired again, by conforming to a certain preferred method, for example an experimental method, a philosophical method, a method of religious meditation etc. Thus, to give a simple example, my belief that careful counting of the number of books in my library justifies my belief that their number equals the number resulting from my count is a justificatory practical belief. In the case of more complex justificatory practical beliefs it may be highly controversial whether the method involved in the justification is correctly described, in particular whether it in fact ensures the results it is supposed to ensure. Philosophical accounts of the so-called scientific method are especially open to doubt and controversy.

Yet both the so-called deductivist and the so-called inductivist account of scientific inquiry rightly stress the important rôle played in it by justificatory practical beliefs. According to the deductivist account, whose foremost modern proponent is Karl Popper, belief in the acceptability of a theory is justified so long as we can believe that it has not been falsified in spite of the most serious attempts at doing so by experiment and observation. The practical pro-attitude towards attempts at empirical falsification clearly characterizes the deductivist belief in the acceptability for the time being, of a theory as a practical belief – even if the deductivist notion of falsification suffers from some obscurity caused by neglecting the difference between the logical and conceptual structure of the falsified theory on the one hand and the statements describing the falsifying experience on the other. (For details, see Körner 1966.)

Contemporary, so-called inductivist accounts are mostly based on some statistical theory and thus indirectly on some theory of probability, whether objective or subjective. Both types of theory insist that the justification of a scientific belief – and hence the justificatory belief that the scientific belief is for the time being acceptable – involve practical preferences for some procedures over others. In the case of objective theories, especially frequency theories, the procedures are mainly concerned with ensuring the randomness of samples. In the case of subjective theories the procedures are mainly concerned with ensuring the 'fairness' of assigning utilities and probabilities to the possible outcomes under consideration (see chapter 3).

A third class of practical beliefs consists of cognitively and morally free beliefs – a belief being cognitively and morally free if it is chosen from a number of equally plausible beliefs, the adoption of none of which would involve cognitive incoherence or immorality. An example of such a belief would arise from a situation in which a person is resolved to act in one of two morally indifferent ways (e.g. to attend one of two concerts); in which his choice would depend on his having one of two beliefs (e.g. that one of the concerts will be more enjoyable); in which the evidence for either belief exactly balances the evidence for the other; and in which adopting neither would result in inaction. If it be objected that a person in such a situation is not really choosing a belief, but choosing to act as if he had this belief, the proper answer is not to deny the distinction, but to insist that as a matter of fact one is often unable to make it.

Another somewhat different example arises from situations in which a person chooses to adopt rather than to reject a very general scientific or metaphysical principle when its adoption or rejection are equally undecidable in the light of the best available knowledge, when neither adoption nor rejection involves cognitive incoherence or immorality, and when he adopts the principle for the simple reason that – other things being equal – he prefers adopting to rejecting it. This, as he tells Max Born in a letter, was Einstein's situation when he asked himself why he refused to believe 'in the dice playing God' of orthodox quantum mechanics. If it be objected that a person in such a situation is not really without a reason other than his simple preference, but merely not conscious of it, the proper answer is, as before, not to deny the distinction, but to insist that as a matter of fact one is often unable to make it.

A fourth class of practical beliefs consists of cognitively, but not also morally, free beliefs – a belief being cognitively, but not also morally, free if it is chosen from a number of equally plausible beliefs, if the adoption of none of them would involve cognitive incoherence, but if the adoption of at least one of them would be immoral while the adoption of at least one other among them would not be immoral. An example would be the rejection rather than the adoption of Galileo's cosmological hypothesis by Bellarmin on the charitable assumption that in his view the evidence for adoption exactly balanced the evidence for rejection, that neither involved cognitive incoherence, but that adoption would be immoral, e.g. by leading to religious or moral decay. Even without recalling the particular example, the dangers inherent in arguments for the adoption of cognitively free and moral, practical beliefs and for the rejection of cognitively free but immoral, practical beliefs should be obvious. They are bound to remain among the favourite arguments of those who are engaged in the persecution or forcible 'reeducation' of religious or political dissenters and in attempts at justifying this activity.

From the analysis of the interdependence of cognitive and practical coherence to speculations about the primacy of one over the other

By exhibiting the dependence of both cognitive and practical coherence on principles which are susceptible to change, and by analysing the interdependence of cognitive and practical coherence, some light is thrown on the structure of practical systems and their relation to categorial frameworks. The analysis implies, and goes beyond the

8-2

fairly obvious observation that at least some beliefs involve practical attitudes and at least some practical attitudes involve beliefs. Yet even this obvious observation is seemingly denied by philosophers who following Kant assert the ultimate 'primacy of the practical reason over the theoretical' and by philosophers who take the opposite view. Each of the opposing views employs a highly speculative notion of having and acquiring a belief or a practical attitude, which is not used in the preceding analysis of cognitive and practical coherence, and of their interdependence. To say this is not, of course, to condemn such speculations as futile.

According to one of these extreme speculative views, which might be called 'pure constructivism', all cognition is awareness of constructions, i.e. of implemented practicabilities; all apparent facts are constructs; all thinking is mental (as opposed to physical) construction, which in some cases is a substitute of, or a reflection of, physical construction; and lastly, believing a statement (proposition, judgment or whatever is the object of a belief) is to be aware of a construction and of a statement describing it – the statement and the belief being true and justified if, and only if, the description is correct. Pure constructivism is most plausible when – after the manner of Brouwer, Heyting and the other mathematical intuitionists – it is restricted to mathematics, that is to say to mathematical cognition, constructions, thinking and to true and justified mathematical beliefs.

For the intuitionists the nature, the intuitive clarity and reliability of a mathematical construction are as indubitable as the Cartesian indubitabilities were for Descartes. And they have equally no doubt about the relation between a mathematical construction and a mathematical statement which is mathematically justified or proved by the construction. Once these intuitions are accepted as indubitable, one can accept Heyting's doctrine: that a mathematician's justified assertion that a mathematical proposition is true, amounts to his stating sincerely that he has 'effected a construction F in his mind which proves f'; that a mathematician's justified assertion that a mathematical proposition is false, amounts to his stating sincerely that he has 'effected a construction G which deduces a contradiction from the supposition that the construction F has been brought to an end'; and that other justified mathematical assertions have to be similarly interpreted. If these definitions are accepted then the principles of intuitionist logic (see chapter 1) and the theorems of intuitionist mathematics are indeed nothing but linguistic reports on mathematical constructions – the logical theorems being not so much reports on specific mathematical constructions as reports on general features common to all mathematical constructions so far formed by the person reporting on them.†

As the field of constructivist thinking is expanded beyond mathematics, the nature of the constructions – as well as the relation between them and the linguistic reports on them – becomes less clear. Thus while Kant's account of mathematical thinking anticipates the constructivism of the intuitionists, his account of the rôle of the Categories of the understanding and of the Ideas of reason, especially of freedom, is a constructivism according to which the non-mathematical constructions of the Understanding and of Reason are performed by the transcendental ego, giving form to what cannot be known without it. Since these constructions are only inferred and not apprehended, Kant cannot, and does not, claim that true statements express awareness of these constructions. It might help to avoid confusion if one reserved the name of pure constructivism to the doctrines which imply that all true statements within a restricted or unrestricted field are reports on apprehended constructions and *not* on constructions whose existence is inferred, but which cannot become the objects of awareness.

Other kinds of constructivism which claim the accessibility of the relevant constructions fall far short of the clarity with which the intuitionists have characterized mathematical constructions. Thus operationalism, which holds that all true scientific statements are reports on physical operations or constructions, is not at all clear about the nature of mental operations (e.g. about mathematical computations or theory constructions) which it describes as 'paper-and-pencil operations' (see Bridgman 1943: pp. 7, 114). Again, Marxism is not clear about the demarcation of the nature of social and economic life, i.e. the totality of all socially significant constructions, which at a certain time determine the beliefs held in a certain society – especially as to which of these beliefs are merely 'ideological' and thus only apparently true and which are trans-ideological and thus true *simpliciter*. It might, to give one last example, be argued that Wittgenstein's conception of a form of life was meant to play a central part in a constructivist philosophy which would extend the intuitionist account of mathematics to all thinking. Yet even if this

† For details on intuitionist logic and mathematics see Heyting (1956); for a criticism of the intuitionists' notion of mathematical intuition see Körner (1960: ch. 7).

exegetic conjecture were true, it must be emphasized that Wittgenstein's later philosophy is – as he knew and admitted – far from clear. All the positions mentioned are versions of pragmatism in the wide sense of the term which ranges from pure constructivism to the view that cognitive coherence depends on practical coherence.

If pure constructivism is one extreme speculative view about the relation between practical attitudes and beliefs, what might be called 'pure cognitivism' is the other extreme. According to this view all cognition is awareness of preexistent or predetermined facts; all apparent constructs are such facts; all thinking is an unfolding awareness of preexistent or predetermined facts; and lastly, believing a statement (proposition, judgment or whatever is the object of belief) is to be aware of a fact and of a statement describing it – the statement and the belief being true and justified if, and only if, the description is correct. Pure cognitivism is most plausible when – after the Platonic fashion of most mathematicians – it is restricted to mathematics conceived as the apprehension of timeless mathematical facts.

As the field of pure cognitivism is expanded beyond mathematics to temporal facts, the nature of the facts and the relations between them become less clear. If we assume that all awareness is awareness of preexistent facts, then change and time are merely characteristic of awareness and not of reality, so that time and change is an illusion – a philosophical position which has been attractive to philosophers as ancient as Parmenides and as recent as McTaggart. If some facts are preexistent while others are merely predetermined, then time and change are less illusory than they are on the view that all facts are preexistent. And the view of time and change implied by the doctrine that some facts are preexistent, others predetermined but all facts are either the one or the other is in turn very different from the view of time and change implied by pure constructivism.

The various versions of pure constructivism and of pure cognitivism are speculations about reality which go beyond the interdependence of practical and cognitive coherence as it appears in our awareness of our beliefs and practical attitudes. All these speculations are consistent with the apparent interdependence. But so is another speculation, namely that their appearance corresponds to reality and that reality contains preexistent and predetermined facts and also leaves room for genuine constructions, i.e. the implementation of alternative practicabilities. This speculation will, in due course, be briefly elaborated (see p. 256).

CHAPTER 17

ON ARGUMENT AND EVIDENCE
IN MORALS

This chapter is devoted to an examination of moral reasoning, as manifested in two kinds of moral argument: arguments which are conducted on the assumption that the relevant moral principles are not in question; and arguments in which the issue is the adoption, rejection or modification of one or more moral principles. The chapter starts with a brief discussion of moral arguments based on practical implications, logical implications and deontic implications and proceeds by briefly examining practical plausibility arguments within the limits of practical and factual coherence. The discussion then turns from arguments using moral principles as premises to arguments about the adequacy or inadequacy of the adopted moral principles themselves. This is done by first examining a variety of arguments about principles in other fields and by then using the results of the examination in the analysis of arguments for the rejection or modification of adopted moral principles.

Moral arguments based on practical, logical and deontic implications

In discussing moral arguments based on practical, logical and deontic implications it seems best for our purposes to discuss specific examples. Consider, then, a person S who has adopted a certain moral principle, i.e. who has a practical attitude of at least second level, which is undominated, circumstantially general and personally universal, simple and essential (see pp. 118f). To be more specific, we consider a person S who has adopted a rather crude form of utilitarianism characterized by his pro-attitude towards a personally universal pro-attitude towards the maximization of the gross national product of his nation. Schematically,

(a) $S + [U + \text{Max}]$.

This practical attitude ascribed to S is opposed to (because jointly unrealizable with) any practical attitude ascribed to him by denying that he has an anti-attitude towards a personally universal practical anti-attitude towards the maximization of the gross national product. Schematically,

(b) $\gamma\, (S - [U - \mathrm{Max}])$.

Because (a) and (b) are opposed we have by the definition of practical implication (p. 99)

(c) $S + [U + \mathrm{Max}] \lessdot \cdot S - [U - \mathrm{Max}]$.

Next, we assume – what does not *logically* follow from (a) and (c) – that S's practical attitudes are all practically consistent and that it is true to assert of him that

(d) $S - [U - \mathrm{Max}]$.

The practical attitude ascribed to S by (d) is clearly practically inconsistent with the first level practical attitude ascribed to S by

(e) $S - \mathrm{Max}$

(because (e) is discordant with or negatively dominated by (d)). From this practical inconsistency it follows, again by the definition of practical implication, that

(f) $S - [U - \mathrm{Max}] \lessdot \cdot \gamma\, (S - \mathrm{Max})$.

To the examples (c) and (f) of practical implication others might be readily added. But our two examples are sufficient to show the use of practical implication in arguments to the effect that a moral principle practically implies, and thus morally justifies, the presence of a first level practical attitude which may in fact be absent or the absence of a first level practical attitude which may in fact be present.

The utilitarian of our example may, of course, find that while his utilitarian moral principle practically implies a practical pro-attitude towards the maximization of his nation's gross national product, he himself has a practical pro-attitude towards his own enrichment even when it involves a decrease of the gross national product. He may even sincerely believe that his personal circumstances in conjunction with a well-confirmed scientific theory logically imply his not having the practical attitude which is practically implied by his moral principle. There is no need to repeat that the spirit may be willing, but the flesh weak, and that the willingness and the weakness all too often conflict and are resolved in favour of the flesh; and there should be no need to repeat that the conflict is not logical. Yet as has been pointed out earlier an impression to the contrary may arise through confusing practical implications employed in moral arguments with logical implications employed in arguments about the course of nature.

This does not mean that arguments about the course of nature may not play an important part in moral arguments. Thus the utilitarian of our example will have to know whether a certain type of conduct, in conjunction with what he believes to be true commonsense or scientific assumptions, logically implies the maximization of the gross national product. If such assumptions are not available he may have to rely on probabilistic reasoning and thus on logical implications of probability statements by probability statements.

In either case – that of purely deductive and that of probabilistic arguments about the course of nature – the employment of the logical implications is auxiliary to the employment of practical implications. For the need to employ the former arises not in determining a practical attitude towards a practicability of a certain kind (e.g. the maximization of the gross national product), but in determining whether a certain practicability is of this kind (e.g. whether a practicable change in taxation would increase the size of the gross national product).

A third type of implication which, apart from logical and practical implications, enters arguments from moral principles to practical attitudes consists of deontic implications, based on a code of conduct (see p. 31). Their employment in moral arguments is again auxiliary in at least two different ways which depend on whether they are used within the framework of a deontic morality or whether they are used for the purpose of simplification. First, in a deontic morality, such as the morality based on a moral pro-attitude towards the Decalogue, inferences from the regulations of a code of conduct to code-dependent obligations depend on deontic implications. Second, in a purely axiological morality it may be morally justified to use a code of conduct as a simplification of some parts of the morality, that is to say to use code-dependent deontic in place of practical implications (see chapter 11).

Moral plausibility arguments

A person may be certain about his moral principles, but uncertain about the moral acceptability, i.e. morality or moral indifference, of some of the courses of action which he believes to be open to him. The reason for his moral uncertainty may lie in the competitiveness of some of his moral principles which in some cases leaves room for, and

223

even demands, *ad hoc* intuitions, in the inexact demarcation of the courses of action which are the objects of his moral attitudes, or in the sheer complexity of his moral principles. In a similar way, a person may be certain about the principles defining his categorial framework, but uncertain about the theoretical rationality or ontological possibility of some of his factual beliefs. In both these cases he can only resort to plausibility arguments which take the form of thought experiments of various kinds – in the factual case, for example, by taking part in an imagined lottery played in the Ramsay-deFinetti–Savage fashion (see chapter 3), in the moral case by making an imagined appearance before the court of his conscience and judging himself in *foro interno*.

In the internal lottery the plausibility of a factual proposition's being true may sometimes be measured by imagined 'fair' bets, and ranges from a minimum to a maximum which are conveniently fixed as 0 and 1. A proposition f is judged to have minimal factual plausibility within a categorial framework F if $\square_F 7 f$ (if f is ontologically impossible with respect to F) and maximal factual plausibility if $\square_F f$ (if f is ontologically necessary with respect to F). Moreover, the betting rules defining the fairness of any bet make the scale of measurement an interval scale. The plausibility arguments consist in establishing that – given a set of sincerely made bets, the framework principles (which are usually taken for granted), and the rules of fair betting – the bets *are* fair and that the plausibilities assigned by them are correct.

Moving from the internal lottery to the internal court of conscience, it seems clear that a person who has adopted a set of moral principles, say, Π and is trying to judge the plausibility of a practical attitude ascribed to himself by, say, the statement that a is morally acceptable, will judge this plausibility to be minimal if $\square_\Pi 7 a$ (if a is practically impossible with respect to Π) and maximal if $\square_\Pi a$ (if a is practically necessary with respect to Π). It is less clear how one might judge a moral plausibility to be greater than minimal and smaller than maximal. There is, in particular, no one single activity the rôle of which in the moral sphere would be clearly analogous to that played by fair betting in the factual sphere and which would, in particular, be governed by rules of fairness ensuring that the range of moral plausibility is an interval scale.

There is, however, a variety of thought experiments, conducted by a person *in foro interno*, which serve the assessment of moral plausibility to a set of mutually exclusive and jointly exhaustive practical attitudes ascribed by himself to himself, say the statements $a_1, ..., a_n$, when none of them is judged to be either minimal or maximal. In the conduct of these thought experiments the following stages can be distinguished. (1) Imagining for each of the practical attitudes that it has been implemented and turned out to be immoral – after the fog of passion had lifted, time had been found for deliberation, etc. – so that to each of them there corresponds a mistake, say, $m_1, ..., m_n$. (To imagine that the implementation of every practical attitude has turned out immoral is, of course, to entertain a fiction.) (2) Comparing the imagined mistakes with respect to their seriousness, i.e. applying a relation 'x is at least as serious as y' to any two of them. (3) Judging that one practical attitude, say that denoted by a_r, is morally more plausible than another practical attitude, say that denoted by a_s (that it is more plausible for the implementation of a_r to be morally accept-able than for the implementation of a_s) if and only if the imagined mistake, say, m_r corresponding to a_r is less serious than the imagined mistake m_s corresponding to a_s.

The general description of the imagined proceedings before the court of conscience allows for different relations of comparative seriousness and, consequently, different orderings of practicabilities with respect to their moral plausibility. Thus one might regard a mistake as more serious than another if, considered in the court of conscience, it appears to be more blameworthy, to be more shameful, to cause greater feelings of guilt, to be aesthetically more repellent, etc. As regards the type of ordering established by applying one of these comparative notions, this will depend on one's imagination and discriminatory powers and may range from a quasi or $\Re$–$\mathfrak{X}$ ordering to a measurement on an interval scale of shame, guilt-feelings etc. (see pp. 59 ff.).

Only a fairly elaborate psychological discussion might succeed in dispelling the aura of unreality surrounding these remarks on the appraisal of moral plausibility. But since a judge in an ordinary court of law may clearly find himself in a position in which he must consult his conscience in the manner described, one may hope that the metaphor of the court of conscience and its imagined proceedings may to some extent replace a lengthy digression into introspective or descriptive psychology. The metaphor should also help in avoiding the confusion between statements to the effect that one immoral action or kind of action is more immoral than another (e.g. that, to borrow terms from law and theology, a felony is more immoral than a misdemeanour or that a mortal sin is more immoral than a venial one) with statements to the effect that it is more plausible that of two mutually exclusive actions one rather than the other is immoral.

On various kinds of argument about principles of thought and conduct

From arguments about moral acceptability, inacceptability and plausibility, which employ accepted moral principles as premises, one must distinguish arguments which aim at justifying the acceptance of hitherto accepted or newly proposed moral principles, their rejection or modification. A person's acceptance of a hitherto accepted or newly proposed moral principle or conjunction of such principles is justified if, and in so far as, it is 'adequate to' his previous experience and remains adequate to other actual or imagined experiences. To argue for the adoption by somebody of a hitherto accepted or newly proposed moral principle is to demonstrate its 'adequacy to' his previous experience and to other new or imagined experiences adduced in the course of the argument. The cogency of the argument depends of course on the range and variety of the adduced actual or conceivable experiences, the class of which is in the nature of things an open class. To argue successfully for the rejection or modification of a person's moral principle is to demonstrate 'its inadequacy' to his previous experience or to other new or imagined experiences – where one such experience *may* suffice for the conclusiveness of the argument. Thus while adequacy of a principle cannot be conclusively demonstrated, inadequacy can. For this reason, as well as to avoid unnecessary elaboration, we shall be mainly concerned with attempted demonstrations of inadequacy.

The main obstacle to the analysis of arguments for the adoption, rejection or modification of a moral principle lies in the opaqueness of the notion of its inadequacy (or adequacy) to an experience. Yet it is fairly easy to see what it is *not*. It is not a logical inconsistency or incoherence between beliefs – because a moral principle is not a belief. Nor is it a practical inconsistency between a moral principle and a practical attitude – because this would simply mean that the principle practically implies the negation of the practical attitude and would by itself cast no doubt on the adequacy of the principle.

In attempting a positive characterization, it is worth noting that the inadequacy of principles, the discovery that principles which seemed adequate turned out not to be so, and the employment of arguments intending to show this, are not peculiar to moral thinking, but are familiar in other fields of human endeavour and reflection. Among them are the natural sciences, mathematics, linguistics, and criticism of the arts, all of which abound with arguments in which the confrontation of principles with – actual or imagined – relevant experiences is used to discredit the principles. The nature and the effects of such confrontation differ both between and within the various fields. For our purpose it will be useful to examine a variety of examples ranging from tests whose nature and effects are clearly determined to tests where any attempt at precise definition would amount to misrepresentation. At one extreme are the refutations of empirical laws by counterinstances and of mathematical postulates by reductions *ad absurdum*, at the other are various ways of weakening the claims of aesthetic standards.

Perhaps the most transparent and most convincing arguments against scientific or commonsense empirical principles are those which consist of attempts at refuting empirical generalizations of form 'All Ps are Qs' by appealing to apparent counterinstances of form 'This P is not a Q'. An attempt, say, at refuting the belief that all swans are white, by confronting its holder with an apparently black swan, is very likely to succeed. But its success is not absolutely guaranteed since the addressee of the argument, though entirely convinced that 'This swan is black' logically implies the negation of 'All swans are white', may yet distrust the apparent counterexample. He may, for example, have accepted a dogma about the whiteness of all swans which convinces him that his perception of an apparently black swan is an illusion, or that the bird has been painted black by the devil etc. Thus even in the most straightforward confrontation of an empirical principle with an experience which is adduced to demonstrate the inadequacy of the principle, the pressure of the (apparently) discrediting experience towards rejecting or modifying the principle is not irresistible.

If the pressure of the apparent counterinstance is directed not against a single empirical principle, but against a conjunction of principles, such as a conjunction of hypotheses or a whole empirical theory, its pressure is distributed among the components. This possibility, which was emphasized by Poincaré and Duhem, can be described in less metaphorical terms by considering a conjunction of adopted or proposed hypotheses, say, $H_1, ..., H_n$ which together with certain initial conditions, say o_1, logically imply a certain occurrence, say, o_2. (More precisely, $o_1 \wedge H_1 \wedge ... \wedge H_n \vdash o_2$, where, moreover, every component is essential to the logical implication.) If faced with an apparent counterinstance which, if it were real, would be formulated as $\neg o_2$, one may resist its pressure on any particular hypothesis, say, H_1, not only by regarding the apparent counterexample as an illusion, but also by exempting H_1 from the pressure. (Since by contraposition $\neg o_2 \vdash \neg o_1 \vee \neg H_1 \vee ... \vee \neg H_n$ the falsehood of o_2 logically implies the falsehood of o_1 or H_1 or ... H_n, but *not* that of every – or any particular – member of the disjunction.) The more complex the antecedent of the logical implication, the more possibilities there are for protecting one or more of the principles against the pressure of an apparently discrediting experience.

The characteristic mathematical method of discrediting adopted or proposed principles is to show that they are internally inconsistent, i.e. to deduce a contradiction from them. This method is on the whole more cogent than the empirical method, since there is less danger or suspicion of illusory deductions than there is of illusory perceptions. Yet, though normally more cogent than the production of an empirical counterexample, the method of mathematical *reductio ad absurdum* is not sufficient to discredit single mathematical postulates. This is so because an internally inconsistent mathematical principle is logically equivalent to a conjunction of at least two internally consistent principles, none of which can by itself be blamed for the internal inconsistency of the conjunction. Thus, even though a *reductio ad absurdum* exerts absolute pressure towards the rejection or modification of a conjunction of mathematical principles, its pressure against each of the conjuncts is again resistible.

In the case of arguments intended to demonstrate the inadequacy of a grammatical rule the force of the discrediting experience may vary even more widely in strength than in the case of empirical falsification or mathematical *reductio ad absurdum*. This is particularly so with arguments in which a person who has accepted, or is considering, a principle of grammar is confronted with a sentence or other linguistic expression which, though it conforms to the principle, nevertheless appears odd (bizarre, inappropriate etc.) to him. The relation between a discrediting linguistic counterinstance and a discredited rule of grammar has a prominent feature which is absent from the relation between empirical and mathematical counterinstances and the principles whose adequacy they are meant to demonstrate. While in the empirical and mathematical case, if principle and counterexample are clearly established, the principle must give way, there is, in the linguistic case, no similarly clear preponderance of counter-example over principle. In the linguistic case it is on the contrary not at all unusual that the appearance of oddity may be regarded not as showing a short-coming of the rule but of the person applying it. Thus a person brought up to speak a certain English dialect may find that some of his correct sentences sound odd to him and may take this as a sign that he has not yet fully succeeded in replacing his dialect by the Queen's English – an endeavour which for all sorts of reasons may seem worthwhile to him. (A person trying to unlearn the Queen's English and to learn a particular dialect may find himself in a similar position for reasons which may seem equally laudable, contemptible or indifferent to his fellows.)

The last type of argument – if it can still be regarded as such – which deserves consideration as inviting comparison with arguments about moral principles, is found in aesthetic criticism. It consists not of the confrontation of a principle with instances by which it is discredited, but of a new point of view or vision which deprives it of its force. Although aesthetic standards such as Aristotle's or Boileau's dramaturgy or the rules for composing a fugue or a sonnet are intended only as approximative, necessary conditions for the creation of a play, fugue or poem or for judging these works of art, they may govern artistic creation and critical reflection – so long as they, however incompletely, express a vision which does not admit of complete expression. A play which does not satisfy the requirement of Boileau's three unities of place, time and action has very little chance of being judged successful by anybody whose literary taste is approximately expressed by Boileau's canons. Yet once the vision expressed by them changes, the doctrine of the three unities becomes pointless to the artist and the critic.

Examining aesthetic standards in the light of a changed aesthetic vision, sense of proportion, insight or whatever else one might call the object of the change, is not by itself to argue about aesthetic standards. But it can turn into an argument when one feels a conflict between the observation of aesthetic standards adopted before the conversion to new standards, but still habitually observed, and the new vision which rendered them pointless; and when one feels the need to separate the force of habitual obedience to standards from the pointlessness of the standards themselves. In such situations the argument for the rejection or modification of the old standards, such as the requirement of the three unities, might take the form of an admonition to remember one's conversion, to examine the old standards 'on their merits', to abandon conservativism for its own sake, etc.

On arguments intended to demonstrate the inadequacy
of a moral principle

From examining arguments about principles in fields other than moral thought and conduct, two lessons can be learned which help one to understand the nature of arguments about moral principles, especially of attempts at demonstrating their inadequacy. The first lesson is that none of the attempted inadequacy demonstrations outside morals are irresistible. This should forestall any temptation to deny the status of arguments to moral arguments about principles on the ground that they lack absolute cogency. The second relevant lesson is that arguments about non-moral principles can be divided into two classes, namely those which, so to speak, refer to 'pressures from below', i.e. from cases which in some way are covered by principles, and those which refer to 'pressures from above', i.e. to a vision which can at most only imperfectly approximate to a principle or set of principles. Recognizing this difference leads one to note a similar division in attempts at demonstrating the inadequacy of a principle of morality.

The kind of pressure which lower level practical attitudes may exert on the moral principles by which they are covered depends, as do the analogous pressures in other fields, on the relation between the principle and what it covers. In the case of moral principles this is the relation of practical domination. In order to describe the general manner in which these pressures work, it will be sufficient to consider our earlier example of the gross-national-product utilitarian whose one moral principle will again be schematically expressed by

(1) $S_0 + [U + \text{Max}]$.

(The subscript will be needed to distinguish him from other members of the universal class U.) Now if S_0 has a pro-attitude towards everybody's having a pro-attitude towards maximization of the gross national product of the nation to which he belongs, he *ipso facto* has this pro-attitude towards his own pro-attitude. That is to say, schematically,

(2) $S_0 + [S_0 + \text{Max}]$.

If in addition he has a first level pro-attitude towards the maximization, i.e. if

(3) $S_0 + \mathrm{Max}$

then his first level attitude will strengthen his moral attitude, or at
least, not exert any pressure towards its rejection or modification.
But it is a fundamental fact about practical systems, that a person's
lower and higher level practical attitudes may be in discordance with
each other. Thus, in spite of his pro-attitude towards everybody's
having a pro-attitude towards maximization, S_0 may himself be
indifferent towards it or even have a practical anti-attitude against it,
that is to say that possibly

(4) $S_0 \pm \mathrm{Max}$

or even

(5) $S_0 - \mathrm{Max}$.

By itself the discordance between S_0's first level practical anti-
attitude (5) and his moral attitude ((1) as instantiated by (2)) does not
necessarily involve a pressure towards its rejection or modification.
It might even be that the discordant first level practical attitude is
accompanied by feelings of guilt and shame which reinforce the
adherence to the principle. In order to see under what circumstances
the opposite pressure could arise – and be emphasized in attempts at
demonstrating the inadequacy of the principle – it seems best to
consider an example. Assume, then that S_0 finds himself in a situation
in which by implementing his utilitarian principle he would help to
depress the living standard of some of his fellow citizens or of some
member of another nation below the level of starvation. He might then,
though still holding to his principle, admit that these persons, say,
$S_1, ..., S_n$, not only have a practical anti-attitude towards the maximization of the gross national product, i.e. schematically

(6) $(S_1, S_2, ..., S_n) - \mathrm{Max}$

but have a practical pro-attitude towards this anti-attitude, i.e.

(7) $(S_1, S_2, ..., S_n) + [(S_1, ..., S_n) - \mathrm{Max}]$.

He might even admit that this attitude of theirs can turn into a moral
attitude, i.e. schematically

(8) $(S_1, S_2, ..., S_n) + [U - \mathrm{Max}]$.

Clearly, the admission of *other* people's practical anti-attitude

231

towards maximization of the national gross product (6), and the further admission that for them the anti-attitude might be positively dominated (7) and even dominated by a moral principle (8), may become a strong force towards rejection or modification of the crude utilitarian principle (1). And if it makes S_0 renounce the principle, he may, when engaged in moral argument, try to lead others through the various stages through which he himself passed before acknowledging the principle's inadequacy. The manner in which S_0's first level anti-attitude towards starvation discredits his earlier utilitarian principle is analogous to the manner in which the perception of a black swan discredits the empirical generalization about the whiteness of swans. Both discrediting cases are resistible; and in both cases their discrediting force is increased by the consensus of others – their common perceptions in one case and their common attitudes in the other.

It is not difficult to think of realistic examples of moral arguments based on pressure from below, which – as in the case of empirical and mathematical theories – are directed against conjunctions of principles, so that the force exerted against the members of the conjunction can be distributed among them in a variety of ways. Thus we may assume that S_0 has adopted not only the crude utilitarian principle of the previous example, but also a further moral principle expressing his undominated practical pro-attitude towards everybody's having a practical anti-attitude toward allowing any human being to starve. We may further assume that according to the hitherto available scientific and technological knowledge the two principles were not empirically opposed, but that a new scientific or technological discovery made it possible to treble the gross national product of every nation provided that about one man in every ten thousand would die from starvation as the result of certain economic or chemical changes brought about by any successful attempt at trebling the gross national product. If the conjunction of the crude utilitarian principle and of the anti-starvation moral principle is discredited by the practical anti-attitude of S_0 towards a situation in which the gross national product is trebled and in which, as an unavoidable consequence, one man in ten thousand dies of starvation, then the conjunction of the two principles may yield in favour of one of the two conjuncts or a modification of either.

Our last example of pressure from below is intended to bear some analogy to the manner in which a linguistically odd locution discredits by its oddity a rule of grammar to which it conforms. The example is that of a person S_0 who, together with his fellow citizens, has adopted the crude utilitarian principle in a society which is so organized that conforming to the principle leads to a constant increase in the wealth of a small minority while leaving the economic situation of the rest unchanged; and who finds himself disturbed by the growing inequality. In such a case it is difficult to decide if, and when exactly, a practical anti-attitude towards an odd irregularity of negligible proportions has turned into a practical attitude which exerts some pressure against an adopted moral principle by which it is negatively dominated; and if, and when exactly, a practical attitude which up to a certain time had been negatively dominated has ceased to be so dominated, but has become positively dominated by a moral principle which has replaced the original one.

It must be emphasized that by comparing various kinds of pressure exerted by practical attitudes on moral principles with the pressures exerted by apparent counterinstances, logical absurdities and linguistic oddities on empirical, mathematical and linguistic principles, one is not committed to any claim to, or search for, a precise and complete classification of the ways in which lower level practical attitudes can be – and can be adduced as – evidence for the inadequacy of moral principles. To provide such a classification would, moreover, be of little use since the results in the case of all these successful arguments from below are the same. They are, in particular, the recognition of a general exception to a moral principle; the recognition that two principles which seemed to be strict and mutually consistent are in fact competing (see p. 116); the recognition that one's moral principles leave room for gaps which have to be filled by *ad hoc* intuitions; and lastly the recognition that an old moral principle has to be replaced by a rather different new one.

From the discrediting pressure of lower level practical attitudes on moral principles and from arguments based on them, one must distinguish changes of moral principles which are due to a change of vision or point of view and arguments which appeal to such a change when it seems in danger of being obscured by old habits or otherwise neglected. Although such changes of moral vision are familiar from biographical, autobiographical and imaginative works describing moral conversions, one cannot, it seems, characterize their structure in a general and precise manner. Perhaps all that can be usefully done about them in a philosophical essay is to contrast them with other changes of vision and to indicate schematic examples which rely for completion on experience and empathy.

Although a change of moral vision may be initiated by a worrying counterinstance, it is total or, at least, more comprehensive than the changes so far discussed. Thus if the crude utilitarian of our early examples were faced with starving people sacrificed to the relentless pursuance of economic growth, he might not merely revise his utilitarianism, but be converted to a form of Christianity or Buddhism involving a wholly non-utilitarian morality. However, the moral conversion may, like some radical changes in a person's aesthetic vision, be independent of his religious beliefs or his lack of them. Many examples of changes of a person's moral vision are *ipso facto* changes of his view of himself and can be schematically represented by statements of the following form: And suddenly S saw himself no longer as... (a fighter for a better world, a resolute upholder of the ancient virtues, etc.) but as... (a self-indulgent aesthete, a repellent mixture of Tartuffe and Cato, the Censor, etc.). How S's new vision of himself and of a morally acceptable life may lead him to a radical change of moral principles, is not merely another story but a kind of story which does not belong in this and, possibly, any philosophical enquiry. To point out, however, that appeals to moral conversions may form a legitimate part of moral reasoning and argument is to make a philosophical point.

CHAPTER 18

ON UNDERSTANDING OTHER MORALITIES AND ON THE LIMITS OF MORAL PLURALISM

To have a morality is by its very nature to understand the practical attitudes of others. This understanding may range from the weak assumption, implicit in the form of every moral attitude, that the people to which it refers are like oneself capable of having certain practical attitudes (schematically, that the members of U in $S * [U * X]$ are capable of the same practical attitude $* X$), to the very strong assumption that there is no difference between their morality and one's own (schematically, that the place of S in $S * [U * X]$ can be taken by any member of U). The strong assumption is highly implausible, and implies three consequences which appear even less plausible. One of them is that there is no point in arguments intended to change a person's moral attitudes. This consequence conflicts both with our experience of conducting and being exposed to such arguments and with the analysis of such arguments given in the preceding chapter.

The other two consequences of assuming the identity of all moralities are first, that one understands the morality of other people as well as one understands one's own, and second, that one, consequently, knows the extent of the agreement (i.e. that there is complete agreement) between one's own and everybody else's moral attitudes. Yet experience, often in the form of painful disappointments, shows these statements to be false or highly improbable and raises the philosophical problems of the nature of one person's understanding another's morality and of the extent, if any, to which all moralities are in substantive agreement, that is to say the extent to which all human beings share the same moral attitudes. This chapter begins with a brief examination of what is involved in one person's understanding another's cognitive position, in particular his ontology. It then discusses the nature of understanding an alien morality within an ontology which coincides with one's own, and of understanding an alien morality within an alien ontology. The chapter concludes by considering the extent to which all human beings share the same moral attitudes or, to put it differently, by considering the limits of moral pluralism.

On understanding an alien ontology

In order to understand another person's moral attitudes, i.e. higher level practical attitudes which via lower level practical attitudes are directed towards practicabilities, one must understand a great deal about the world in which he believes himself to be placed and in which, whether on the spur of the moment or in accordance with more or less elaborate plans, he chooses between practicabilities and implements his choices. Although a detailed inquiry into the nature of one person's understanding of another's beliefs is here out of question, it is, even for our present limited purpose, necessary to distinguish between different species of such understanding and to pay some special attention to the understanding of an alien ontology. It will be most convenient to present the different species of understanding another's beliefs in decreasing order of perfection and illustrate them by a sequence of examples. A common feature of all the examples is that they refer to situations which involve two persons, say S (Sextus) and Q (Quintus), in which S believes a certain proposition f, say, that some schizophrenics are possessed by daemons – schematically

$$(\exists x)\,(\exists y)\,[(x \in \text{sch}) \land (y \in \text{daem}) \land (x \operatorname{poss} y)]$$

– and in which Q understands S's believing f. The situations differ in the species or degree of Q's understanding of S's belief.

There is no doubt that Q understands S's belief that f if Q like S believes f to be true. Yet Q's belief that f is true is not a condition of Q's understanding what S believes in believing f. Q understands S's belief just as well if he differs from S in not believing that f is true, but believes that as a matter of fact f – the *same f* which S believes to be true – is false, as yet undecided, or even undecidable. If Q considers f to be contingently false, we may distinguish between the case where he believes all the attributes occurring in f ($x \in \text{sch}$, $y \in \text{daem}$, $x \operatorname{poss} y$) to be applicable, but at least one of them to be misapplied, and the case where he believes at least one of them to be inapplicable. In neither case do Q's grounds for believing that $\rceil f$ affect his understanding of S's belief that f. Similar remarks apply to Q's belief that f is undecided or undecidable.

Difficulties in Q's understanding of S's belief that f arise if S's and

Q's categorial frameworks differ from each other (see p. 207). Thus it may be ontologically impossible or incoherent with respect to Q's categorial framework to assume that daemons exist as independent particulars or substances or that daemons exist at all. Using Q not only as an abbreviation of Q's name, but also as an abbreviation of the conjunction of his framework principles and abbreviating the union of Q's *summa genera* of his independent particulars or substances by sub, we may express the ontological impossibility of the assumption that daemons are independent particulars by

(1) $\neg \Diamond_Q (\exists x) ((x \in \text{daem}) \land (x \in \text{sub}))$

and the ontological impossibility of the assumption that daemons exist either as dependent or as independent particulars by

(2) $\neg \Diamond_Q (\exists x) (x \in \text{daem})$.

These statements of ontological impossibility should be contrasted on the one hand with statements expressing the factual inapplicability of an attribute, e.g.

(3) $\neg (\exists x) (x \in \text{daem}) \land \Diamond (\exists x) (x \in \text{daem})$

which present no difficulty to Q's understanding of the statement that there are daemons whether or not he believes it to be true; on the other hand with statements expressing the logical inapplicability, and consequent unintelligibility, of certain attributes such as 'being and not being a daemon', schematically $(x \in \text{daem} \land \neg (x \in \text{daem}))$, which of logical necessity is empty, i.e.

(4) $\vdash \neg (\exists x) (x \in \text{daem} \land \neg (x \in \text{daem}))$.

Q may overcome the obstacle expressed by (1) by recognizing that while for S daemons are independent particulars, he himself can regard them as dependent particulars to which reference can be made only by syncategorematic terms such as 'possessed by daemons' or 'believing in daemons' in a sense in which asserting of anything that it possesses such an attribute is *not* to imply the actual existence of daemons. Another way of overcoming the obstacle presented by (1) is for Q to 'put himself completely into S's cognitive position' – something that is very much easier said than done. Complete empathy would, of course, overcome any obstacle to Q's understanding of S. But this is obvious and need not be repeated whenever less ambitious, though perhaps more successful, attempts at ontological understanding are considered.

The obstacle presented to Q's understanding of S's belief by (2), that is to say by Q's belief that the existence of daemons as independent or as dependent particulars is ontologically impossible, cannot be overcome by using the distinction between dependent and independent particulars. One way of overcoming it is to regard daemons as fictitious particulars, about which statements can in certain contexts and for certain purposes be identified with statements which from the point of view of Q's categorial framework are free from obscurity. Thus both the obstacles, expressed by (1) and (2), to Q's understanding of S's belief that f, can be overcome by Q's modifying f in a suitable fashion and by incorporating the so-modified f into his own categorial framework. It is worth noting that both ways of adjusting statements of an alien ontology to one's own were well known and often used by Leibniz, who regards statements conflicting only with (1) as describing *phaenomena bene fundata* and statements conflicting also with (2) as expressing *fictiones bene fundatae*. There are other ways in which two categorial frameworks may diverge, in which this divergence presents obstacles to one person's ontological understanding of another's belief and in which these obstacles may be surmounted. The general method of achieving ontological understanding is, however, the same, namely transposing a suitably interpreted belief from an alien into one's own categorial framework.

The ontological difficulties which Q may have in understanding S's belief that f must be distinguished from any linguistic difficulties to which Q may also be subject – whether or not he and S speak the same language. Thus Q may not understand at all how to translate the words 'schizophrenic', 'daemons' and 'possessed by daemons' and yet, as he may find out after learning the translations, think in the same, or a very similar, categorial framework as S. On the other hand, Q may speak the same language as S and yet completely fail to understand how S interprets the relation 'possessed by' – which for Q holds only in works of fiction – as holding between schizophrenics inhabiting the actual world and daemons which like the characteristic 'possessed by' belongs to fiction only.

It might, with some justification be objected that the distinction between ontological and linguistic understanding is not clear because even if 'ontological understanding' is defined in terms of the fairly clear notion of a categorial framework, 'linguistic understanding' is not defined in terms of any similarly clear notion of a language. The force of the objection can, however, be considerably weakened either by appealing to our usual, unanalysed notion of a language which allows us to say that the very different ontologies of, say, Leibniz,

Kant and Marx can be expressed in the same language or else to suggest that the distinction made in model theory between the sentence of a formal language and the structures in which they 'hold' can be extended to cover the distinction between the sentences of a natural language and the structures (including categorial frameworks) in which they 'hold'. And if language is conceived of in some such manner, the analysis of linguistic understanding is better left to enquiries into the nature of language than to an enquiry into the nature of ontologies, moralities and their interrelations.

On understanding an alien morality in a familiar ontology

To the distinction between the linguistic and the ontological understanding of another's factual beliefs there corresponds a similar distinction between the linguistic and the moral understanding of another's moral attitudes. Thus just as Q may linguistically understand the statement that S believes schizophrenics to be possessed by daemons and lack any ontological understanding of a categorial framework in which daemons may exist as independent or even as dependent particulars; so Q may linguistically understand the statement that S has a moral pro-attitude towards maximizing the gross national product in all circumstances and yet lack any moral understanding of a morality in which the phrase 'in all circumstances' is taken literally, and thus as possibly covering the starvation of a large number of citizens. And just as the obstacles to Q's ontological understanding of S's belief in daemons may be more or less successfully overcome by so modifying S's belief that it can be incorporated into Q's categorial framework (e.g. by the demotion of daemons from actual particulars to useful fictions), so the obstacles to Q's moral understanding of S's moral attitudes, may also be more or less successfully overcome by their modification and subsequent incorporation into Q's morality.

In trying to analyse some of the ways in which moral understanding can be achieved by such modification and accommodation, it will be convenient to distinguish between situations in which the ontologies of Q and S are fairly similar or in which their differences do not matter, and situations in which both the ontologies and the moralities of Q and S differ greatly. The distinction is not sharp and cannot be made absolute because a person's system of beliefs and his practical system are not independent of each other. Nor should it be taken to imply that a similar ontology makes it always easier to bridge the gap in the understanding of a different morality. Thus a Catholic might find it easy to understand why it had been considered moral by a group of shipwrecked head-hunters to live on human flesh and very difficult to understand that a group of shipwrecked Catholic theologians could ever come to the same conclusion.

Let us then consider the example of two persons Q and S whose ontologies are very similar and whose moralities are very different. To ensure the similarity of their ontologies we assume that Q and S are two agnostic materialists who share not only the same categorial framework, but all their factual beliefs about what courses of nature are empirically possible and practicable. To ensure the difference in their moralities we assume, as before, that S is a crude gross-national-product utilitarian and that Q lives by a moral principle which requires him to love his neighbour as he loves himself or, at least, to act *as if* he so loved his neighbour. (Without going into further details we assume that Q is neither a masochist nor, in general, a person of 'abnormal' first level practical attitudes.) We further assume that Q does not doubt the sincerity of S's moral convictions and that, while incapable of 'putting himself completely into S's position' and dissatisfied with a purely linguistic understanding of S's morality, he tries to understand it by accommodating it to his own with a minimum of modification. Since S's and Q's factual beliefs are assumed to agree, what have to be modified are S's practical attitudes.

S's crude utilitarianism would be exemplified by his having a practical pro-attitude towards everybody's having a practical pro-attitude towards the maximization of the gross national product, even if such maximization causes the death by starvation (s) of n people out of every thousand, where n is obviously greater than zero and smaller than 1,000 since otherwise there would be no nation and hence no gross national product – schematically

$$S + [U + \text{Max} \land \text{Max} \to s = n/1000].$$

Q, who finds this second level attitude morally reprehensible (practically inconsistent with his moral principle of benevolence) may try to understand it by making one or more fictitious assumptions about S's practical system which would make it morally acceptable (i.e. moral or morally indifferent). In doing so he resembles a Newtonian physicist who treats a freely falling body *as if it* were a Newtonian particle, an adherent of the Leibnizian metaphysics who treats the

physical world *as if* it were a Democritean universe subject to me-
chanical causes only, and many others whose thinking and conduct
in certain contexts and for certain purposes might be expressed by
the motto *fingo ut intelligam*.

Following in their footsteps he might fictitiously modify either the
object of the universal attitude (schematically

$$\text{Max} \wedge [\text{Max} \rightarrow s = n/1000]$$

or its subject (schematically the class U). The idealization or fictitious
modification of the object of the universal attitude may be quantitative, qualitative, or concern the relevance of its characteristics. Thus
if in the cases under consideration their moral reprehensibility lies
only in the connection between maximization and starvation, Q may
try to overcome this obstacle to his moral understanding of S by
making n very small, negligibly small or 'infinitely' small. In other
words, being unable to understand S's utilitarianism when it leads to
the starvation of some people, he feigns blindnesss to this aspect of S's
morality in order to understand it. A fictitious modification in quality
of the object of the universal attitude might, for example, consist in
replacing the starvation of a certain proportion of people by their
occasionally feeling hungry or in replacing – in the cases under consideration – the unavoidable connection between maximization of
the gross national product and the starvation of some members of the
nation by a merely probabilistic connection of low or very small
probability. Lastly a fictitious modification which would concern a
relevant feature of the object of the universal attitude would pretend
that the essential connection between maximization and starvation
is a merely inessential coincidence as would be the coincidence of
maximization in a country as a whole with floods, earthquakes or
other acts of God in some parts of it.

The fictitious modification of the class of human beings (U), which
is the subject of the first level practical attitude towards which S's
second level practical attitude is directed may affect either the
membership of the class or the nature of its members. Thus Q might,
in order to understand S's utilitarianism, resort to the fiction that
those human beings who starve as the result of maximization do not
really exist – a fiction which is easier to uphold when one is surrounded
by well fed neighbours than when one is surrounded by hungry
beggars in the slums of a developing country with a crudely utilitarian
government. Fictions affecting the nature of the membership of the

class of human beings, which are the subject of the first level and part of the object of the second level attitude, consist in Q's assuming that he has adopted S's rather than his own qualifications for membership in this class. A sincere defender and a sincere opponent of abortion can morally understand each other if the former assumes that human embryos are and the latter that they are not human beings. A sincere defender of the view that blacks should be the slaves of whites and a sincere defender of the view that whites should be the slaves of blacks can morally understand each if the former excludes blacks and the latter excludes whites from the class of human beings. They might, having made their fictitious assumptions, even praise each other should they find that each of them is a great animal lover and an even greater lover of quasi-humans who are unfortunate enough to have been born with skins of the wrong colour.

The last examples raise specifically and forcefully two questions which in a more general form also arise from reflection on moral reasoning and moral arguments. One is the question of deciding where to draw the line between human embryos and lower organisms and between human embryos and human children. This kind of question is not peculiar to moral understanding or practical thinking and is one of the reasons for developing logical theories which admit inexact attributes (see p. 20). The second question is whether anybody is able sincerely to exclude any member of the zoological species *homo sapiens* from the class of human beings to which his moral attitudes are directed, or whether such exclusion can always be explained by moral weakness and bad faith. There can be little doubt that these frequent human shortcomings may, and often do, create the illusion of unusual moral attitudes, where there are none. To admit this is, however, not to imply that there can be only one morality and that moral pluralism is not only limited, but wholly mistaken.

On understanding an alien morality in an alien ontology

If Q differs from S not only in his morality but also in his ontology, then Q's ontological understanding of some of S's factual beliefs may well be a precondition of Q's moral understanding of some of S's practical attitudes. Indeed without a prior ontological understanding Q may not even be able to decide whether S's morality and his own are not very much less different than they appear because of their different ontological surroundings. To illustrate this possibility we may assume that Q lives by the same principle of benevolence, as he did in the previous example, and that S is on the face of it a gross-national-product utilitarian even though he is convinced that maximization leads to starvation of a certain percentage of the population. Yet because now S's ontology is assumed to be radically different from Q's the appearance that their moralities are also radically different, may be wholly deceptive.

Depending on the content of S's ontology and his other beliefs, his morality may in fact be guided by the same principle of benevolence as Q's. He may, for example, admit daemons as (dependent or independent) particulars into his ontology; hold the religious belief that only death by starvation can exorcise a daemon and thus open a possibility of eternal bliss which is closed to those who are possessed by daemons; believe in a daemonological economic theory according to which the maximization of the gross national product leads unavoidably to the starvation of those, and only those, who are possessed by daemons (an assumption which reminds one of the manner in which some economic *laissez-faire* politicians tended to deal with those who became the victims of perfect competition); and have certain other beliefs which clearly imply that what seemed crude utilitarianism, when put into the Procrustean bed of Q's categorial framework, coincides with, or comes very near to Q's own morality, when left in the categorial framework of S.

The difficulties of understanding an alien morality in an alien ontology – of modifying alien ontological beliefs and moral attitudes and adjusting them to one's own ontology and morality – are great enough even when there are no linguistic obstacles to overcome. Yet concentrating on the obstacles to linguistic understanding may obscure the nature of the obstacles to ontological and moral understanding, especially where both of them are combined. It is, therefore, even more important to separate linguistic from ontological-cum-moral understanding than it is to separate linguistic understanding from purely ontological or purely moral understanding. A German Jew or a liberal may have linguistically understood what the Nazis meant by 'Ariertum' as well as the late Professor Evans Pritchard linguistically understood what his Nuer hosts meant by 'kwoth' (Spirit) and 'cak' (Creation). Yet for neither of them does linguistic understanding guarantee an understanding of the alien ontology or morality.

Assuming linguistic understanding, moral misunderstandings of an alien morality may arise from a great variety of sources among which the following are particularly important. One is, of course, to see identities in ontology, morality or both where there are none. Another source of misunderstanding is to make the opposite mistake of seeing differences where there are identities. A German Jew or a liberal may, for example, succeed in assuming that his 'Aryan' neighbour is acting in accordance with a sincerely held Aryan morality in betraying their friendship by denouncing him to the secret police, when in fact he and his neighbour share the same morality and his neighbour is merely a miserable coward. A third source of misunderstanding is an excessive inclination to assume that the person living by an alien morality must be assumed to conform to it, however strange his conduct. Some adherents of so-called functionalism in recent anthropology seem prone to making this mistake when they try to avoid the imposition of their own ontology or morality on the communities which they try to understand. A fourth source of misunderstanding is the opposite inclination to assume that the person living by an alien morality is acting morally only in so far as his conduct is moral from the point of view of a familiar ontology and morality. This mistake could easily be made by those who regard alien ontologies and moralities as 'primitive' in a sense which implies that primitive people somehow try to think in our categorial framework and to live by our morality, but – being primitive – fail more or less completely.

Yet no classification of possible ontological or moral misunderstandings is likely to do justice to all the possible kinds of interconnections between a person's ontology and his morality which, so to speak, intersect in the conception which he has of himself as an individual in an ever changing cognitive and practical position. Statements describing such a conception abound in self-references and attributes which relate different aspects of a person to each other and the world. If S makes a statement of form, 'I have a moral attitude...towards one of my practical attitudes...towards one of my practicable courses of action...in a world with characteristics... in which I believe $myself$ to have existed since...' and Q is interpreting the statement as expressing part of S's morality, he must make particularly sure that he understands those of S's constitutive and individuating principles which are associated with the concepts of an agent and of an action.

The constitutive and individuating attributes of S's concept of an agent determine the equivalence class of all those, and only those, interveners in the course of nature which are representative of S or, equivalently, from which S is abstracted (see p. 76). And the spread of the temporally distinct members of this equivalence class – over the lifetime of S's body, over part of his lifetime, over the life of his and other bodies, etc. – partly determines the beliefs, moral attitudes and actions which S ascribes to himself. Thus a Hindoo accepts responsibility for interventions in the course of nature which preceded his birth, while a modern believer in psychoanalysis may reject it even for interventions preceding the curative insight into a certain inner conflict between his id, ego and superego. The ascription of beliefs and practical attitudes to S via the members of the equivalence class is necessary, though not sufficient, for deciding whether *his* beliefs are cognitively consistent and coherent and whether *his* practical attitudes are practically consistent and coherent. A difficulty in arriving at such a decision is that it is often not clear which of the beliefs and attitudes, though rightly ascribed as having once been his, can be considered as still being his.

Just as the constitutive and individuating principles which S associates with the concept of an agent characterize his conception of his place in the world, so the constitutive and individuating principles associated with his concept of an action characterize his conception of his sphere of influence in the world and thus also of the world. The key notion in a person's conception of the nature and reach of his sphere of influence is his conception of predetermination – causal, probabilistic or other (see chapter 5). And it is clearly not possible to understand another person's moral attitude to his or other people's practicabilities without an ontological understanding of this notion. The concepts of an agent and of an action have already been considered in some detail in order to exhibit the structure of practical systems. It was nevertheless necessary to consider them briefly once again in a somewhat different manner for the purpose of analysing, not one's own practical system or the general structure of practical systems, but the nature of understanding an alien morality by building various kinds of bridge from one's own to another's ontology and morality.

On the limits of moral pluralism

In trying to determine the limits of moral pluralism it is important to avoid certain tempting cul-de-sacs. Among them are stipulative definitions, except when they are explicitly used to save the repetition of cumbersome and obvious qualifications and are easily eliminated; so-called transcendental arguments, which attempt to prove the uniqueness of a certain morality either incorrectly from premisses from which it does not follow or correctly from premisses whose uniqueness is no less in doubt than that of the morality; and, of course, many other fallacious arguments which are used in metaphysics and have acquired some spurious respectability. The appropriate method for determining the limits of moral pluralism is exhibition analysis (which was briefly explained and contrasted with other philosophical methods in the Introduction, p. 2). It consists in identifying and in exhibiting the structure of various more or less comprehensive systems of beliefs or practical attitudes, such as mathematical, scientific, or metaphysical theories or of standards of prudential, legal and moral conduct. The method is anthropological in so far as it tries to identify these systems on the basis of documentary and other empirical evidence; and philosophical in so far as in analysing the systems it uses analytical tools which, like the various systems of logic, are especially familiar to philosophers or, like the distinctions embodied in the notion of a categorial framework, have been discovered by them.

The method has been extensively used in this essay and has led to the recognition of some general limitations of moral pluralism, which are conveniently recalled by referring to the schematic representation of moral attitudes, namely $S * [U * X_1 \wedge \ldots \wedge X_n]$ or, if the condition of circumstantial generality is not satisfied, $S * [U * f]$. The limitations with which a logico-philosophical enquiry is most concerned and into which it is well equipped to enquire, are the structural limitations of moral attitudes. The preceding enquiry has shown that moral attitudes are practical attitudes of at least second level which are undominated, personally universal, essential and simple and stand in various relations of consistency and inconsistency with other practical attitudes of the same or lower level. These general structural constraints on moral pluralism are by no means negligible. They far exceed, for example, the requirement of 'universalizability', which is sometimes thought sufficient to establish the moral duties of all people in all situations.

In emphasizing that the subject (S) of a moral attitude is a member of a class (U) comprising the whole zoological human species, or at least a subclass of it, our analysis moreover acknowledges the psychological constraints imposed on every bearer of a moral attitude by the physical and psychological characteristics of the class to which he belongs. The common human features – physical and psychological – which demarcate the range of any person's first level practical attitudes and thus the objects of his moral attitudes are a case in point. Because human beings have no *practical* attitudes towards doubling their size at will, towards using more than seven eyes or towards changing themselves into birds, there are no moral standards which would govern these activities. But it is a far cry from this truism to a psychological theory of the manner in which common human needs and abilities, under all or certain specific circumstances, demarcate the range of practical attitudes of first level whose presence is a necessary condition for the presence of moral attitudes.

Similar remarks apply to the interrelations of the class U, especially of those of its members which form various social groups of which S is a member, and to the physical surroundings in which they live. If there is an abundance of water and of food, one will expect the way of life of S's community, its public morality (see p. 181) and the private moralities of its members, to be other than if there is a shortage of water and food. But this truism is again a long way removed from a sociological theory which would explain the manner in which social organization and natural surroundings are interdependent as well as the manner in which and the extent to which they determine the moralities of the members of a society and the development of these moralities.

The preceding examination of the structure of practical systems and of moralities thus acknowledges two kinds of constraints on moral pluralism, namely (1) specific structural constraints expressed by relations between a person (S), his conception of the class of human beings (U), his higher level attitudes directed to this class $(*U)$, his lower level attitudes $(*X_1 \wedge \ldots \wedge X_n$ or $*f)$ and his conception of practicable and, hence, empirically possible situations (characterized by $X_1 \wedge \ldots \wedge X_n$ or described by f); and (2) some very general psychological, social and physical constraints which are implied by the common, empirical features of the entities which qualify as terms of these relations. The examination also leaves room for, and invites, further empirical enquiries into what as a matter of fact is common to all moralities.

It is not the task of a philosophical enquiry into the structure of, say, scientific systems to determine the extent to which, independently of their common structure, all known scientific systems have as a matter of empirical fact the same elements. It is similarly not the task of a philosophical enquiry into the structure of practical systems and moralities to determine the extent to which, independently of their common structure, all moralities contain as a matter of empirical fact the same moral standards. This division of labour between philosophical analysis and empirical enquiry implies no conflict between them. And the philosopher, who is not specially equipped to determine whether, for example, all known moralities contain principles which express a moral pro-attitude towards feeding one's children and a moral anti-attitude towards incest, is well advised to leave this enquiry to others. But he is equally well advised not to ignore its results. For even though they may not affect the validity of his analysis, they may involve the discovery of new cognitive or practical structures or of as yet unidentified features of familiar ones of a kind which demand, and are capable of, philosophical analysis.

CHAPTER 19

ON THE ANALYSIS OF MORAL SYSTEMS AS A TOPIC FOR SPECULATION AND A SOURCE OF MORAL GUIDANCE

Beyond the questions which can be answered by philosophical analysis, conceived of as the exhibition of the structure of systems of beliefs and practical attitudes, lie the questions of speculative philosophy about the place of these systems, not just within wider systems of various kinds, but within the whole of reality. An essay devoted to the analysis of practical systems unavoidably raises speculative questions. But while so far no definite answers have been suggested, the border between analysis and speculation will be deliberately crossed in this chapter. In doing so two subsidiary aims will also be served. One is to illustrate the relation between analytical and speculative moral philosophy, the other is to show how philosophical analysis, by revealing its own limitations, legitimizes and encourages philosophical speculation. The chapter starts by briefly considering the nature of speculative questions and the conditions which have to be satisfied by acceptable answers. It goes on to suggest speculative answers to the interdependent problems of the adequacy of any cognitive and of any practical position to reality and to give a speculative defence of moral freedom. The chapter and the book conclude with some modest remarks on the analysis of moral systems as a source of moral guidance.

On the speculative metaphysics of morals

Of the propositions, which are commonly regarded as metaphysical, only one species has so far been considered in any detail, namely the principles which define a person's categorial framework and, thereby, what for him is ontologically possible (coherent), impossible and necessary. A person's framework principles have also been called his 'principles of cognitive rationality' to distinguish them from his moral principles or principles of practical rationality. From the principles of cognitive and practical rationality we must distinguish principles of a very different kind which might be called 'principles of metaphysical reality'. These principles are speculative conjectures about reality as a whole, including man's place in it, his apprehension of it and his actions upon it.

This distinction between principles of rationality and principles of reality corresponds to Kant's distinction between two classes of metaphysical principles – even though Kant held that the membership of either class is unchangeable. The metaphysical principles which he regards as the necessary conditions of objective experience are principles of theoretical rationality; the categorical imperative is his principle of practical rationality; and lastly those metaphysical propositions which he regards as the result of illegitimate attempts at making a transition from the awareness of infinite sequences of conditions to the knowledge of the unconditioned, are principles of metaphysical reality. Such principles cannot be known, although they can be speculatively conjectured. As to his own principles of metaphysical reality – that man is free, that his soul is immortal, that there is a god – Kant (1787: Preface) claims that they can be the objects of rational faith which, though less certain than knowledge, is more secure than mere speculative conjecture.

A person's speculative conjectures must satisfy the necessary conditions of logical consistency, of cognitive coherence and of moral acceptability. It would thus be a logical mistake to hold that reality is and is not wholly spiritual. It would be incoherent to adhere both to a principle of theoretical rationality according to which not every action and, hence, not every event is completely determined and also to the speculative conjecture that time is an illusion and that events merely reveal some aspects of an unchangeable reality. And it would be morally unacceptable to adopt a Christian morality and to hold that reality requires that genocide be acknowledged as a moral duty.

The strength of these constraints on a person's speculative conjectures about reality depends, of course, on the strength of his adherence to a particular categorial framework or a particular morality. If, for example, he vacillates between two contrary framework principles, then incoherence will consist in logical inconsistency with their disjunction. If, like a theoretical counterpart of Buridan's ass, he is perfectly undecided between two contradictory framework principles, his speculation will be unconstrained by either or constrained by both. That a person's speculative conjectures must be consistent with his logic, his categorial framework and his morality does not exclude the possibility that these very systems of beliefs and practical attitudes are themselves the objects of his speculations. Nor does it exclude the possibility, that a speculative conjecture which is logically consistent, coherent and morally acceptable may yet help to undermine one's adherence to a categorial framework or a morality in favour of its replacement by another.

As to the positive requirements which a person's principles of metaphysical reality have to fulfil one can say little more than that they should give intellectual and emotional satisfaction to him. Both kinds of satisfaction arise from the incorporation of his beliefs and attitudes into an all-embracing reality which is not merely all-embracing, but endowed with more specific characteristics. The source of his intellectual satisfaction is that this more specific, speculative characterization of reality implies answers to questions which are otherwise unanswerable. The source of his emotional satisfaction is that this more specific characterization provides him with a more suitable, because more specific, object for what might be called his 'cosmic emotions' such as confidence in, despair about, awe of, reverence for, or indifference towards the reality which embraces himself and all that exists. Although these cosmic emotions play a central rôle in some metaphysical systems, there is no need to attempt their description. Indeed this brief incursion into speculative metaphysics does not presuppose an answer to the question as to whether every human being has these emotions or is capable of having them.

From ontological pluralism to a perspectivist metaphysics

Because of the interdependence of practical attitudes and factual beliefs, the metaphysical problems of the practical adequacy of a morality and of the cognitive adequacy of an ontology to reality are also interdependent. Before turning to the problem as to which practical position, if any, is adequate to reality, it will be well to consider the parallel problem as to which cognitive position, if any, is adequate to reality. This problem confronts one in two parts, namely, on the one hand as a problem of the adequacy of those beliefs which are held when, or in so far as, one does not question the adequacy of one's categorial framework; on the other hand as a problem of the adequacy of the categorial framework itself. The possible answers to the first and comparatively easy part of the problem suggest possible answers to the second, much more difficult part.

As regards the first part of the problem it is useful to recall that a person who thinks within a categorial framework (see chapter 16, p. 207) explicitly or implicitly distinguishes between three kinds of false proposition, namely logically impossible propositions, which violate the logical principles underlying the framework, ontologically impossible propositions which violate the non-logical principles defining the categorial framework, and propositions which, while being logically and ontologically possible, are false on other grounds. The difference between ontologically impossible and simply false propositions is that the former not only misdescribe the actual world but – by violating the framework principles – distort its structure. Yet, as has been pointed out before (p. 191), even a categorial distortion of the actual world can illuminate its nature if it simplifies or idealizes it in such a manner that for certain purposes and in certain contexts the idealizing distortion can be identified with a correct, but too complex or otherwise unmanageable, representation of the actual world.

Consider, for example, a person who thinks within the Kantian categorial framework (as described on p. 214), but who at the same time uses indeterministic quantum theory as his physics and the classical economic theory of perfect competition as his economics. For such a person his physics and his economics will be categorial distortions of the actual world. Yet if he holds that without his physics and his economics his understanding of the worlds' physical and economic features would be even more defective, it is reasonable for him to employ these sciences rather than to forego their employment. Again, a person of a rationalist cast of mind might consider only a particular science, such as physics, to be categorially undistorted and yet use commonsense and other sciences to apprehend features of the world which to him are otherwise not, or not easily, accessible. And one can think of many other examples.

A person's logically possible beliefs which are inconsistent with his categorial framework and thus ontologically impossible are, even if cognitively useful, categorially distorted. Yet these beliefs could be accommodated to some other categorial framework – whether already available or constructed for the purpose. In this case the second categorial framework or, more precisely, its defining principles would be categorially distorted with respect to the first and vice versa. That different categorial frameworks are with respect to each other onto-logically impossible and, even if cognitively useful, distorted, leads to the more difficult part of our problem about the adequacy of categorial frameworks to reality. To this problem two speculative answers offer themselves: namely, on the one hand a metaphysical correspondence theory according to which one, and only one, categorial framework is adequate to reality, and on the other hand a perspectivist metaphysics according to which every categorial framework is a distortion of reality although different frameworks distort it in different ways.

Although the decision between these two and other possible metaphysical positions is a matter for speculation, it may nevertheless be worthwhile to adduce some considerations in favour of perspectivism. First, since all thinking within categorial frameworks rests on a differentiation between particulars and attributes and since this differentiation is not unique, it makes sense to assume that any such differentiation, and hence any categorial framework, is a distortion of a reality which is not so differentiated. The assumption would be supported by any legitimate claim to some more direct awareness of this reality. It is – among others – made by Nicolaus de Cusa and Spinoza both of whom hold that there is, apart from perception and discursive understanding a third kind of cognition which yields an awareness of reality as a whole and of every aspect of it in its interconnection with the whole. Yet even without laying claim to Cusanus' *intellectus* which reveals reality as the *coincidentia oppositorum* or to Spinoza's *scientia intuitiva* which reveals every aspect of it *sub specie aeternitatis*, one may reasonably regard certain metaphysical moods, religious feelings and aesthetic experiences as yielding through the 'fleshly dress' of a categorial framework 'bright shoots of everlastingness' as envisaged by Cusanus (1488: book I, ch. IV) or Spinoza (1882: *Ethics* pt II, prop. XIVff.).

Another point in favour of perspectivism is the experience of intellectual enrichment from gaining the ontological understanding of a hitherto wholly alien categorial framework – an experience familiar to scientists, historians and anthropologists (see p. 236). This experience is plausibly explained as the grasp of a new aspect of reality which, however distorted it may be, it is preferable to attain than to miss. A third point in favour of perspectivism is the not uncommon moral experience of not merely having a practical attitude towards everybody's having a certain practical attitude, but of identifying oneself with everybody in a way which seems to transcend the separateness of particulars – especially of persons – which is presupposed by discursive thinking, that is to say by the application of attributes to particulars. If one grants the logical consistency, cognitive coherence and moral acceptability of metaphysical perspectivism, then the three points adduced in its favour may serve to indicate why it can give the intellectual and emotional satisfaction required of speculative theses.

From moral pluralism to a metaphysics of self-transcendence

Moral, like ontological, pluralism raises the problem of adequacy to reality in two parts. There is the comparatively simple problem of the moral adequacy of a person's practical attitudes when or in so far as he does not question his morality. And there is the much more difficult problem of the adequacy of his morality. As in the case of ontological pluralism answers to the first problem suggest answers to the second.

Starting, then, with practical attitudes which are immoral with respect to a person's morality (his moral principles or his moral attitudes which lack circumstantial generality) we can distinguish three kinds of immoral attitudes: practical attitudes which are immoral because they are decomposable into opposed or incongruent practical attitudes of which at most one is morally acceptable; practical attitudes which are immoral because they are opposed to, or incongruent with, the person's moral attitudes and are in this sense distorting it; and practical attitudes which are immoral because negatively dominated by a moral principle (or by a practical attitude which differs from a moral principle only by not being circumstantially general).

We have seen that, for example in scientific thinking, the employment of categorially distorted principles may be justified if it illuminates features of the world which are otherwise overlooked. In a similar way the employment of morally distorted principles may be morally excused if it serves morally approved ends, in particular moral co-operation. One may thus, for example, judge an action which conforms to the law of the land or public morality to be immoral (have a moral anti-attitude towards the action) and yet judge it morally excusable (have a pro-attitude towards refraining from punishing the agent or from imposing otherwise appropriate sanctions). Again, one may judge immoral and yet morally excuse the replacement of a complex moral set of legal regulations by a morally slightly distorted simpler one. In all this one must, of course, guard against the danger of self-deception and remember that just as a cognitively illuminating but categorially distorted belief remains false, so a morally excusable but immoral practical attitude or action remains immoral (see pp. 195 ff.).

254

That the moralities of different persons may not be practically incompatible but excusably distorted with respect to each other raises – as was the case with categorial distortion – the second part of the problem of the adequacy of a person's morality, namely its adequacy to reality. As before at least two speculative answers offer themselves, namely, on the one hand a metaphysics of morals according to which one, and only one, moral system is adequate to reality, and on the other hand a metaphysics of morals according to which every morality is a distorted expression of a person's attempt to transcend the limitations of his separate self-hood which makes him appear a member of a class rather than a part of a whole or – to use appropriately metaphorical language – which makes him appear 'an Island entire of himself' rather than 'a piece of the continent, a part of the main'.

Of the considerations which might be adduced in favour of a metaphysics of morals which conceives moralities as attempts at self-transcendence the following seem worth mentioning, First, just as the apparent experience of moral self-transcendence was used to support a metaphysical perspectivism according to which any differentiation of the world into particulars and attributes is a distortion of reality, so metaphysical perspectivism, i.e. the conception of any categorial framework and any differentiation of the world into particulars and attributes as a distortion of it, can in turn be used to support the metaphysics of moral self-transcendence. Metaphysical perspectivism implies or at least strongly suggests moral self-transcendence for Nicolaus de Cusa, Spinoza, and other thinkers. Second, it makes speculative sense to regard – with Schopenhauer among others – the personal universality of moral attitudes (schematically expressed by $S*[U*...]$) as a conceptualized counterpart of a deeper personal identification of oneself with all other human, or even all other living, beings. Third, what has been said about moral understanding as falling short of ideal empathy (see p. 237), may be taken to point to an analogous distinction between a distorted awareness of a class of human beings and a direct awareness of undifferentiated humanity.

It should be emphasized again that a perspectivist metaphysics combined with a speculative ethics of self-transcendence is, at best, compatible with our analyses. It gives emotional and intellectual satisfaction to some people, but will no doubt appear too soft and mystical a vision to those who like their speculations to seem as tough and down to earth as mathematical deductions from indubitable premisses or uncontroversial reports of transparent experiments. The speculative position of, say, a cognitive and a moral correspondence theory, according to which one and only one categorial framework and one and only one moral system are adequate to reality, gains its aura of toughness from a tacit assumption that one can compare reality as apprehended through a categorial framework and a moral system with reality as apprehended independently of them. Yet it is this very assumption of a direct, unconceptualized access to reality which the adherents of a metaphysical correspondence theory find most abhorrent in metaphysical perspectivism and the ethics of self-transcendence. It seems, moreover, that while the latter metaphysical position can be content with glimpses of a directly apprehended reality, the correspondence theory must presuppose a more perfect direct knowledge of it if reality as apprehended by a categorial framework and a moral system is to be compared with reality as it exists independently of them.

The metaphysical problem of freedom

Although the preceding remarks about a speculative metaphysics of perspectivism and a speculative ethics of self-transcendence are not only meant to exemplify the transition from analysis to speculation, but also to indicate a viable speculative position, any elaboration of it would here be out of place. As outlined, it can appeal to what is common ground between Spinoza's pantheism and Cusanus' Christian theology but does not, for example, imply any definite answers to the three Kantian questions about the existence of God, about personal immortality and about moral freedom. Of these the last plays a special rôle in moral thinking where even the mere description of an action or other practicability implies the agent's acknowledgement of his *apparent* freedom effectively to choose between more than one practicable course of events (see p. 65). So much is agreed between philosophers as different as the determinist Hume and the libertarian Kierkegaard towards whom our analyses – including the analysis of various kinds of determinism and libertarianism – have preserved an appropriate analytical neutrality. In dropping it by indicating a speculative case for libertarianism one does, of course, no more than once again propose a metaphysical position which satisfies the requirements of logical consistency, cognitive coherence and moral acceptability and which, one hopes, will be intellectually and emotionally as satisfactory to others as it is to oneself. A brief outline is all that is needed. (For a somewhat more detailed exposition see Körner 1971*b*: ch. 14.)

Considerations adduced for, or against, libertarianism and the corresponding notion of moral responsibility are usually based on introspection, on the nature and content of science, and the nature and content of logic. Of these three sources introspection is the least variable while the dominant views of science and logic may change radically, and have undergone such changes in our century. That introspection, when unaided or unhindered by science, logic or metaphysics, seems to support libertarianism is admitted even by Hume (in section VIII of the *Enquiry Concerning Human Understanding*). He points on the one hand to the 'seeming experience which we have, or may have, of liberty or indifference, in many of our actions', on the other hand to our making a clear distinction between bestowing aesthetic praise or blame on a person whom we do not hold responsible for his bodily features and bestowing moral praise or blame on a person whom we hold responsible for having acted as he did and not otherwise.

As matters stood in the days of Hume both science – which was wholly deterministic – and logic – in which the law of excluded middle was valid without exception – contradicted the introspective data. As matters stand today both science and logic are compatible with them: science, if one regards indeterministic quantum mechanics as representative of its content or if one accepts an analysis of the structure of scientific theories according to which they are in any case not descriptions but idealizations of experience (see Körner 1966); logic, if one considers a logical theory without the law of excluded middle no less acceptable than classical logic so that libertarianism instead of being excluded by that logic might be a reason for rejecting it (compare chapter 1 on the relations between classical and constructive logic).

Thus the small voice of introspection raised in favour of libertarianism and audible even to Hume is no longer drowned by the heavy guns of classical physics and classical logic. It is reinforced by our feelings of guilt and bad conscience and our natural interpretation of them as not necessarily pathological but as deriving from the instinctively accepted assumption that it is sometimes possible to choose effectively between living by one's morality and violating it and between making oneself a better or a worse person, as judged in the light of this morality. It is further reinforced by our analysis of discordance as a species of practical inconsistency which appears to be removable by implementing the dominating moral attitude rather than the dominated lower practical attitude.

Two further considerations may be adduced in favour of libertarianism: a pragmatic one, which presupposes in its addressee a moral anti-attitude towards excusing immoral conduct (except when the excuse is morally justified as in the situations mentioned on p. 196); and a metaphysical one, which presupposes that its addressee has adopted a version of metaphysical perspectivism combined with a version of the ethics of self-transcendence. The pragmatic argument distinguishes between the possibility that determinism is true and the possibility that libertarianism is true. If determinism is true then one's whole life including one's excuses for one's immoral conduct are predetermined. If libertarianism is true then determinism may provide one with excuses which are not available to the libertarian. Hence the number of excuses for immoral conduct which is available to the libertarian is at most equal to the number of such excuses available to the determinist. And in so far as the availability of a smaller number of such excuses is preferable to that of a larger number of them, libertarianism is preferable to determinism.

Metaphysical perspectivism and the speculative ethics of self-transcendence make it appear natural to regard oneself as a part of reality – a part which though enormously constrained by the whole yet makes a small constraining contribution to the being or becoming of the whole. This speculation fits in well with one's instinctive conviction that although one cannot effectively choose one's destiny, one has a limited choice between different versions of it, of the world in which it is realized and, thus, of oneself. By adducing this and other speculative considerations in favour of libertarianism one usually reaches only the converted. But even the converted may need, or welcome, some fortification of their metaphysical conjectures. It goes without saying that determinism too may be defended as logically consistent, as coherent with a variety of categorial frameworks, as morally acceptable in the light of a variety of moralities and as intellectually and emotionally satisfying. But if one finds it intellectually and emotionally wholly unsatisfying and if one finds the considerations which are adduced in its favour wholly unpersuasive, it seems appropriate to leave its advocacy to others.

On the analysis of moral systems as a source of
moral guidance

The analysis of practical and, more particularly, of moral systems
interacts not only with philosophical speculations about the place of
morality in the scheme of things, but also with the actual choices –
introspected or observed from the outside – which have to be made by
human beings in the course of their lives. While these choices must
obviously be taken into account if the analysis is to be realistic, it
may be less clear how the analysis may, in turn, be a source of moral
guidance. Without aiming at too systematic or too comprehensive
a presentation of the ways in which the philosophical analysis of moral
systems can serve the solution of one's moral problems, it is natural to
distinguish between help which is derivable from the analysis of the
formal structure of practical systems, help which is derivable from the
distinction between different types of morality and help which is
derivable from an analysis of the relation between moralities and
systems of other standards guiding human conduct, such as legal
systems.

The formal analyses – especially of constructive thinking, of practical preference and of codes of conduct – have the same kind of
relevance to the solution of actual problems about one's conduct as
any logical or mathematical theory has to the solution of problems
falling within its range of competence. A simple instructive example
is classical propositional logic, the application of whose rules is in
complex situations less fraught with the danger of howlers than the
reliance on instinct and intuition. One can, without difficulty and
almost at random, select structural features of practical systems and
principles corresponding to them which have been brought to light
by our analysis and can be applied to problems which otherwise would
be tackled less effectively.

One important structural feature of practical systems is their
stratification. This enables one to analyse the notion of practical
inconsistency as opposition, discordance or incongruence and to forma-
lize the notion of practical implication between attitudes. It further
shows that, and why, definitions of rationality as the maximization
of first level preferences are counterintuitive and lead to paradoxical
consequences (see p. 175). Again, the analysis of the structure of
codes of conduct and the reduction of deontic to ordinary semantic
relations should facilitate complex deontic reasoning and secure it

against error. Together with the analysis of the structure of practical preferences and attitudes it should further help us to avoid various confusions between, and conflations of, preferential and deontic reasoning. Among them is the mistaken assumption that having a moral pro-attitude towards a certain option logically implies acknowledging a code-dependent or code-independent moral obligation towards realizing this option.

Turning to less formal matters one might mention the taxonomy of moralities and the analysis of one person's moral understanding of another's morality in a similar or different ontology. Thus the distinction between axiological, deontic and mixed moralities and various species of these types may help one in articulating one's own morality by raising questions which are easily ignored – for example, whether a certain moral principle is strict or competing, whether a certain code of conduct represents a deontic morality or a convenient simplification of an axiological morality under 'normal' circumstances. Again, the analysis of the nature of moral understanding is likely to improve one's actual ability to understand others, as well as one's actual ability to make oneself understood by them through a suitable formulation of moral arguments.

Lastly, the analysis of the nature and interrelation of moral and other standards of conduct is likely to prove relevant to some actual moral problems. By showing, as has been done, how the morality of judges and administrators is received into the law of the land through official legal channels as well as through the interstices of the legal system, one excludes various simple-minded accounts of the relation between law and morality. Thus one may conceive of extreme situations in which it may be moral to conform to a law which would be immoral if it were not part of a legal system which as a whole is moral, as well as extreme situations in which it may be immoral to conform to a law which would be moral if it were not part of a legal system which as a whole is immoral.

The number and variety of examples illustrating the relevance of moral theory to moral practice could be greatly increased since almost every thesis of the preceding enquiry could be matched by a principle capable of practical application to actual moral problems. To show this in detail would, however, be tedious and unnecessary. It would also be painful because any attempt at matching a thesis with a corresponding applicable principle is likely to reveal shortcomings in the formulation of the thesis, in the argument leading to it or both in the thesis and the argument. And yielding to the natural and laudable temptation to remove these shortcomings might all too easily make the end of the enquiry coincide with that of the enquirer.

REFERENCES

Arrow, K. J. 1951. *Social choice and Individual Values*. New York.

Bertalanffy, L. von. 1968. *General System Theory*. New York.

Brentano, F. 1889 etc. *Vom Ursprung sittlicher Erkenntnis*. Leipzig.

Bridgman, P. 1943. *The Nature of Thermodynamics*. Cambridge, Mass.

Butler, J. 1736 etc. *The Analogy*. London.

Chisholm, R. M. & Sosa, E. 1966. 'Intrinsic preferability and the problem of supererogation', *Synthese* vol. 16, pp. 321–31.

Cleave, J. P. 1973/4. 'An account of entailment based on classical semantics', *Analysis* vol. 34.

Cleave, J. P. 1974. 'The notion of logical consequence in the logic of inexact predicates', *Z. für Math. Logik und Grundlagen der Math.* vol. 20, pp. 307–24.

Cusa, Nicolaus de. 1488 etc. *De docta ignorantia (Opera)*. Strassburg.

Descartes, R. 1641 etc. *Meditationes de prima philosophia*. Paris.

Durkheim, E. 1906. 'La détermination du fait moral', *Bulletin de la Société Francaise de philosophie* vol. 6.

Durkheim, E. 1951. *Sociologie et Philosophie*. Paris.

Dworkin, R. 1970. 'Is law a system of rules' in *Essays in Legal Philosophy* ed. R. S. Summers. Oxford.

Fellner, W. 1965. *Probability and Profit*. Homewood, Illinois.

Field, G. C. 1949. *The Philosophy of Plato*. Oxford.

Føllesdal, D. & Hilpinnen, R. 1971. 'Deontic logic: an introduction' in *Deontic Logic: Introductory and Systematic Readings* ed. R. Hilpinnen. Dordrecht.

Gödel, K. 1933. 'Zum intuitionistischen Aussagenkalkül', *Ergebnisse eines math. Kolloquiums* no. 4.

Grzegorczyk, A. 1964. 'A philosophically plausible interpretation of intuitionistic logic', *Indagationes Mathematicae* vol. 26.

Heyting, A. 1956. *Intuitionism – An Introduction*. Amsterdam.

Kant, I. 1787 etc. *Kritik der Reinen Vernunft*, 2nd edn. Riga.

Kant, I. 1788 etc. *Kritik der Praktischen Vernunft*. Riga.

Kant, I. 1797 etc. *Metaphysische Anfangsgründe der Rechtslehre* (2nd part of *Die Metaphysik der Sitten*). Königsberg.

Kemeny, J. G. 1955. 'Fair bets and inductive probabilities', *Journal of Symbolic Logic* vol. 20, no. 3.

Kemeny, J. G., Schleifer, A. Jnr., Snell, J. L. & Thompson, G. L. 1965. *Finite Mathematics*. Inglewood Cliffs, N.J.

Körner, S. 1955. *Conceptual Thinking*. Cambridge.

Körner, S. 1960. *The Philosophy of Mathematics*. London.

Körner, S. 1966. *Experience and Theory*. London.

Körner, S. 1971*a*. *Abstraction in Science and Morals*. Cambridge.

Körner, S. 1971*b*. *Fundamental Questions in Philosophy*. London.

Körner, S. 1971*c*. *Categorial Frameworks*. Oxford.

Körner, S. 1973. 'Material necessity', *Kant-Studien* vol. 64, no. 4.

Kyburg, H. E. & Smokler, H. E. (eds.) 1964. *Studies in Subjective Probability*. New York.

Leibniz, G. W. 1714 etc. *Essay de Théoricée*.

Locke, J. 1690 etc. *Two Treatises on Government*. London.

Merleau-Ponty, M. 1954. *Phénoménologie de la perception*. Paris.

Montague, R. 1960. 'Logical Necessity, Physical Necessity, Ethics and Quantifiers', *Inquiry* vol. 4. Reprinted in *Formal Philosophy* ed. R. Thomason. Yale U.P. 1974.

Mostowski, A. 1966. *Thirty Years of Foundational Studies*. Oxford.

Nelson, L. 1917. *Kritik der praktischen Vernunft* (Abhandlungen der Friesschen Schule, N.F., reprinted Hamburg, 1972).

Ossowska, M. 1971. *Social Determinants of Moral Ideas*. London.

Perelman, C. 1945. *De la justice*. Brussels.

Rawls, J. 1972. *A Theory of Justice*. Oxford.

Schlaifer, R. 1969. *Analysis of Decisions under Uncertainty*. New York.

Sen, A. K. 1970. *Collective Choice and Social Welfare*. Edinburgh.

Sen, A. K. 1974. 'Choice, Ordering and Morality' in *Practical Reason* ed. S. Körner. Oxford and Yale.

Sohm, R. 1884 etc. *Institutionen des römischen Rechts*. Leipzig. (Translated by J. C. Ledlie, 3rd edn. Oxford 1907.)

Spinoza, B. 1882 etc. *Opera*, ed. Vloten and Land. The Hague.

Strawson, P. F. 1966. *The Bounds of Sense*. London.

Streeter, B. H. 1932. *The Buddha and the Christ*. London.

Weber, Max 1922. *Gesammelte Schriften zur Wissenschaftslehre*. Tübingen.

Williams, Glanville 1961. *Criminal Law*, 2nd edn. London.

INDEX

actions, *see also* interventions; agents
  their ascription, 81–3
  their demarcation, 83–5
  their external and internal perspectives, 85–7
adequacy of a system of regulations, *see also* codes of conduct defined, 29–31
  loss and restoration, 36–8
actus reus, 87
agents
  defined, 78–9
  as persisting subjects of interventions, 76–8
  and persons, 79–83
analysis, distinguished from speculative philosophy, 2–3
anti-attitudes, *see* practical attitudes
application of a theory, 6, 194
arguments
  about the adequacy of moral principles, 230–4
  about aesthetic standards, 229–30
  about empirical principles, 227–8
  about grammatical rules, 229
  about mathematical principles, 228
  based on moral plausibility, 223–6
  based on practical, logical and deontic implications, 221–3
Aristotle, 7, 103, 153
Arrow, K. J., 173, 175, 194, 262
attitudes of practical indifference, *see* practical attitudes
Austin, John, 180
axiological systems of morality, 142–4

beliefs, *see also* practical beliefs and practical attitudes, 88–92
Bellarmin, R., 217
Bentham, J., 212
Bertalanffy, L. von, 83, 104, 262
bodily conduct, 65–7
Born, M., 71, 217
bourgeois morality, 193
Brentano, F., 102

Bridgman, P., 219
Brouwer, L. J., 218
Buddhism, as an ideal way of life, 201
Butler, J., 163, 262

categorial frameworks
  as distortions of each other, 252
  structure and function, 208–10
character, 109–11
Chisholm, R. M., 62, 262
choice, *see* also interventions
  conditions of effective choice, 67–9
Christianity, as an ideal way of life, 201
circumstantial generality, 115 and *passim*
classification, *see also* equivalence classes
  of just interests, 152–4
  of prudential values, 164–5
codes of conduct
  formal structure, 27–38
  and justice, 151
  social function, 108
  supreme, 132–6
cognitivism in mathematics and metaphysics, 220
coherence
  of beliefs, 26–7, 208–10
  interdependence of cognitive and practical coherence, 213–21
  of practical attitudes, 99, 210–13
commonsense, *see* specialist thinking; idealization and specialist thinking, 5–7, 191–7
competing principles, *see* evaluative principles
complementarity of practical attitudes, 96
Comte, A., 107
constructivism in mathematics and metaphysics, 218–20
contract theories of justice, 157–60
Cusa, N. de, 253, 255, 262
customary law, 184

deductive abstraction, 6, 194